Visual Aids and Photography in Education

Visual Aids and Photography in Education

A VISUAL AIDS MANUAL FOR TEACHERS AND LEARNERS

by MICHAEL LANGFORD FRPS FIIP
Tutor in Photography, Royal College of Art, London

FOCAL PRESS
London and New York

ISBN 0 240 50717 7

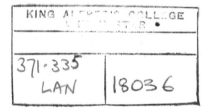
Filmset in Photon Imprint 11 on 12 pt. by
Richard Clay (The Chaucer Press), Ltd, Bungay, Suffolk
and printed in Great Britain by
Fletcher & Son Ltd, Norwich

Contents

Chapter 9 Photographic Project Work   266

Acknowledgements

Preparing this book was made easier and considerably more enjoyable through the help and advice received from educationalists, manufacturers and A–V experts. Thanks are particularly due to H. M. I. Frank Hawkins and to the many teachers in British schools and training centres who gave up time to talk or write to me, or to supply illustrations. Most of the best ideas for utilising photography are theirs.

Among manufacturers Kodak Ltd (Education Service); Agfa-Gevaert Ltd; Rank Audio Visual Ltd; 3M Ltd; Encyclopaedia Britannica Ltd; Educational Productions Ltd; and Macmillan Educational Ltd were particularly helpful. Those sources of independent advice, the National Audio Visual Aids Centre and the National Reprographic Centre for Documentation gave invaluable aid in arbitrating sales claims and answering queries on points of detail.

At Focal Press Percy Poynter did tremendous work making my diagrams fit to reproduce in a book on visual aids. Finally, thanks to Michael Clarke of London University who first suggested the need for a practical manual of this kind.

Introduction

THE TREND AWAY from the 'print-dominated approach' in modern methods of education and training makes it obligatory for the teacher to have some practical knowledge of the whole field of audio-visual (a.v.) techniques. This book has been conceived as an essentially practical guide to the educational use of equipment most educational establishments can sooner or later expect to possess—photographic cameras and associated gear, document copiers, duplicators and projectors, and software of various kinds. It sets out to show in detail how today's equipment can be used by teachers themselves to make aids, and by learners to expand their knowledge and develop individual creative abilities. The book is therefore intended for everyone concerned with education—students in Colleges of Education, schoolteachers, technical instructors, lecturers, a.v. technicians, administrators and LEA subject organisers, not forgetting the learners themselves.

Starting from the assumption that the reader accepts the validity of visual aids and has an interest in photography and image reproduction processes, no practical knowledge is expected (beyond perhaps holiday snaps and simple records). Technicalities are simplified into step-by-step procedures. These show how to translate a variety of original material into visual aids software, organise facilities in a school environment, and plan class and individual projects using photography. Incidentally many of the educational principles and a.v. technology sections of the City & Guilds Audio-Visual Aid Technicians Certificate (Subject 419) are covered here.

The first section of the book is concerned with hardware. I am conscious that one of the cornerstones of visual aid philosophy is that it should begin with the education problem, not the hardware. Developments in educational ideas easily pass unnoticed when one is overabsorbed by the equipment and materials. But in planning this book I felt that an early description of the range of hardware and its purpose and function has the merit of allowing objective assessment of what each type of equipment will (and will not) do, and establishes the terminology used to discuss visual aids production and presentation.

If you are already familiar with the tools for showing and making visual aids, pass straight through to Chapter 3, which begins the main section of the book, and deals with planning and buying or making software to solve specific teaching problems. Here combinations of artwork, photography, cinematography and document copying are used to devise educationally effective aids.

Educational television is not included *per se*; at present TV facilities are still limited and live TV production still essentially a team job, whereas this book is primarily aimed at the individual teacher and his class group. Nevertheless much of the practical description of movie film production, artwork preparation and still photography is equally applicable to images for eventual transmission through a TV channel, and specific references are made to this medium wherever special requirements apply.

The biggest demands for visual aids are from flat copy originals such as drawings, magazine clippings and books, etc., and a 'do-it-yourself' reference section is included in Chapter 5 giving many alternative procedures for turning any of these originals into various forms of aid. Planning software begins with assessing need but must also look ahead to conditions of presentation and the way in which an aid will integrate within a teaching scheme. A chapter on presentation therefore completes the software section. References to sources of commercial hardware and software, suppliers of materials, plans and requirements for setting up photographic workshops, copyright considerations, further reading and a glossary of all technical terms used in the text are included in the Appendices.

The final section on student participation could have filled a whole book. As it is I have attempted to show in practical terms how photography can be and is being applied by students through discovery projects spanning a wide range of hitherto separate disciplines, from art to science. The future here at all levels of education is exciting, despite the familiar old handicaps of lack of money and facilities. Some ways around these problems are suggested.

In short, here is a blend of image production techniques, hints, tips and applied educational principles which may be of help in the communication of ideas. The choice and validity of these ideas remain very much the province of the teacher. In the last analysis, when the door shuts, he is faced with a room full of eager, interested, bored or indifferent individuals. By gathering together his knowledge and various manipulative and organisational skills (including more than a touch of 'show-biz'), it is his privilege to develop interest and discovery in this raw material. Photography in particular can be made a valuable and popular ingredient in such a situation—not, as some teachers consider, as mere icing on the educational cake, but as a medium as universally applied throughout the curriculum as the written word and drawn illustration.

1. Equipment for displaying images

THE PHYSICAL form a visual aid is to take is inevitably conditioned by the equipment available. Before going very far, therefore, we should be reasonably familiar with most basic forms of visual aids presentation hardware currently used in teaching—display devices and projectors of all kinds. This does not mean that this chapter becomes a glorified manufacturers' catalogue, but more an opportunity to outline mechanical principles and discuss pedagogic strengths and weaknesses of various items. Not least, we can establish the meaning of names and terms which will crop up again when the choice and preparation of aids are discussed. Comparisons can also be drawn between equipment in terms of practical design features, capital and running costs, size and format of the software they accept, and their inter-relationships within the context of teaching.

EQUIPMENT FOR PROJECTING STILL IMAGES

Slide projectors

The old magic lantern is probably the earliest optical visual aids machine. With its splendidly decorated brass lamphouse, polished rosewood slide carrier and huge lens, the magic lantern was entertaining and informing audiences in smoky village halls a generation before the cinema. Today, under the updated title of slide projector, these machines are a great deal more compact and efficient.

The slide projector in its simplest form consists of a bright light source and simple lens (called a condenser) to concentrate illumination through the transparency or lantern slide, supported in a sliding carrier (Fig. 1.1). Beyond the carrier a multi-element lens projects the image of the brightly illuminated slide on to a screen or wall. The projection lens can be moved forwards and backwards to focus the image sharply on the screen.

Most projectors have a small built-in electric fan to prevent the lamp (and slide) from overheating; this, plus the small size of today's

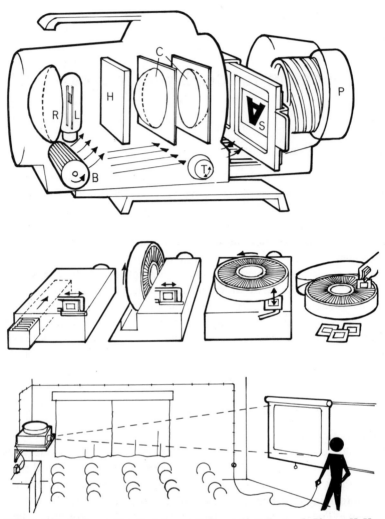

Fig. 1.1. Slide Projector. *Top:* Basic layout. L, Lamp. R, Reflector. B, Blower. H, Heat filter (absorbs heat and requires ventilating). C, Condenser lenses. S, Slides. P, Projection lens. T, Tilting control. *Centre:* Various forms of magazine-loading projectors. *Bottom:* Semi-permanent classroom arrangement using magazine projector and remote control.

tungsten halogen lamps allows the lamphouse to be very compact. (Never accidentally obstruct the air circulation vents—e.g. with a carelessly draped curtain or cloth—as the heat build-up can destroy the lamp and distort the lamphouse.) Usually a piece of heat-absorbing glass is also located in some well-ventilated position between the lamp and slide carrier.

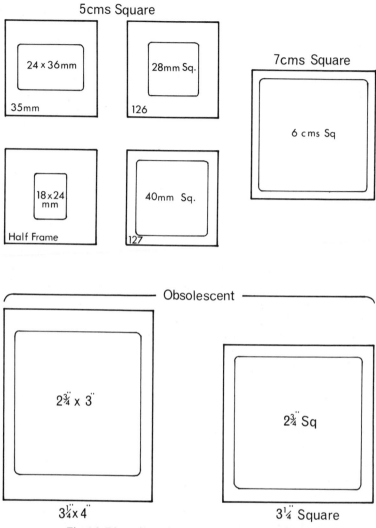

Fig. 1.2. Dimensions of current and obsolescent slides.

Most slide projectors on the market are designed to accept slides with 5 × 5 cm * outside dimensions. As shown in Fig. 1.2, these commonly comprise colour or black-and-white transparencies, in horizontal, square or vertical picture format on 35-mm-wide film. Film material is bound up in cardboard or plastic mounts. The 5 × 5-cm slide is now the accepted standard in British schools.

* The precise standard is 50·8 mm (2 in.) square.

15

A few manufacturers make projectors scaled up in size and designed to accept another international standard—slides 7 cm square. This means that colour transparencies taken with a 6 × 6-cm rollfilm camera can be mounted in card or plastic frames and projected. The 7-cm-square projector usually has an adaptor allowing the slide carrier to be masked down to accept 5 × 5-cm slides too.

The oldest types of slide projector, and the accepted British standard until about 15 years ago, were made for slides $3\frac{1}{4}$ in. square. Many projectors of this size are still in use, although now usually adapted to one of the modern sizes. In the United States, large oblong slides $3\frac{1}{4}$ in. × 4 in. are still occasionally used.

A basic slide projector is operated by hand—the carrier accepts two slides side by side, so that while one slide is being projected another can be loaded or unloaded. A much better arrangement for teaching is to use a magazine-loading projector (Fig. 1.1). The plastic magazine, which may hold up to 80 slides, is pre-loaded with all the slides required for a class or lecture, and simply clipped to the machine. Not unlike a juke-box playing a record, a mechanism in the projector withdraws each slide in turn, projects it and returns it to the magazine. At the end of the session therefore the set of slides is all ready for use again. The teacher can prepare and store sequences of slides at home instead of struggling with loose transparencies in the classroom.

Most magazine-loading projectors are made for 5 × 5-cm slides and a few for 7 × 7-cm slides; almost all have a motorised slide carrier so that the operator has only to press a button to change to the next slide. This button control can be on a long extension lead so that the teacher can control the presentation when standing in front of the class near the screen. Often another small motor is built into the machine and operated by another switch on the same remote control to move the lens gently backwards and forwards for focusing.

Any classroom where slides are frequently used can therefore be fitted with a projector shelf on the wall at the back of the room, wired for mains and permanently wired to the other end of the room for remote control. The machine is stored in a cupboard but brought immediately into use simply by locating it on the shelf, clipping on the magazine and plugging in the two leads.

Slide projector accessories

Any projector with push-button control can also be operated by an automatic timer accessory—the number of seconds interval between slides being pre-set on a dial. This regular cycle of picture changing is of more use in exhibitions than classroom situations. A more important

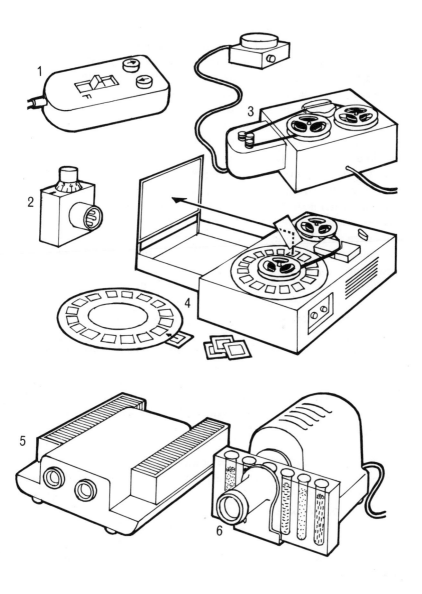

Fig. 1.3. Special purpose slide projectors and accessories. 1, Remote control offering forward and backward progression of magazine, and lens focusing. 2, Automatic timer. 3, Synchronisation attachment to tape recorder, to control projector. 4, Projector with built-in tape recorder (transparencies load into disc magazine). 5, Dual image or stereo projector. 6, Projector designed to show specimens of solutions, etc., in test tubes.

feature is that the projector may be operated by a tape synchroniser (Fig. 1.3). This is a tape recorder which will play back recorded commentary and music and (on a separate inaudible track) cue signals which cause the projector to change slides. Some a.v. slide machines have a cassette tape recorder and speaker built into the same unit as the projector. The teacher can pre-record commentary and cues at home for later use by himself and others, or borrow a complete 'package lecture' from a visual aids library.

For any given size slide the size of the image projected on the screen depends on the distance of the projector and the focal length of its lens. The *shorter* the focal length the *larger* the image (Table 8.2). Therefore a second interchangeable lens (e.g. of shorter focal length than the standard lens) is useful if the machine can only be placed close to the screen in one classroom and a long way back in another. Some projectors have variable focal length or zoom lenses—with these the picture size may be enlarge or reduced to fill the screen without moving the projector.

Occasionally it is helpful to use two slide projectors together, e.g. when making direct comparisons between two images, such as paintings. A few dual projectors are made with twin lamphouses and lenses, and accepting two magazines. Such projectors will show two images side by side, or a single image, or, by simultaneously fading out one slide and fading in the other, allow images on the screen to dissolve smoothly one into the other instead of following each other with the usual brief gap. It is also possible to buy dissolve shutter units to fit over the front of two separate conventional projectors. These devices are further discussed under 'Presentation' on page 287.

Advantages and disadvantages of slide projector

In use, the slide projector has certain advantages and disadvantages, such as:

1. *Almost unlimited sources of material.* Millions of 5 × 5-cm slides are available from producers and libraries (page 316) covering an ever-growing range of subjects. Anything that can be photographed by the teacher himself or by students can easily be made into a colour slide (Chapter 5).

2. *Low cost.* Good projectors cost between £25 and £80, less than a movie projector or epidiascope; 35-mm colour slides can be made for a few pence each.

3. *Student attention.* The brilliance and crispness of the image, and excellence of colour reproduction focuses attention. A large number of images can be presented in a short period of time.

4. *Ability to adapt sequences.* As each slide remains a separate unit, the quantity and order of slides can be adapted to suit the needs of a particular group. This is particularly valuable in revision work, and wherever a subject is taught to several groups at differing levels.

5. *Blackout.* To do full justice to image quality and impact, the projector should really be used in a blacked-out room. The larger the screen the more important this becomes. However, if blackout is poor or non-existent the contemporary slide projector will still give a readable image, but keep the image small. The use of a highly reflective screen or a modern back-projection screen (page 255) permits acceptable projection in a well-lit room.

6. *Mechanical simplicity.* The straightforward manually operated projector is extremely simple to master, with only slide changing, focusing and occasional lamp changing to worry about—a characteristic that may more than compensate for the need to change slides by hand. Good-quality magazine-loading machines are also generally reliable—but may occasionally jam owing to the slide not being returned to the magazine properly. This is something to check when choosing machines; mostly it is avoided by using slide mounts which do not buckle or jam.

7. *Auxiliary uses.* A slide projector can be used as a spotlight for photography and also as a simple enlarger (see Chapter 9). For methods of making black-and-white and colour transparencies for slide projectors, see pages 159–72. A few slide projectors have adaptors for special jobs such as projecting an image of the contents of test tubes (Fig. 1.3) or microscope slides (page 23).

Filmstrip projectors

The filmstrip projector differs from the 5 × 5-cm slide projector in only one important detail—it is intended to project a set of transparencies printed along one continuous length of 35-mm film. Instead of slide carrier the projector has a pair of plastic bobbins or spools (Fig. 1.4). The filmstrip, 35 mm wide and a metre or so long, is loaded completely on to one spool and the leader passed between two spring-loaded glass pressure plates and attached to the second spool. Turning the spool draws the film through the glass sandwich, allowing one frame after another to be projected, until the end of the filmstrip is reached.

Filmstrips have sprocket holes along both edges and carry images in one of two sizes—double or single frame (see Fig. 1.5). All projectors are designed to project 36 × 24-mm double frames although most filmstrips are printed with single-frame pictures. A small metal mask is

19

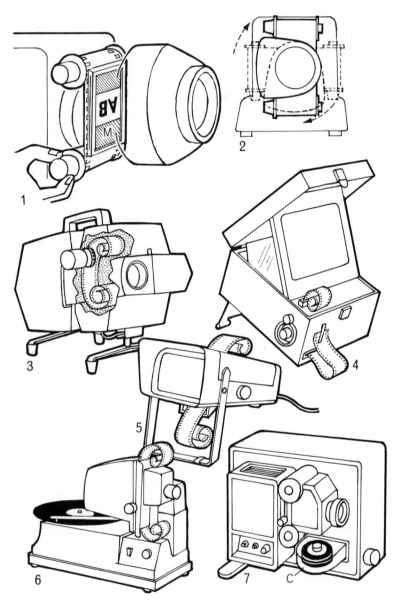

Fig. 1.4. Filmstrip Projector. 1, Simplest method of transporting film. Note single frame mask (M). 2, Lens/carrier rotation to change from horizontal to vertical images. 3, 4, 5, Equipment for operation by students. 4 gives a 6 × 8-in. image on a back-projection screen. 5, Battery-operated hand viewer. 6, Auto sound-linked projector using disc player. 7, Auto projector using loop of magnetic tape in plug-in cassette (C) to provide sound.

inserted to cut down the size of the picture aperture. The whole filmstrip carrier is also swivelled from horizontal to vertical film direction when changing from double to single-frame filmstrips, owing to the different orientation of the image printed on the film (Fig. 1.5).

Filmstrip carriers are interchangeable with 5 × 5-cm slide carriers on some slide projectors; other projectors are made for filmstrips alone. Some filmstrip projectors have a hand-operated or motor-driven claw or sprocket wheel to pull the film along by one frame each time a button is pressed. Again this signal may come from magnetic tape.

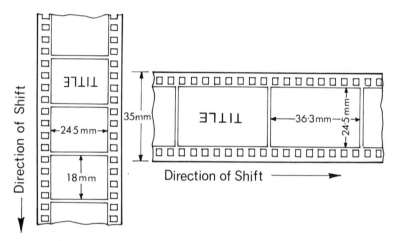

Fig. 1.5. Filmstrips. Dimensions of single and (*right*) double-frame image formats on the film itself. (Most projector gate aperture dimensions are 0·3–0·5 mm less than this.) Title is as seen from the *back* of the projector.

The filmstrip projector is the most widely used item of visual aids equipment in British education, largely because:

1. Complete filmstrips cost about 25p, as they can be produced in quantity at low cost.

2. Filmstrips are extremely compact (100 pictures roll up into one 3·5-cm-diam. tin).

3. Individual pictures cannot be lost or misplaced—the order of presentation never varies and strips are well suited to fully mechanised aids.

4. The projectors themselves are inexpensive, often cheaper than slide machines.

5. They are very simple to handle and can even be operated by young children.

Choosing between filmstrip and slides for particular teaching tasks is further discussed in Chapter 3, and practical preparation of filmstrips on page 187.

When choosing a slide or filmstrip projector, the following points should be checked:

1. Does the machine give an image of suitable *size* (see page 253) when positioned at the most convenient distance from the screen?

2. Will the image be sufficiently *bright*, bearing in mind the lighting conditions in the room and type of screen to be used? Check this by projecting a colour transparency having a rather dark image.

3. Will the lens sharply focus both the centre and corners of the picture at the same time? (Assuming that the film is sandwiched flat between glass and not bowed in a cardboard mount.)

4. Does the slide or strip become uncomfortably hot if projected for more than a few seconds? Overheating can damage colour transparencies and permanently warp film.

5. Is the slide evenly illuminated or is there a bright 'hot spot' at the centre of the screen? Check by first focusing a slide and then removing it from the carrier.

6. Does the design of the machine allow easy operation, if necessary *in the dark*, and is the magazine likely to jam? If so with what type of slide mounts?

7. Is the blower fan acceptably quiet?

8. Is the machine *safe* mechanically and electrically if used by children: their fingers are small.

Evaluation in brief: The slide/filmstrip projector opens as many new windows on the world as the sound projector and TV, but often with less class disruption. A 'must' for teachers interested in making their own visual aids, or at least accumulating a collection of bought transparencies.

Handviewers for filmstrips or slides

Apart from projectors as such, simple individual handviewers (Fig. 1.4) are available for filmstrips or slides. Used together with cassette-loading playback tape recorders these form excellent units for individual study. A strip viewer may advance the film by one frame whenever a lever is pressed; most viewers have a built-in lens and a battery system, or operate through a transformer system from the mains.

Microprojectors

Also known as a projection microscope, the microprojector fulfils a specialised role. It accepts a live or inert specimen on a standard microscope slide, projecting part of it as a greatly enlarged image (e.g. 2000 times) on to the screen. Alternatively it will project a brighter, smaller image at about 300 times magnification on to a tabletop or a built-in back-projection screen (see Fig. 1.6). Room blackout is essential.

Thus a microprojector becomes a valuable tool for group instruction in biology, science and natural history subjects. The machine is essen-

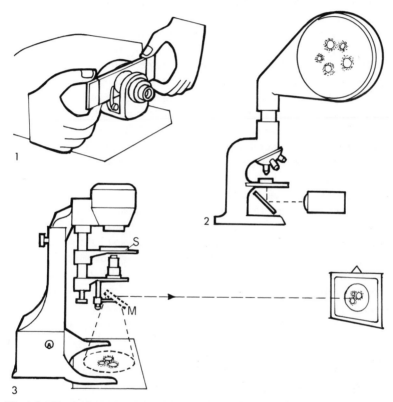

Fig. 1.6. Microprojectors. 1, Special slide stage and lens attached to conventional type projector. 2, Back-projection screen attachment to a microscope. 3, Microprojector for direct (downward) projection on to table-top or, via mirror (M) to wall screen.

tially a high-quality microscope with a compact, high-intensity light source. It may have a range of objective lenses for achieving different degrees of magnification. By dimming the projection lamp and changing lenses the microprojector can also be used for direct viewing—like any other microscope.

A few micro attachments comprising a special slide stage and lens system are made as accessories for conventional 5 × 5-cm slide projectors, and are therefore cheaper than a separate microprojector. However, unless these attachments are well designed it is sometimes difficult to achieve satisfactory image brightness at high magnifications.

Overhead projectors

The overhead projector (OHP) is one of the relatively new items of visual aids hardware. Developed during the Second World War, it really only came into general use in British schools in the 1960s when improvements in design greatly decreased its size and cost. The OHP is now the biggest growth area of the visual aids equipment market.

The machine is intended to project large (250 × 250 mm) transparencies * over a short distance, to give a big screen image. Unlike other projectors, however, the teacher operating it can sit or stand at the front of the class, facing the students. It is possible to write, draw and add coloured areas to the transparency while it is being projected. Thus the projector combines the versatility of the chalkboard with some of the features of the slide projector. It works particularly well with diagrams and line drawings, either pre-drawn or photocopied from sources such as books, on to film. The cost of the machine is approximately equal to that of a roller blackboard.

Mechanically the projector comprises a light box with a horizontal glass stage and containing an intense blower-cooled light source and a condenser or mirror system to concentrate the light upwards (Fig. 1.7). Thirty centimetres or so above the centre of the glass stage, and supported on a column, a lens and a 45° mirror image a silhouette of whatever is placed on the stage, projecting it on to a screen behind the teacher. A 2 × 2-metre screen can be filled from a distance of about 3 m (see Table 1.2). The image is usually focused by moving the lens/mirror unit slightly up or down the column.

Thus the teacher can use the OHP stage as a writing desk without looking at the screen, knowing that whatever he writes with a grease pencil or transparent coloured ink felt pen will appear, greatly enlarged, behind him (see Fig. 1.8). Writing is made on acetate film stretched over the glass—usually a 15-m-long scroll of 25-cm-wide acetate is provided, rolled up on one of two large spools either side of the stage. Drawings and note headings can be prepared in outline form on the scroll and unrolled across the stage as required, then finished and annotated in front of the class.

Even more important, permanent transparent outline maps, graphs

---

* Transparencies used for overhead projectors are also known as 'transparentals', 'projectuals' or 'foils'.

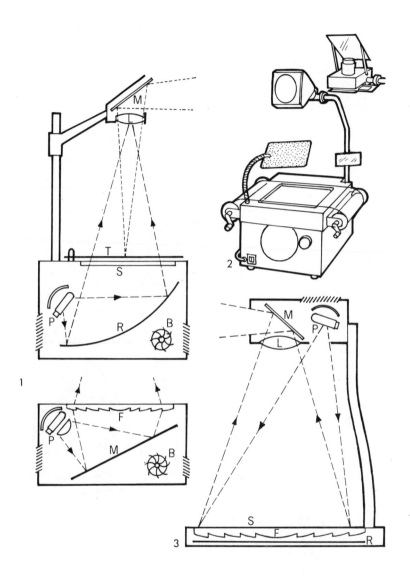

Fig. 1.7. 1, Overhead projector design. P, Projection lamp. R, Reflector. B, Blower. S, Stage. T, Transparency. M, Mirror, and L, Projection lens. More common arrangement (*lower left*) uses plane mirror with fresnel lens (F) above to concentrate light up to projection lens. 2, General layout, showing scroll attachment, teacher's anti-glare visor and small driving mirror to check projected image behind him. Also alternative head unit for projecting 5 × 5-cm slides. 3, An OHP model using a lamp in the head and fresnel lens backed by highly reflective surface (R). This machine folds up into briefcase form.

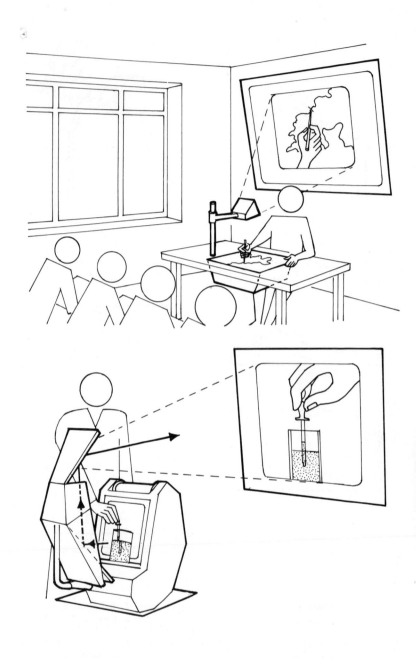

Fig. 1.8. Overhead projector. *Top:* General arrangement in formal classroom. *Bottom:* OHP tilted and fitted with accessory mirrors to allow liquids, etc., to be imaged.

and copies of documents can be prepared within minutes on a heat copier or made photographically from books and other sources. They are also published commercially. Coloured areas or lettering on a separate film sheet can be overlaid on these basic diagrams at the point in the lesson where the information is introduced. In theory, there is no limit to the number of films that can be overlaid on each other to build up information, a piece at a time. In practice, however, the contrast of the image begins to suffer after five or six overlays.

Transparent Perspex models (e.g. gearwheels) can be moved about on the OHP stage to show relationships in the teaching of mechanics,

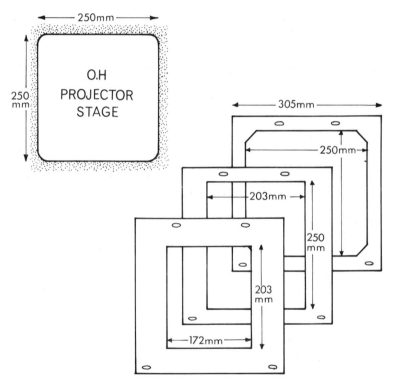

Fig. 1.9. Aperture dimensions of the most commonly used OHP transparency mounts.

geometry, etc. Similarly, crystals can be shown growing, iron filings tracing the paths of magnetic forces, and skeletons of snakes, lizards, etc., be enlarged as giant silhouettes on the screen or chalkboard. A shallow glass dish of water laid on the stage can be used to show the action of wave-fronts in optics (Fig. 1.10), and parts of diagrams incorporating bits of polarising filter can be made to appear to move or change colour when a polarising filter is rotated under the lens (see motion simulation, page 242). One model of the overhead projector (Fig. 1.8) allows vertical objects such as liquids in open test tubes to be imaged. Another has an adaptor to allow projection of 5 × 5-cm slides. Two further OHP accessories deserve mention. A smoky plastic visor on a flexible arm can be used to shade the teacher's eyes from the

Fig. 1.10. Some ways of utilising the overhead projector stage. 1, Pre-written information on scroll. 2, Diagrams with detail added by overlays (in any order). 3, Transparent plastic models. 4, Water in a flat-bottomed glass dish—ripples and other waveforms project as dark lines. 5, Single transparency shown one section at a time using 'revelation masks'. 6, Overdrawing additional information on a sheet of acetate laid over an existing transparency, without damaging this base image. See also polarising technique, Fig. 7.16.

glare of the stage (more necessary on some models than others). Also a small driving mirror clipped to the OHP lens support post allows a quick check on what is appearing on the screen, without having to turn around.

Advantages and disadvantages of overhead projector

The main advantages and disadvantages of the overhead projector in practical terms are as follows:

1. *No break in communication.* The teacher continues to make visual contact with the class in the normal way. The transition from verbal discussion to projected visual information and back again is an even less conscious disruption than the use of the chalkboard.

2. *No blacking out.* The projected image is bright enough to be seen clearly in a normally lit classroom. Only when strong daylight is directly reaching the screen or a particularly dark OHP transparency is being projected will shading of the screen be necessary.

3. *Mechanical simplicity.* There is little to adjust other than the focusing and tilt of the head unit.

4. *Visual appeal.* Effectively used, the equipment gives a more dynamic image than a slide or filmstrip projector. The progressive disclosure of one part of a diagram at a time, the sudden addition of colour to key areas and introduction of written annotations by prepared overlay, along with the teacher's easy emphasis of detail by pen or pointer as he speaks, can all be made positive factors in holding students' attention.

5. *Versatility.* The OHP can be used to project images from transparent film, transparent models, silhouettes of opaque objects, ripple tanks and test tubes. It can even be used in making OHP transparencies (see Fig. 4.15).

6. *Skill in use.* Although the projector is superficially easy to use, some practice is essential, such as learning how to make on-the-spot handwriting of appropriate size and legibility. The projected image itself cannot be constantly checked unless the teacher uses a mirror.

7. *Preparation.* The type of illumination system used tends to make any part of a transparency which *diffuses* the light appear black on the screen. Transparencies must therefore be prepared on film; even the

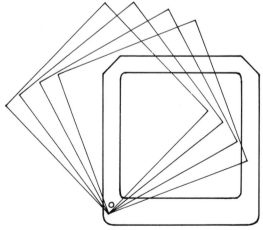

Fig. 1.11. OHP transparency with base image mounted in card frame, and four pivoting overlays.

thinnest paper acts as if opaque. Coloured lines or areas must be made with spirit ink, clear dye or pieces of stick-on transparent tint. Coloured grease pencilling (and even faint scratches on the acetate) project as if black in most machines.

When choosing an overhead projector the following features should be checked:

1. Does the machine deliver an image which is sufficiently large, bright, and evenly illuminated when used under the limitations of actual room conditions?

2. Does the lens resolve detail sharply enough for lettering to be read clearly—out to the edges of the image? Do odd patches of unexpected colour appear?

3. Does the stage grow hot (rather than warm) when the machine has been on for a few minutes? This can cause OHP transparencies to buckle and parts then to project as out of focus and distorted. Transfer lettering will detach itself from acetate and writing in spirit ink dries too quickly and cracks. Grease pencil writing melts.

4. Does the illumination from the light box glare uncomfortably into your eyes when using the machine? A visor may be essential.

5. Does the fan create a nuisance by the volume and pitch of the noise it makes? Does its vibration cause image shake on the screen?

6. Can the lamp be changed quickly and easily if it fails in the middle of a lecture? (Some machines have a standby lamp which can be instantly switched in as replacement.)

7. Is the mirror/lens unit high enough to allow room for manipulation of hinged overlays on the stage?

Teaching evaluation in brief: A flexible, useful tool which, if not the magical replacement for the chalkboard, is worthy of experiment by every teacher whatever his subject. Confidence in its future is shown by the number of publishers now issuing OHP transparencies.

Making OHP transparencies and overlays by photography and document-copying devices is described on pages 172–81.

Episcopes (or opaque projectors)

So far, all the projectors described have been designed to project from *transparent* images on film or glass. The episcope projects images direct from books, drawings and from photographs on paper, and most other opaque-based originals. It is one of the older visual aids devices and has long had a rather bad reputation for the dimness of the image it produces (see image brightness comparisons, Table 1.1).

The episcope is set up near the middle of the classroom and forms images on a wall screen. The book or document is usually placed face

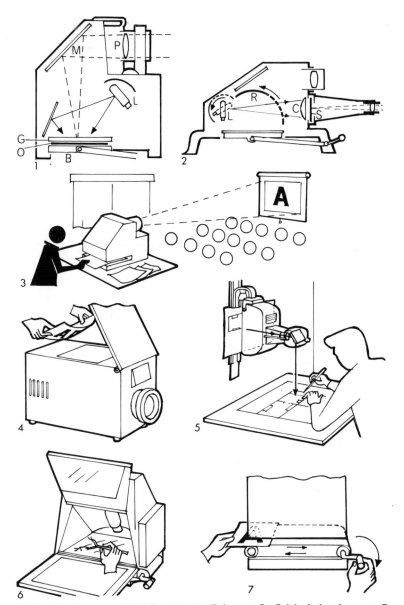

Fig. 1.12. Episcopes and Epidiascopes. 1, Episcope. O, Original drawing, etc. B, Backing plate (spring-loaded). G, Glass top plate. L, Lamp. M, Main mirror. P, Projection lens. 2, Epidiascope, shown set for showing slides (dia-positives). R, Rotating mask. C, Condenser lens. S, Slide. 3, Classroom arrangement, note blackout. 4, Portable episcope. 5, Wall-mounted episcope. 6, Some episcopes give easy access to the *top* surface of the glass window, allowing simple three-dimension objects to be imaged. 7, Quick conveyor method of feeding and removing material.

31

up under a horizontal glass window near the base of the machine (Fig. 1.12). Here it is brilliantly illuminated by a lamp or lamps enclosed inside the projector, the light reflected from the page being received by an internal 45° mirror and lens at the top of the episcope, and focused to form a sharp image on the screen.

Some machines have a slide carrier and second lens system located at the front of the unit; by covering the episcope lens and adjusting the lamp the machine is converted into a slide/filmstrip projector. (Projectors serving this dual function are known as epidiascopes.)

Advantages and disadvantages of episcope

The main advantages and disadvantages of the episcope in practical terms are as follows:

1. *Immediacy.* Material seldom has to be specially prepared. The episcope works directly from the teacher's books, maps, magazine articles, stamps, photographic prints in black and white and colour. Even coins and other fairly flat subjects such as leaves and butterflies can be projected. However, subjects do tend to grow hot and this restricts its use for living things.

2. *Limited visual impact.* Its weak light output (inherent in a system using illumination reflected from the original picture material) means that the image is much dimmer than filmstrip and slide projectors. You should not try to fill a large screen with this machine. A smaller image is always brighter.

3. *Blackout.* Owing to the weak light output, a good classroom blackout is essential, particularly if finest detail and colour is to be clearly observed.

4. *Limited acceptance.* The largest area of original material the machine will project at one time is limited by the dimensions of the window—usually 250-mm square. Larger originals (e.g. maps) may have to be projected one section at a time.

5. *Auxiliary uses.* The episcope serves the important additional function of allowing a drawn design or other piece of artwork to be enlarged or reduced in size, simply by projecting it at the required size and then tracing over the image by hand, or using some form of photographic enlarging paper. When choosing a machine try to pick one which allows the lens to focus out sufficiently to give same-size images or reductions—only a few makes do. An episcope is also useful for previewing the projected appearance of diagrams destined to be made into slides and OHP transparencies, e.g. is it too overloaded with data for clear comprehension?

Teaching evaluation in brief: The episcope is the sort of machine which sounds perfect in theory but is often disappointing in practical performance. It is benefiting from developments in new light sources and applied optics, but currently much of its function has been taken over by the more effective overhead projector. In many schools and teachers' centres it is now used primarily to alter the size of drawn artwork.

EQUIPMENT FOR PROJECTING MOVING IMAGES

If a series of slightly dissimilar still pictures is rapidly presented to the eye, the individual pictures are seen as one continuous image with dissimilar bits moving. When pictures are presented at slow rates the eye is conscious of their individual character but, because the human eye gives slight persistence of vision after an image has been removed, pictures presented faster than about 18 per sec blend into an apparently continuous image with a barely perceptible background flicker. Faster rates give progressively less flicker. The function of a moving film projector is therefore to project a long series of still pictures at a rate sufficiently fast to utilise this persistence of vision effect, but not so fast that it is ruinously expensive in film. The way this job is performed is worth understanding, for it has a direct bearing on the proper handling of the machine.

Motion picture film projector
Optically a motion picture projector is built in the same way as a slide projector, but instead of the slide carrier a special mechanism feeds film one frame after another in quick succession—and holds each one quite still for the brief instant it is projected.

As Fig. 1.13 shows, powerful illumination from a blower-cooled lamp passes through a heat filter and condenser lenses which concentrate it through a rectangular aperture in polished metal guides called the film *gate*. The gate aperture coincides with one frame of film, and it is this frame which is imaged by the projector lens on to a distant screen. A metal claw device, also in the gate, engages in the film perforation holes and pulls the film down in jerks, frame by frame. Each frame is left stationary for a moment while the claw retracts, rises and re-engages with perforations higher up, ready for the next pull-down. Linked up with the claw a little disc with a cut out sector rotates across the light beam and blocks the illumination while the film is moved, so that only *stationary* frames are projected on the screen.

The only other mechanical problem is delivering and collecting film from the gate at a rate fast enough to keep pace with the claw. This is

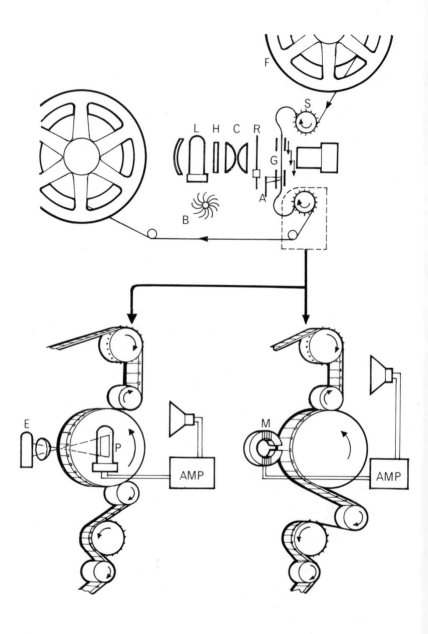

Fig. 1.13. Motion picture projector layout. L, Main lamp. B, Blower. H, Heat filter. C, Condensers. R, Rotary shutter. G, Gate with aperture. A, Claw. S, Sprockets. F, Feed spool. Sound replay may be optical (*bottom left*) or magnetic (*bottom right*). E, Excitor lamp. P, Photo-cell. M, Magnetic play head.

done by fitting motor-driven sprockets above and below the gate to draw film smoothly off a top feed spool and supply it equally evenly to a power-driven take-up spool below.

As the claw gives *intermittent* movement to the film and the sprockets impart *continuous* movement, the film is made to form loops before and after the gate to absorb these differences. The standard film speed for silent film projectors is now 18 frames per sec (fps) (recently changed from an older standard of 16 fps). Sound films are projected at 24 fps to obtain sound of adequate quality.

Reproducing and recording sound on film

Sound can be reproduced from film in one of two ways—from an optical or a magnetic soundtrack.

Film with an optical soundtrack has a strip along one edge carrying a photographic image of light and dark areas (Fig. 1.14). To reproduce sound from this track the projector must have a reading head between the lower sprocket and take-up spool (Fig. 1.13) containing a small 'exciter' lamp behind a slot, which directs light through the track and on to a light-sensitive valve known as a photo-electric cell. As the moving film allows more or less light to reach the cell, electrical signals are set up which are played through the amplifier and loudspeaker.

Film having a magnetic sound track carries a narrow strip of ferrous oxide (as used on recording tapes) along one or both of its edges. On the projector a magnetic pick-up head in a position similar to an optical head 'reads' the film passing over it, and reproduces the recording through an amplifier and loudspeaker system; this part of the projector is virtually a tape playback machine. Most magnetic sound projectors fulfil the complete function of a tape recorder and allow sound to be recorded as well as played back. A microphone or gramophone turntable is plugged into the amplifier and the magnetic head then records on the striped film. This latter feature is one of the great attractions of magnetic sound projectors—sound can be added to films with ease (page 232).

Optical tracks were the earliest of the two methods of putting sound on film. Sound reproduction is so poor at a film speed of 18 fps that 24 fps is considered the minimum to allow a reasonable frequency range. Even then quality is inferior to a magnetic track. Optical sound projectors cannot be used for recording sound—the making of optical soundtracks is highly complicated and certainly beyond the scope of the teacher film-maker.

Why, then, have optical sound projectors? For many years optical

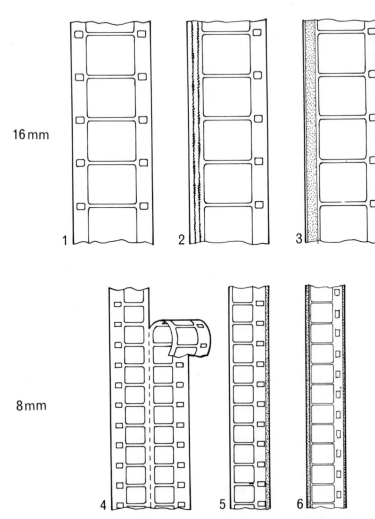

16mm

8mm

Fig. 1.14. Movie film sizes. 1, 16-mm silent. 2, 16-mm optical sound. 3, 16-mm with magnetic sound stripe. 4, Standard 8-mm double run. The (16-mm) camera film is split after processing. 5, Standard 8-mm with magnetic sound stripe. 6, Super 8-mm (magnetic sound). Note the balancing stripe in 3 and 6. 16-mm double perforated film can be run on a sound projector (amplifier switched off). It can be useful for special film techniques, Fig. 7.14.

sound recording was the only way to put sound on film; it is also still the cheapest and most convenient system whenever a large number of copies of a film are being issued. Consequently the bulk of films in film libraries have optical tracks. Libraries are also concerned at the possibility of accidental erasure of a magnetic track by a careless projectionist switching to 'record' (although most magnetic projectors have a special lock to guard against careless switching).

As most of the films put through a school projector are likely to be from library sources the provision of an optical head remains important. Several 16-mm sound projectors are fitted with both types of sound head, and can be switched from one to the other with ease.

Movie film sizes

Projectors are made for film widths of 70 mm, 35 mm, 16 mm, 9·5 mm and 8 mm. The 70-mm and 35-mm projectors are used in the cinema industry and are restricted to permanent installations such as theatres. The 9·5-mm gauge, popular in the past, is becoming disused in favour of other gauges, and materials are now very restricted. This leaves only 16 mm and 8 mm, the latter being currently available in Standard-8 and Super-8 forms, Fig. 1.14.

Standard-8, which dates from the 1930s, is derived from cut-down 16 mm. The 16-mm-wide film is exposed down one-half of its width and then run through the camera again to expose the other half in the opposite direction. After processing, the film is slit down the middle and joined end to end.

However, the popularity of narrow-gauge films led to a desire to improve image quality and get more light on to the screen without having to widen the film. Since 1967 a redesigned form of 8-mm film has come into use under the name of Super-8. The film is 8 mm in width and each frame is about 50% bigger in area than the double-8 frame. The result is sharper, brighter pictures on the screen because less enlargement is needed and more light can be concentrated through the larger gate aperture. But to achieve this, sprocket hole shape and separation has been changed so that *Super-8 cannot be projected on a Standard-8 projector, and vice versa.* For some years it will be possible to buy conversion kits to allow Standard-8 projectors to run the new film; a few dual-gauge machines are available.

Some care is needed in threading both 16-mm and 8-mm projectors with film (particularly when surrounded by young critics longing to point out that a picture is upside down, backwards or stationary and scorching in the middle). Details vary with individual projectors, but the main points to watch appear in Appendix VIII. Manufacturers are acutely conscious of the fact that most people find film-threading fiddling, and self-threading and cassette-loaded projectors are now common.

Film for projection comes in spools of various capacities. The standard sizes for the various gauges and the running times of the film they

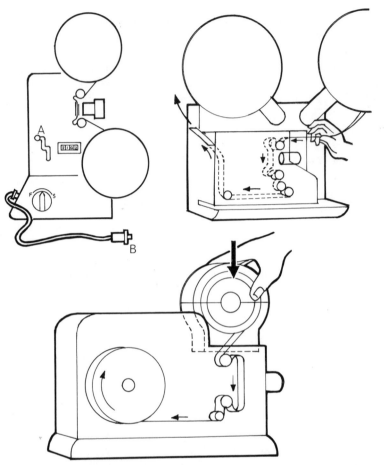

Fig. 1.15. Movie projector variations. *Top left:* Analytical 16-mm projector with (A) multi-speed gear box and (B) remote control for single frame hold. *Top right:* 'Feed in' automatic threading projector. *Bottom:* Cassette (cartridge)-loading projector. The film is automatically withdrawn and rewound back into the cassette after showing.

contain are shown in Fig. 1.16. All but the cheapest movie projectors are today equipped with a means of using the motor to rewind film back on to the feed spool at the end of the film. Like cleaning the chalkboard this is important teaching practice unless the film library specifically requests return of film in an unwound state.

Some of the more expensive projectors offer features such as ability to stop the film transport and so hold the machine projecting a single frame. Similarly some projectors will project film in reverse direction at the touch of a switch. Neither facility is needed for more than a tiny percentage of presentations, because subjects justifying this sort of

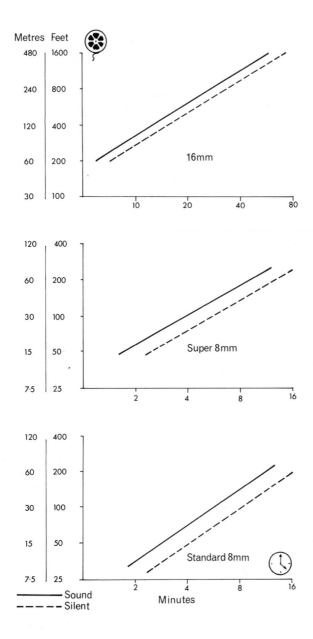

Fig. 1.16. Running times for movie film at sound (24 fps) and silent (18 fps) speeds.

analysis are usually more effective if presented on loop films (see below) or on filmstrips. One specialised 16-mm silent projector (Fig. 1.15) allows film to be shown at various controlled speeds down to 2 fps, and has frame counters to allow accurate measurement from filmed records of subjects such as traffic flow, and animal locomotion.

Automatic threading is perhaps the most time-saving refinement in sound projector design. Some machines, for example, just require the leading end of the film to be fed into a slot. When the motor is started film is drawn correctly past sprockets, claws and sound drum, and reappears at the back of the machine ready for attachment to the take-up spool (Fig. 1.15). However, on some models once the film is safely in the projection path it is fiddling trying to get it out again until the whole film has been run. This may be a hurdle to the active use of film, i.e. selecting only one or two sequences relevant to the subject under study. Other 'self-threader' machines have an open slot path into which the film is pushed just like loading a domestic tape recorder. Mid film unlacing is then possible. This projector may also offer rapid 'in path' rewinding—again like a tape recorder.

Another development, now in use for 8 mm, is to use film enclosed in cartridges and never touched by hand. The cartridge is just placed in a recess in the front of the projector; mechanism in the projector then withdraws the film, threads it to a built-in take-up spool, and returns it into the cartridge after presentation.

Motion picture replay through television
Another way of showing motion pictures is by means of a special playback machine which is simply plugged direct into the aerial socket of the school's television receiver, whereupon the film appears as if a TV programme. Several standard receivers can be fed simultaneously (Fig. 1.17). One such system—Electronic Video Reproduction (EVR)—converts photographic images on special 8·75-mm unperforated film into electronic signals, 60 min of material occupying a 7-in.-dia EVR telecartridge. Sound is recorded on magnetic stripe. Like enclosed cartridges for 8 mm, the EVR film requires no threading and remains untouched by hand.

An important advantage over normal movie film, EVR film moves continuously through the teleplayer. This, plus its electronic image scanning, makes it easy to skip, repeat, run action at various speeds, and hold single frames, via controls like a tape recorder. The tele-cartridges are also cheaper than movie film giving equivalent screen time and tend to have a longer life. The system is well suited to private study as well as group viewing.

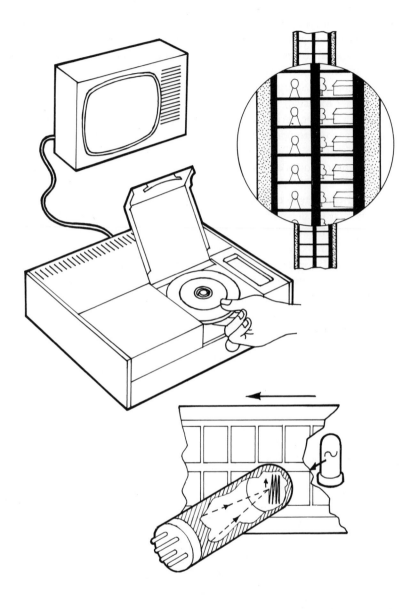

Fig. 1.17. EVR. *Centre:* Auto-threading telecartridge being placed in player which feeds ordinary TV set. 8·75-mm EVR film (*top right*) carries two rows of images, and two magnetic tracks. *Bottom:* Film moves continuously past light source, and is scanned by electronic tube similar to TV camera tube.

Rival new systems include video-discs—thin vinyl discs looking like records and played on a 1500 rpm turntable supplying a TV set. Less flexible in usage, programmes are very low cost and the system is more likely to appeal to the popular entertainment market.

Yet another source of TV images is the video (VTR) magnetic tape recorder/player. Several of these are on the market, using $\frac{1}{2}$ in., or $\frac{1}{4}$ in. tape (less expensive). VTR machines replay commercially produced tapes with similar vari-speed, single frame facility as EVR. In addition one can record transmitted (e.g. Schools TV) programmes and self-prepared material. Tapes can be wiped and re-used. Table 1.1 summarises these modes of TV presentation.

The loop (or single concept) film projector

Whenever it is beneficial to demonstrate a simple sequence several times (e.g. tennis strokes, use of a pipette in chemistry or some handicraft skill) a short loop of film has teaching value. In its simplest form this can just be several feet of film, sufficient to contain one or more cycles of the action, with its two ends spliced together and allowed to

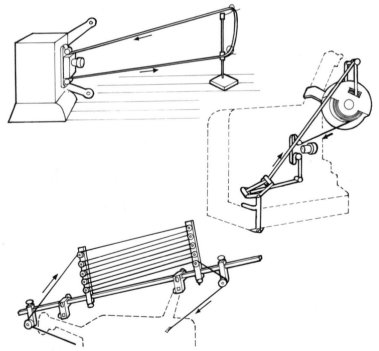

Fig. 1.18. Loop attachments for conventional projectors. The multi-pulley arrangement is suitable only for short lengths, owing to the build-up of friction.

run continuously through an ordinary projector. Of course some means must also be provided for supporting the main body of film without having it flop into the light beam or scratching (Fig. 1.18).

The disadvantage of this method is the time and trouble required to set up the equipment just for a minute or so of illustration. Within the last five years manufacturers have designed new 8-mm projectors specifically for loop film. The film is formed into a loose coil (Fig. 1.19)

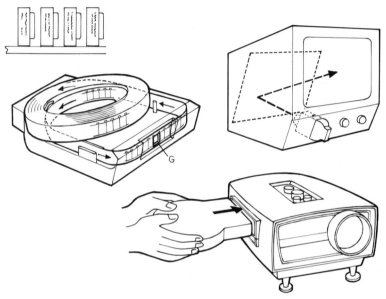

Fig. 1.19. 8-mm loop cassette and projectors. *Left:* Transparent plastic container, open only at the gate (G). Underside of cassette behind gate is recessed—allowing mirror system in projector to rear illuminate film frame in the gate, which is then projected by a lens in front. *Top right:* Back-projection machine. *Bottom right:* Front-projection machine (this one accepts large Technicolor 8-in. diameter cassettes).

and is drawn from inside the coil and returned to its perimeter. Thus, the whole coil can be permanently housed in a plastic cassette. The small section of film appearing in the gate of the cassette automatically engages with the projector transport mechanism and illumination system so that one has only to insert the cassette into the machine and switch on, and the film will run continuously until switched off again. A loop projector is therefore simple to use, even for the most untechnically minded.

Although originally made for Standard-8, most loop projectors today are designed for Super-8 film, the smallest standardised cassettes containing any length of film up to about five minutes cycling time.

TABLE 1.1
Summary—Equipment for displaying images by projection

Equipment	Main teaching characteristic	Relative image brightness*	Skill needed to use	Portability	Availability of commercial software	Ease of preparing own software	Safe for children to handle alone
Slide projector	Ease of adapting pic sequences High image quality	Blackout not essential	Slight	Very portable	Extremely wide range	Very easy	Yes (non-auto models)
Film strip projector	Low cost of images Fixed sequences —easy to link with audio aid	Blackout not essential	None	Very portable	Extremely wide range	Fairly difficult	Yes
Handviewer for slide/strip	As above, applied to individual study	Normal lighting	None	Extreme portability	Extremely wide range	Fairly difficult	Yes
Micro-projector	Specialist applications—group study of micro phenomenom	Preferably blackout	Moderate	Fairly portable	Limited	Microscope specimens	Older children
Overhead projector	As versatile as chalkboard. Teacher facing class, maintains communication	Usually blackout unnecessary	Slight	Very portable	Moderate	Very easy	Yes
Episcope	No special preparation of software	Poor, blackout important	None	Not very portable			Yes
Movie sound projector	Complete 'package'. Movement, realism	Preferably some blackout	Moderate	Not very portable	Extremely wide range	Expensive	No
Loop projector	Repetitive action. Links easily with exposition, or for individual study	Intended for small group viewing small screen usually requires no blackout	None	Very portable	Moderate	Fairly easy	Yes
VTR video cassettes	As film, but easier selection, stop frame, etc		Slight		Growing	Fairly easy (incl. taping of broadcasts)	Older children
EVR video cassettes	As VTR but second image track allows optional 'cross-cutting' Suitable individuals as well as groups	(TV set blackout unnecessary)	None	Together with TV set, not very portable	Growing fast	Impossible	Older children
Video-discs	As (short) films but also easy stop-frame and place finding		Slight		Still prototype stage	Impossible	Older children

* Are against some projected image size

Several machines accept magnetic-striped sound loop films. (There are, however, distinct advantages in having *silent* single concept loops so that the teacher can use the machine to illustrate what *he* is saying.) An extensive range of commercially made loops is now available; alternatively several firms (page 320) offer a service for sealing teachers' own Super-8 films into loop cassettes.

The projected image is either thrown on to a separate screen or some models project on to a back-projection screen forming part of the same unit—and looking rather like a TV receiver. Loop projectors are essentially designed for small group viewing. They will adequately illuminate a 50-cm-wide image in competition with normal room lighting but shaded from direct daylight.

One form of continuous loop sound projector (the Technicolor 1000) uses enlarged cartridges holding up to 29 min of film. Sound is reproduced from an *optical* soundtrack on the film, thus reducing film printing costs. This type of equipment therefore merges the functions of loop projector and conventional sound film projector—offering the convenience of the former with the breadth of material of the latter.

The right film projector for the job

The 16-mm optical sound projector meets the first priority of most schools—namely the ability to draw on thousands of 16-mm titles in National and county film libraries, commercial libraries and government institutions, industry and television organisations (page 316). It can be used for audiences of all sizes. A reliable self-threading model is most likely to encourage the non-technically minded user. Unfortunately this type of equipment is also the most expensive.

An 8-mm loop projector is a more flexible personalised visual aids machine, complementing the 16-mm projector as the slide projector complements the filmstrip. There are few areas of teaching where it cannot be cued in to lucidly demonstrate what the teacher is explaining.

Equally the loop projector can be used by an individual as a teaching or revising machine. Teachers and learners are able to prepare their own mute or magnetic sound visual material for this projector cheaply, using a Super-8 cine camera (page 218).

When choosing a film projector, the following features should be checked:

1. Is it easy to thread and operate (including rewinding)?

2. Is the image bright enough for use in a room with little or no blackout?

3. If so, is the image big enough for the size of the group, and the probable projector-to-screen distance (see Table 8.1).

4. Does it give a steady, well-resolved image, and is the mechanical noise unobtrusive?

5. Is plenty of library film material available to fit the machine?

6. Is it easy to move around from one room to another, and is it safe mechanically and electrically?

Film splicers and other cine camera accessories are discussed on page 100.

Screens

Projection screens for still and cine projectors are divided into two main types—translucent materials for rear projection and opaque

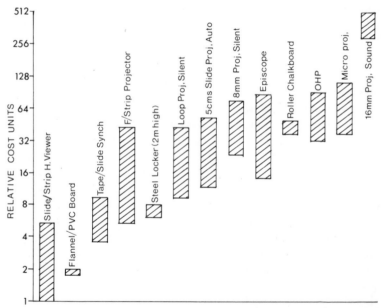

Table 1.2. Capital cost of equipment. Two items of standard school furniture have been included here to allow closer comparison of prices.

materials for front projection. Front-projection screens are made with either a plastic, glass-beaded or other highly directional reflective surface; a silver aluminised surface; or a matt white surface. All these materials can be bought as complete made-up screens, edge masked and ready for hanging, or as raw material for making up.

The main requirement of a screen in a teaching situation is that it should provide the brightest possible picture to the whole class under minimal conditions of room blackout. Unlike some industrial training situations it is seldom practical for a school to have a light-tight room fully laid out for visual aids presentation—the aid must come into the ordinary classroom.

Choice, positioning and size of screens are intimately related to size and shape of room, type of aid and other aspects of presentation, and will all be considered together in Chapter 8, page 250.

SIMPLE EQUIPMENT FOR DISPLAYS NOT INVOLVING PROJECTION

Under this heading come a great miscellany of items, from chalk-boards to three-dimensional models. Here we are concerned with the types of display equipment with which photographic images can be used; as Fig. 1.20 shows, all the equipment is physically very simple.

Flannelgraph (also known as feltboard or flannelboard)

A method of display based on the fact that two pieces of long-fibred material such as felt or flannel will cling to each other. A large piece of baize or flannelette is stretched over a vertical board (e.g. 1·5-cm block-board) and pasted to it or folded and pinned behind. When shapes and symbols cut out in similar material are pressed on to the surface of the flannelboard they adhere there until peeled off again. Thus components in a display can instantly be added or subtracted as a session proceeds. Even more important, drawings and photographs on paper can be individually pasted on to lint backing or griddled flock paper, which allows them to cling to the flannelboard too. It is essential to keep flannelgraph materials free from dust and folds as they then lose their already slight adhesion and keep falling off the board.

Hook and loop (teazlegraph)

A support system similar to the flannelgraph but using pieces of nylon carrying thousands of nylon hooks as the artwork backing. These adhere to a stretched sheet covered with minute nylon loops.

Plastograph

Similar to the flannelgraph but based on the adhesion between thin shiny plastic sheeting. The board can be anything with a smooth glossy

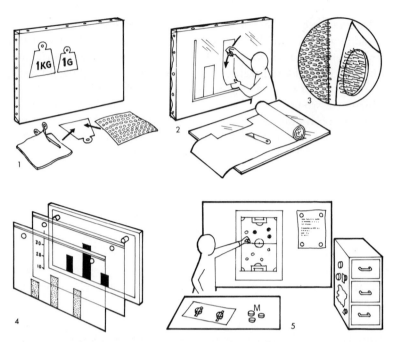

Fig. 1.20. Non-projection display devices. 1, Flannelgraph. Drawing made on paper has flannel sheet or pad attached to rear surface. Board is felt-covered. 2, Plastograph, uses thin PVC in various colours. Board is covered in black PVC. 3, Magnified detail of hook and loop attachment system, board is covered with loops. 4, A compare board. Overlays drawn on thick plastic, hung over base paper drawing. 5, Magnetic board. Small disc magnets (M) cling to steel board—they can be attached to back of paper cut-outs (note storage on metal filing cabinet).

surface, or a background sheet of heavy-gauge PVC of an appropriate colour. Photographs and other paper illustrations can be prepared by sticking several little pads of sheet PVC on the backs. The illustrations can then be placed on the board using a smoothing action, and are peeled off again and returned to acetate storage sheets when not required. Plastograph board and materials must be kept free from dust and scratches.

Magnetic board

Again similar to the flannelgraph, but offering stronger adhesion and able to support heavier illustrative material. The board is essentially a flat steel sheet, painted or covered with coloured plastic. Small flat disc magnets or plastic magnetic strip are stuck on the back of photographs, drawings, etc., making them adhere to the board. More crudely, material can just be clipped to the board *under* magnets. Many magnetic boards do double duty as plastograph or chalkboards, or (if painted white) projection screens.

Evaluation in brief: Flannel/plastic/magnetic boards are cheap and versatile, and although materials have to be prepared they can be as simple as hand-lettered pieces of card. Ideal for the demonstrative method of teaching. Symbols and headings can be rapidly smoothed on to the board as points are made, the teacher hardly turning from the class—an excellent way to summarise a lecture. These aids can be effective with quite large audiences, provided material is drawn boldly enough. Equally they can be used to encourage student involvement in junior school activities, such as language classes.

Always ensure that the adhesive system is working reliably. If bits of display keep falling off, using these aids swiftly dissolves into a music hall act.

Bulletin boards and wallcharts
Most classrooms and corridors have room for display (bulletin) boards and wallcharts. A further extension is a light box containing strip tubes or a window over which tracing paper or opaque plastic may be fitted for displaying transparencies. A great range of wallcharts and posters is available commercially, but often it is necessary for teachers and students to design and make up their own. Small-scale designs can be blown up to full size using an episcope or overhead projector, then tracing on to poster-size paper.

Photographic methods of making pictures on paper or film large enough for flannel/plastic/magnetic or general display boards are described in Chapters 4 and 5.

Models
The importance of models in giving students three-dimensional realism in the concept of an object or environment is well known. The modelling material—usually card or wood—can be made to appear more detailed and realistic when covered with a photographic print showing suitably scaled textures, building façades, control panels, people, interior detail of cutaway models and so on. Prints can form authentic-looking panoramic backgrounds to bought or home-made models. Photography can also be used as a visual notebook when on a field survey of a subject for a future scale model (page 275).

49

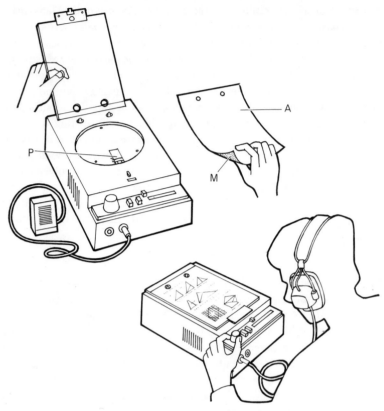

Fig. 1.21. A teaching machine consisting of a special magnetic recorder/replayer with pick-up head mounted in rotating turntable (P). Machine uses ordinary paper (A) rear-coated with magnetic zinc oxide (M). Head follows path like gramophone record, replaying several minutes of teacher's recording. The paper top surface can receive images by any form of duplicator.

Teaching machines

A wide range of teaching machines have been marketed during the past ten years, and many have failed to be adopted. Of the others some offer various opportunities in the use of visual images. The Synchrofax Audio Page (Fig. 1.21), for example, uses sheets of paper coated on the reverse side with a magnetic recording surface. The front surface can be printed upon using a duplicator, or can be used as a mount for cut-out drawings or photographs.

Comparative costs

It is difficult to quote all-important capital cost of equipment in a book, owing to rapid increases in prices which renders the text out of date before it appears. Table 1.2 attempts to show *relative* prices both in terms of visual aids equipment and schoolroom furniture. These should hold good for most comparative purposes. A similar table relating the cost of preparation hardware appears on page 77.

2. Equipment for preparing images

So FAR visual aids equipment has been described which might be used in conjunction with software either commercially marketed or prepared by the teacher himself. Taking self-help a stage further it would be helpful to look at equipment for the actual making of slides and filmstrips, movies and OHP transparencies for projection, or paper prints for hand-outs and displays. The important items here are the document copier and the duplicator, the photographic camera (still and movie) and the enlarger. Later these will be used for specific preparation jobs, described in detail in Chapters 4–6.

EQUIPMENT FOR COPYING AND DUPLICATING DOCUMENTS

The modern office copying machine and the duplicator are tools for producing one or a modest run of reproductions of documents of the same size as the originals. In this role they are successors to the camera and the printing press, and have acquired their own genetic title—reprography. Reprographic equipment enables us to choose or prepare a diagram, graph, table, piece of typescript, etc. (perhaps in a book or cut from a magazine or newspaper), and run off a paper print for the bulletin board, a transparency for the overhead projector or several dozen copies for handing out to students.

The equipment is—or should be—quick and simple to use, able to reproduce anything, but without being cripplingly expensive to buy or to run. The fact that so many varied machines are on the market proves the point that no one piece of equipment meets all these requirements. Sales claims understandably veil product deficiencies and we, the consumers, sometimes purchase as much by confusion as informed choice.

The description of each machine in this chapter begins with a pragmatic explanation of how the process it utilises works. This in turn explains the advantages and limitations of practical performance. Comparisons—particularly in terms of the types of aid a machine can or cannot prepare—form our main theme.

Reprographic terminology

A full glossary of technical terms appears on page 301, but five terms deserve special mention because they will crop up frequently here. A *copier* is generally accepted to mean a machine into which the original document and sensitive material is fed (by hand) each time a copy is required. A *duplicator* contains a master, or stencil, or other form of printing plate brought repeatedly into contact with sheets of ordinary paper automatically fed into the machine. (A few hybrids exist such as certain electrostatic—Xerox—copiers which retain an original document within the machine and issue a pre-set number of copies automatically.) Most copiers can produce a master for use on a duplicator, and this combined use is usually the quickest and cheapest arrangement when a number of hand-outs are needed from a printed document.

Material for copying or duplicating often has solid areas of black (or colour) and clear areas of white. Printed or typed text, maps and pen sketches all fall into this category, to which the term *line* original is given. Actual photographs, paintings and drawings containing a range of subtle tones between black and white are known as *continuous-tone* originals. The latter are less easy to reproduce acceptably because most copying and duplicating processes are designed to give contrasty results which, although enhancing quality when line copying, reproduce continuous tones with a harsh 'soot-and-whitewash' effect.

Photographic illustrations appearing in books, brochures, magazines, newspapers, etc., are *screened*, i.e. when closely examined are found to be made up of dots of solid black (or colour) in various sizes. If the dots are large enough to be easily distinguishable—as in newspapers—the illustration is said to be coarse screened and may reproduce acceptably when copied as if a line original. Photographic materials are available (described in Chapter 5) for converting continuous tone originals into screened pictures for ease of reproduction in a copier or duplicator.

Types of copying machine

A copying machine needs to have some method of accepting an original document, book, etc., usually in tight contact with a sheet of sensitive material. The sandwich is then exposed to light or heat, according to the principle upon which the machine is based. With most types of copier the exposed sensitive material, separated from the original, now requires processing. In some machines this means using a liquid, while others use vapour or a powder.

As Fig. 2.1 shows, the physical arrangements for bringing original document and sensitive material into intimate contact fall into two main physical types. A rotary or roller machine is compact and convenient for originals in sheet form, but cannot of course accept bound books or magazines. A flatbed design (using a glass-topped or air-cushioned light box) is bulkier but allows both separate sheets and bound material to be copied without damage. With the exception of one very expensive electrostatic machine all current copying machines give results in monochrome only.

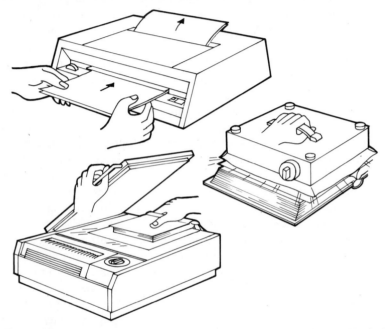

Fig. 2.1. The two basic copying machine designs. *Top:* Rotary type. *Bottom:* Flat-bed type (showing positioning of bound book for reflex printing). *Right:* Unusual portable light box with translucent plastic 'air bag' for reflex printing from undulating surfaces.

So much for general points. We ought now to look at each type of copying process separately. There are really five main types:

1. Copiers using heat: commercial products by 3M (Thermofax) or Block & Anderson (Bandaflex).

2. Copiers using liquid processed photographic materials: products by Kodak (Verifax, etc.), Agfa-Gevaert (Copy Rapid), Dalcopy, etc.

3. Copiers using light to expose and heat to process: products by 3M (Dual Spectrum), etc.

4. Copiers using diazo materials: products by Ozalid, Ilford, etc.

5. Copiers using electrostatic principles: products by Rank-Xerox, Ozalid (Electrofax), etc.

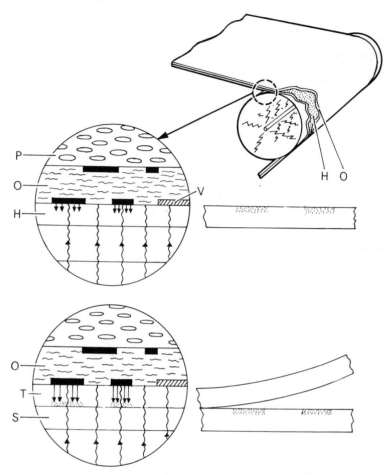

Fig. 2.2. Principle of heat copying. Heat sensitive material (H) passes over drum containing IR source, in tight contact with original (O) backed by pressure pad (P). IR causes inked parts of document to heat up—but not vegetable ink (V). This forms visible image in layer H. *Bottom:* Arrangement using intermediate transfer sheet (T) to form image on non-heat sensitive sheet (S). Some machines do not use intermediates— others use them for particular jobs such as duplicator master making.

Heat copiers

HOW THE PROCESS WORKS. Thin, plastic-based sensitive materials are used which either change colour, deposit dye or alter in some other permanent manner at a certain critical temperature. This material, in contact with the original document for copying, is fed into a rotary machine containing a simple infra-red heat source. As Fig. 2.2 shows, printing ink, pencil (but not vegetable based ink or crayon) on the original absorbs the infra-red radiation and warms up sufficiently to trigger the heat sensitive material in these areas only. Most materials require no further processing. Within 4–5 sec the sandwich is delivered from the machine with the copy in a readable state.

In practice three main types of heat sensitive material are used:

1. Direct printing plastic or paper. The thin plastic gives an image which is viewed through the back to be right-reading, forming an excellent OHP transparency. The paper material forms a black line image on its rear surface (therefore right-reading).

2. Transfer printing material, shown in the lower half of Fig. 2.2, is a thin, carbon-paper type of throw-away transfer sheet placed with its back to the original. This transfers dye on to a layer of ordinary thin paper or plastic wherever parts of the original document heat up. The resulting copy carries a wrong-reading image in dye, ready for immediate attachment to a spirit or ink duplicator. The transfer material can also be used for OHP transparencies and for single prints, although this is more expensive than using direct printing material. As feeding three sheets of predominantly thin material together into a rotary machine can be awkward the sandwich is usually enclosed in an acetate folder (Fig. 2.3).

3. Water-soluble direct printing material. Some film-based materials for OHP transparency production have a coating of coloured, heat-sensitive compounds which become insoluble in water (e.g. Agfa-Gevaert Transparex). After passing through the machine the film is damp sponged to leave a clear positive image the colour of the dye.

WHAT HEAT COPIERS WILL DO. The machine will convert sheets of typed or printed matter or ink/pencil line drawings into spirit masters or ink stencils capable of running off hundreds of paper copies on the appropriate duplicating machine. A heat copier gives acceptable OHP transparencies, carrying either black or (single) coloured line on a clear background, or a 'frosted' line which can be coloured locally by hand, to give a multicoloured transparency, or clear lines on a coloured or black background. It is not therefore difficult to devise and produce overlays as well as base transparencies. Heat copiers give single, thin paper copies of passable quality. Some heat copiers offer an additional function as a laminator—drawings, maps, etc., are fed through in contact with a sheet of heat-adhesive clear film and acquire a protective finish like an LP record sleeve or paperback book jacket.

WHAT HEAT COPIERS WILL NOT DO. The heat process will not reproduce vegetable inks—marks by fibre-tipped pens, markers, colour crayons and dyes, most ball-point pens and some coloured printing

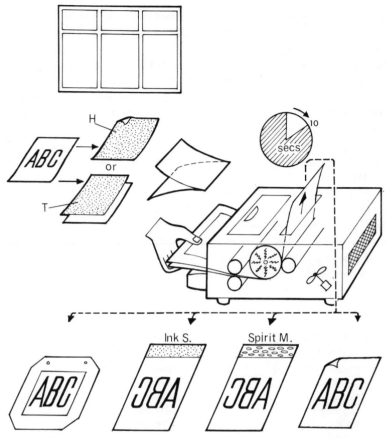

Fig. 2.3. Heat copying. Using direct heat sensitive (H) or transfer (T) materials (in acetate folder for handling convenience) reproduction is possible in four forms—OHP transparency; ink stencil; spirit master; and paper print.

inks (Table 2.1). These vanish completely in the reproduction. As heat copiers are rotary in design, pages from books and magazines can be copied only if detached from their bindings. The paper or thin plastic copies produced are flimsy, tend to curl and have slightly diffused detail. Direct printing materials remain heat sensitive and turn black if strongly heated. Most documents on coloured bases will not reproduce with acceptable contrast. Photographs and other continuous-tone illustrations will not reproduce satisfactorily but crude results are sometimes possible with very coarse-screened pictures. Cost of heat-sensitive material makes the use of this copier for single, direct copies expensive (Fig. 5.24).

To overcome the first two of these limitations manufacturers such as 3M have combined light-sensitive and heat-sensitive processes in two-stage 'Dry Photo' or 'Dual Spectrum' machines. These are discussed shortly, on page 63.

SUMMARY OF PRACTICAL FEATURES. A heat copier is a really valuable adjunct to an overhead projector, and spirit or ink duplicator. It gives transparencies or duplicator masters from suitable sheet originals within seconds—in the preparation room or wherever they are wanted during a session in workshop or classroom.

Thanks to its freedom from chemicals and mechanical simplicity it requires no more skill to operate or time to maintain than a space heater.

Material costs for OHP and duplicator work are modest.

Heat materials are insensitive to light and can therefore be handled and used under bright light conditions.

The user of a heat copier must always remember that some pigments and inks and most coloured documents fail to reproduce and the machine could damage old originals which are vulnerable to heat.

TABLE 2.1
Heat copying—type of original

Originals which will successfully reproduce:	Originals which will not reproduce:
Typewritten matter	Coloured pencil
Pencilled matter	Felt pen
Newspaper text cuttings	China marker
Magazine text and line drawings	Ball-point pen
Ink stencil duplicated matter	Pen ink
Litho duplicated matter	Printed matter on colour paper
Indian ink	Spirit duplicated matter
Photographic line images	

(NB: Paper clips, pins and staples must always be removed from originals before feeding through a rotary copier.)

Photocopiers

HOW THE PROCESSES WORK. Photocopiers use a range of light-sensitive materials (mostly paper but also film) which, although very much less sensitive and more contrasty than the materials used for conventional photography, should not be left around in open packets or handled in bright light. (Domestic artificial light or subdued daylight is harmless during the normal brief handling time between packet and copying machines.)

The material is exposed in tight contact with the original document, book, magazine, etc., in a flatbed-type machine having a glass-topped box containing several light bulbs. The majority of originals are on opaque-based paper, often printed on both sides, and the sandwich of original document and sensitive material is arranged in the order

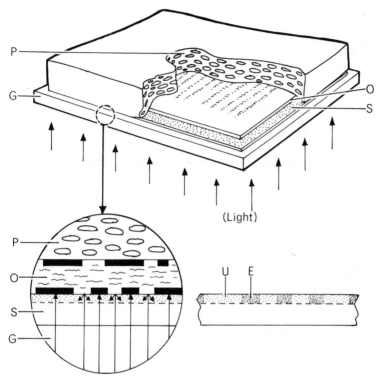

(Light)

Fig. 2.4. Principle of reflex exposing photo-materials to light. G, Glass on top of light box. S, Light sensitive material, sensitive surface *upwards*. O, Original (double sided) document. P, Pressure pad to maintain tight surface contact. Light is reflected back from white parts of original, resulting in extra exposed areas (E) as opposed to lesser exposed areas (U).

shown in Fig. 2.4, for reflex printing. The light first passes through the sensitive material and is reflected back from the white parts of the original (giving the material a 'double light dose').

After the exposure, which is timed by a clock switch on the machine, the light-sensitive material is removed and placed in one or more liquid chemicals to develop its latent image. The functions of these chemicals vary with the machine and type of sensitive material used (see Fig. 2.5). PHOTO-STABILISATION NEG/POS PAPERS. The exposed paper is fed into a processing machine (a separate unit or a processing compartment

59

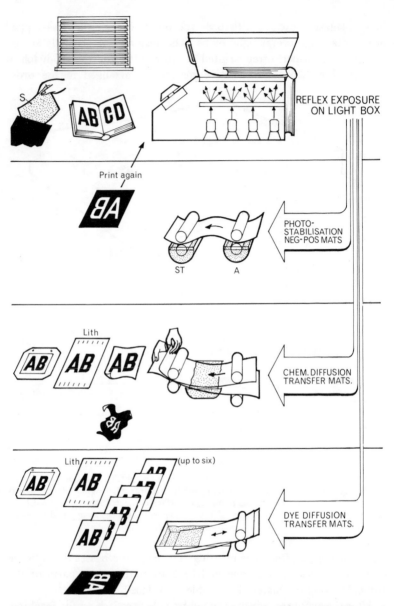

REFLEX EXPOSURE
ON LIGHT BOX

Print again

PHOTO-
STABILISATION
NEG-POS MATS

ST   A

Lith

CHEM. DIFFUSION
TRANSFER MATS.

Lith (up to six)

DYE DIFFUSION
TRANSFER MATS.

Fig. 2.5. Photo-copying. Three forms of photocopier, each reflex exposing light sensitive material (S) to the original on a flat-bed light box. Afterwards each type of machine processes its particular materials in a different way, i.e. photostabilisation material in roller applied activator and stabiliser; and chemical or dye diffusion each in a single solution, sandwiched to a receiving material. Photostabilisation materials are also made for continuous tone contact printing from camera negatives and (projection speed) for enlarging. The processor is therefore rather more useful than appears here.

of the copier) where a coating of alkaline activator causes developer already in the paper to develop up a negative image. The paper immediately passes through a trough of stabiliser to destroy its remaining light sensitivity and it emerges damp dry, having taken a total of about eight seconds to process. We now have a negative, mirror image of the original, which is returned to the light box and contact printed direct on to another sheet of the same material. When this in turn is processed we have a positive, right-reading copy. Many prints can be made from the paper negative, one at a time, and the negative stored for future use. Stabilised negatives and prints have a life of about 4–6 months before they begin to fade or discolour, but they may be conventionally fixed and washed (page 94) at some convenient time, whereupon they become as permanent as any other photographic image.

PHOTO-STABILISATION DIRECT POSITIVE PAPERS. These materials give a positive result (black text reproduced as black text) in one stage. Papers are exposed and processed in the same way as described above. If the original is on a single-side translucent or transparent base it can be copied direct (non reflex) through the back on to this material and gives a readable result.

CHEMICAL DIFFUSION TRANSFER PAPERS, FILM OR FOIL. These are negative materials for reflex exposing to the original in the same way as other photographic materials, but require a rather different processing machine (Fig. 2.5). The exposed but unprocessed paper is fed into one slot in this machine, and a receiving sheet of paper, acetate film or thin metal foil fed into an adjacent slot. Inside, a trough of activator forms a negative image in the exposed paper, damps the receiving sheet and rolls the two into tight contact so that they emerge as a damp–dry sandwich. The two materials are allowed to remain in contact for about ten seconds, during which time simple chemicals in the receiving sheet cause clear areas of the negative (i.e. dark areas on the original) to discharge salts into the receiving sheet, where they are blackened to form a positive image. The two sheets are peeled apart, revealing a positive, right-reading copy on the receiving material. It can be seen how similar this process is to the Polaroid process.

With most chemical diffusion transfer materials one further paper copy can be produced immediately if the negative and another receiving sheet are wetted by passing through the activator, and left in contact for 2–3 times the transfer period of the first copy. After transfer the negative is of no further use and is not therefore filed. By choosing to use acetate film as the receiving sheet an excellent black image OHP transparency or master for diazo prints can be prepared. Equally, transfer can be made on to thick paper or metallic foil to form a printing plate ready for running off several hundred copies on an offset litho duplicator.

DYE DIFFUSION (OR GELATINE) TRANSFER MATERIALS. These are probably better known as Verifax materials marketed by Kodak. The original document is reflex exposed on to the gelatine-coated light-sensitive surface of a sheet of thick paper, which is then completely immersed in a dish of special activator in the base of the machine (Fig. 2.5). Here the sheet takes about half a minute to form a dense black dye overall, the gelatine being hardened in the areas which received most light (white parts of the original). A sheet of *ordinary* paper, or film, or a litho plate is now slid into the solution, the two removed together under a spring-loaded squeegee, and immediately pulled apart. The receiving material now carries a permanent positive right reading copy in black dye. If the receiving material is paper the negative can be returned to the solution with a fresh sheet and the transfer stage repeated until 6–8 paper copies have been pulled. Each copy is progressively slightly lighter. The negative is then discarded.

From the foregoing it can be seen that the equipment for photocopying essentially comprises an exposing unit (normally a light box) and a processing unit which differs mechanically and chemically between three types of material: neg/pos or direct positive; chemical diffusion transfer; and dye diffusion. Machines are marketed with exposing and processing units joined as one unit, or as separate items. The latter will save money if several types of photo-materials are to be used. These can be processed in their various ways but all exposed on the one light box. It might be worth choosing a special type of light box, such as the air-bag (Fig. 2.1) to give best results for the type of work being done.

WHAT PHOTOCOPIERS WILL DO. Used properly these machines give copies of outstanding quality. Copies can be made from a wide range of originals—printing in various colours, in inks, vegetable dyes, pencil, etc., and screened photographic images. They produce first-class OHP transparencies and translucent masters for diazo printing or plates for offset litho (itself the highest-quality duplicating process). Small numbers of direct paper copies can be made in a minute or so using dye diffusion materials. In the case of stabilisation processed materials it is possible to contact print from ordinary continuous-tone camera negatives straight on to low contrast paper made for the purpose. This useful 'extra' is of value in class project work using photography. The processor can also be used in the darkroom to process continuous tone enlargements made on fast photo-stabilisation bromide paper, and the exposing unit to print slides, etc. (Chapter 9).

WHAT PHOTOCOPIERS WILL NOT DO. Originals on coloured bases other than blue or very pastel tints do not reproduce with sufficient contrast. Some materials (stabilisation processed) do not give results with a permanent life unless conventionally fixed and washed. Results are in black and white: monochrome-coloured images are not available direct as with heat and diazo materials. Photocopiers do not give results quite as quickly as other processes such as heat, owing to the two stages involved. Photocopiers do not themselves provide masters for spirit or ink stencil duplicators.

SUMMARY OF PRACTICAL FEATURES. All photocopier processors use chemicals in liquid form, which is a nuisance because it demands regular renewal of solutions and cleaning out. It also restricts portability and is an ever-present potential source of mess. Some solutions deteriorate whether used or not, although many machines now have sachette reservoirs to which solutions drain when not in use, to reduce oxidation. The liquids are pumped up again when the unit is switched on.

Photocopiers are the most versatile of all copiers in terms of the types of original they can reproduce well.

They can give very good-quality results, particularly on paper and film.

They provide excellent translucent prints from which cheaper prints can be run off by diazo; and paper prints from vegetable ink originals which can thereafter be reproduced by a heat copier.

These machines require slightly more skill to use efficiently than other copiers, and single copies take longer to produce than with, say, a heat copier.

As the materials are (weakly) sensitive to visible light the photocopier should not be used near a window: a shaded corner or shuttered preparation room is advisable.

The cost per unit area of light-sensitive photographic materials is inherently high (see Fig. 5.24) because of the silver salts with which they are coated. The cost of, say, half a dozen copies is somewhat reduced when dye diffusion (Verifax) materials are used, for the results are printed on ordinary paper. Greatest cost occurs with neg/pos papers where each receiving paper is just as expensive as the exposing material.

Combined light and heat copiers

HOW THE PROCESS WORKS. The 3M Dual Spectrum and Dry Photo type copiers combine the ability to copy most sorts of originals characteristic of the photocopier, with the speed and solution-free features of the heat copier. As Fig. 2.6 shows, the exposing section is a light box of the same design as a photocopier (in fact, a photocopier light box can be used instead). The original book or document is reflex printed on to a sheet of intermediate paper which is then placed face to face with a sheet of final receiving paper and the two passed through a

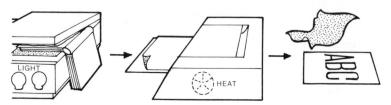

Fig. 2.6. Light and heat (Dual Spectrum) copying. A light-sensitive intermediate sheet is reflex exposed to the original. In the rotary heat 'processing' compartment this intermediate forms a visible image on a sheet of receiving material.

heat processor* forming the second half of the machine. Under heat, unexposed areas of the intermediate sheet react with chemicals in receiving paper to form a positive, right-reading copy on the latter. The intermediate is then thrown away.

Transfer can alternatively be made on to a transparent base to give a direct OHP transparency or master for diazo printing. Having made one paper copy with the light heat process, further copies can be reproduced from this using heat, photo or any other process.

SUMMARY OF PRACTICAL FEATURES. Vegetable and most other originals to which heat-sensitive materials will not respond can be reproduced—even screened illustrations. Copies can be made from bound books and other thick originals unacceptable to rotary copiers.

No liquids are needed and the final copies are permanent: they will not fade chemically or remain vulnerable to heat.

It will produce OHP transparencies and single prints on paper (but is slow and expensive for several copies off, as a new intermediate is needed for each one).

Most machines do not themselves produce masters for spirit duplicators or offset litho plates.

Diazo (Dye-line) copiers

HOW THE PROCESS WORKS. This is the process commonly used by architects and engineers for making working prints from large plans or technical drawings. Diazo materials (paper and film) carry a coating of

---

* The temperature of this heat processor differs from that of direct heat-copying machines. The latter cannot therefore be used to process light-heat materials.

inexpensive yellowish diazo salts which bleach under the action of strong ultra-violet light. The original to be copied must be single-sided on a *transparent* or *translucent* base (e.g. tracing paper, acetate, plastic). Diazo sheet and original are fed together into a rotary machine which passes them in intimate contact around a glass cylinder containing an ultra-violet lamp. (A more crude method is to expose the sandwich for some time to daylight between curved sheets of acetate, Fig. 2.7.)

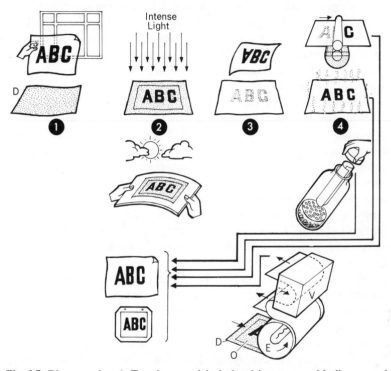

Fig. 2.7. Diazo copying. 1, Translucent original placed in contact with diazo-coated paper or film. 2, Exposure to UV rich light (curved acetate sandwich for improvised printer). 3, Correctly exposed diazo appears bleached in unprotected areas. 4, Dye image forms when sheet has alkali solution applied, or submitted to ammonia vapour— e.g. in sweet jar with ammonia-soaked cotton wool. *Bottom:* Diazo copying machine. Diazo plus original feeds around a UV source in glass exposing drum (E). Diazo sheet alone then passes through vapour processing compartment (V).

Sufficient exposure is given for the diazo under clear parts of the original to bleach white. Remaining diazo (shielded under line or text areas) is now caused to darken and so form a positive print in black or any one of a range of coloured dyes. The method of darkening can be by application of vapour or liquid, different diazo materials being made for each method.

Vapour-processed paper or acetate-based diazo material is simply submitted to ammonia gas. This can take place in a vapour chamber in a motorised machine (Fig. 2.7) or simply using a compartment or sweet jar containing a little ammonia-soaked cotton wool. The room where the processing is carried out should be ventilated. The image appears strongly in a few seconds, its colour being determined by the initial choice of paper or film.

Diazo paper and acetate designed for liquid processing is passed briefly through a trough of 'developer' solution, usually guided by powered rollers, and then squeezed semi-dry. In this case the dye former is contained in the solution itself, so that for the same diazo material different solutions can be chosen to give different image colours. If the result justifies the time (e.g. more often with an OHP transparency than with paper prints) the copy can be processed locally by hand, using different couplers to give a multicoloured result.

WHAT DIAZO COPIERS WILL DO. OHP transparencies and overlays in a variety of brilliant colours can be produced (incidentally with minimum outlay on equipment if sun printing and sweet jar vapour processing is used). Text, ink and heavy pencil drawings up to quite large sizes can be cheaply reproduced on paper because diazo paper is only about one-quarter the cost of other light-sensitive materials (Fig. 5.24). Screened photographic illustrations can also be reproduced, provided that all these originals are also on translucent bases.

WHAT DIAZO COPIERS WILL NOT DO. As these materials cannot be used for normal reflex printing, originals can be copied only if they have single-sided bases through which light can easily penetrate. Another process (e.g. heat or photocopying) will probably have to be used to convert documents into this diazo acceptable form. Diazo results are not fully permanent. The dye image on the copy tends to bleach away if left lying about in daylight—say displayed for several weeks on a bulletin board. Diazo copiers cannot themselves provide masters, plates, etc., for use on a duplicating machine.

SUMMARY OF PRACTICAL FEATURES. The chief attractions are low cost paper prints, variety of image colours, and ability to give excellent OHP transparencies.

The technical simplicity of diazo facilitates the production of results at home with improvised equipment.

A diazo machine is a reasonable method for producing a dozen or so hand-outs which do not justify preparing a duplicator, and would be expensive on photographic materials.

Original artwork must be prepared on translucent or transparent material. If it is in a book or magazine it must first be converted to this form by another process.

Electrostatic copiers

HOW THE PROCESS WORKS. This is an electrical/mechanical process provided by one of two types of sophisticated automatic machine. One type (Xerox) uses an image transfer version of the process; the other (Ozalid) uses direct printing.

With the Xerox type, the document to be copied is either fed *under* (rotary machines) or placed face down *over* a glass plate (flatbed

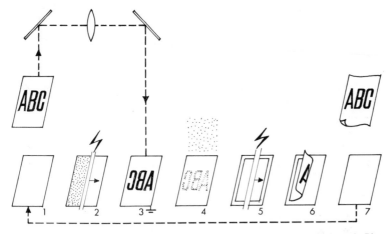

Fig. 2.8. Principle of electrostatic copying. 1, Selenium-coated metal plate. 2, Plate receives static electric charge. 3, Exposure to optical image of original, charge leaks to earth from illuminated areas. 4, 'Developed' with charged ink particles. 5, Ordinary paper placed over surface, image transferred by electrical charge through back of paper. 6, Paper removed (image then heat fused into its fibres). 7, Plate cleaned ready for re-use.

machines). In both cases it does not come into direct contact with sensitive material but is lit by lamps and imaged by a lens on to selenium-coated metal which has received a static electrical charge (Fig. 2.8). The charge leaks away in areas recording 'white' parts of the original document, and the machine next covers the metal plate with a metallic powered ink which adheres only to remaining charged areas, so forming a visible positive image. Next the metal comes into contact with a sheet of ordinary paper (or special film) to which it transfers its image. The paper emerges from the machine carrying a positive, right-reading and very permanent image, while the metal is cleaned and charged again ready for the next copy. On most machines the metal

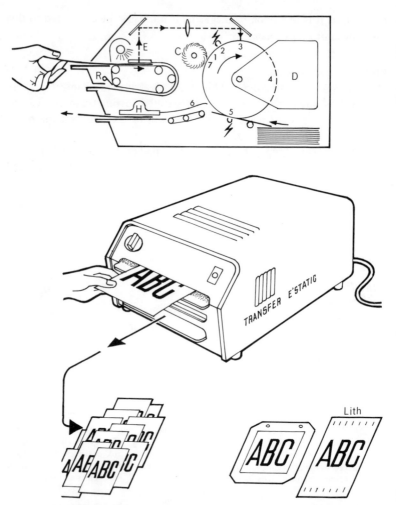

Fig. 2.9. Electrostatic copier transfer (Xerox) type. E, Exposing section with cover glass 'window' and lamp. D, Powder-developing section. H, Heat-fusing section. C, Drum-cleaning section. Numbered stages relate to stages in Fig. 2.8. When repeat flap (R) is dropped original remains circulating in machine, repeatedly reproducing.

surface takes the form of a drum so that the machine approaches the appearance and performance of a duplicator, Fig. 2.9.

The Ozalid type—the second or direct printing family of electrostatic copiers—uses zinc oxide-coated paper instead of a metal surface. The paper is charged, exposed, 'developed' and then emerges from the machine. As Fig. 2.10 shows, one mirror is included in the optical system between the original document and sensitive surface to produce a final result which is right-reading. The original need not be disturbed as successive copies are run off—every rotary machine has a copy retention device—so that again we have a machine which is as much a duplicator as a copier. A few of the more elaborate electrostatic machines (both versions) allow the imaging lens to be adjusted so that copies can be made larger or smaller than the original.

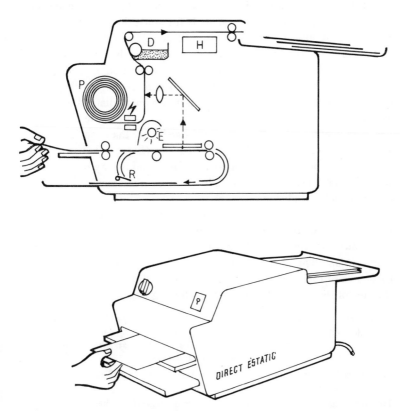

Fig. 2.10. Electrostatic copier, direct type. E, Exposing section. P, Roll of zinc oxide-coated paper, electrically charged just before exposure. D, Liquid developing section. H, Heat fusing. Repeat flap (R) has same function as in Fig. 2.9.

WHAT ELECTROSTATIC COPIERS WILL DO. These copiers have the same sensitivity to colours as panchromatic photographic film and will reproduce any line image even on coloured backgrounds, or on opaque, translucent or transparent bases. They give very permanent black ink copies on paper, and on film base for OHP transparencies, thin metal offset litho plates and translucent-based copies for diazo reproduction. It is even possible to copy a surface of any three-dimensional object which can be stood on the exposing glass of a flatbed machine. Electrostatic copiers are practically automatic in their action—they require no skill and little practice to use successfully.

WHAT ELECTROSTATIC COPIERS WILL NOT DO. They will not reproduce photographic illustrations unless they are coarse-screened. Large areas of black in diagrams, maps, etc., tend to reproduce with full-blooded perimeters but with ink-starved weak and patchy central zones. They will not give masters or stencils for spirit or ink duplicators.

SUMMARY OF PRACTICAL FEATURES. Electrostatic machines are costly to buy and are usually rented, payment being partly based on numbers of copies made. They are a simple-to-use, fast method of producing one or a quantity of copies on paper for hand-outs, from every type of line original. However, unless one of the more expensive flatbed machines is available, bound books and mounted originals cannot be copied. Cost per copy is higher than for diazo, and also higher than copies run off on a duplicator when several dozen are required (Fig. 5.24). The quality of the black and white result can be very clear, and is very permanent. As the light-sensitive surface is totally enclosed, the machine can be used in bright light conditions.

COMPARING THE VARIOUS COPYING SYSTEMS. Intense competition in the world of document reproduction, with every manufacturer striving to extend the usefulness of his particular process, results in considerable overlap. Figures 2.2 and 5.24 summarise and compare the cost performance of each type of copier at the time this book was written. At the risk of over-generalisation, the following conclusions are offered:

If the primary aim in purchasing is:	Consider this type of copying machine:
To produce OHP transparencies	Heat. Photocopier (diffusion transfer)' Diazo. Light-heat. Electrostatic (transfer)
To produce OHP transparencies and overlays in various colours	Heat. Diazo. Light-heat
To produce single paper copies, for wall display, models, feltboard, etc.	Photocopier. Light-heat. Electrostatic
To produce paper hand-outs for seminars (6–8, or occasional dozens)	Photocopier (dye diffusion or photo-stabilisation). Diazo
To produce duplicated hand-outs in conjunction with an existing spirit duplicator, ink duplicator or office offset litho press	Heat. Photocopier (diffusion transfer) for lith
To copy from the widest possible range of originals	Flatbed photocopier, light-heat, or electrostatic
To make paper copies with minimum capital outlay (accepting an element of inconvenience and improvisation)	Diazo materials

Types of duplicating machine

A duplicator is a modest output printing machine. At its heart is a suitably-prepared master (or stencil or plate, according to type of machine) normally attached to the outside skin of a drum. The machine has some system of releasing ink only from those areas of the master carrying the image to be printed, and a means of automatically feeding sheets of paper one at a time into contact with the drum. There are three different forms of duplicator:

1. The spirit duplicator (using masters)—commercial products such as Banda, etc.

2. The ink or cut stencil duplicator—commercial products such as Gestetner, Roneo, etc.

3. The offset litho duplicator (using plates)—commercial products such as Multilith, Rotaprint, etc.

Spirit duplicators

HOW THE PROCESS WORKS. The spirit duplicator (Fig. 2.11) requires a master in the form of glossy paper carrying a mirror image of the matter to be duplicated in thick hectograph-type carbon. There are two methods of preparing the master:

1. Placing special carbon paper face-to-face with the master paper, and then typing or drawing on the *back* of the master paper.

2. Using a thermal carbon transfer sheet between a printed document and special master receiving paper, and feeding them through a heat copier.

The prepared master is clipped to the drum, carbon image side outwards. Turning a handle or operating a motor draws sheets of (semi-gloss) paper individually under a methylated spirit-soaked pad and into contact with the revolving drum. The spirit traces left on each sheet of paper cause a small amount of pigment to be transferred from the master to the paper surface. Between 50 and 300 impressions can be taken before the image on the master becomes too weak to print well.

PRACTICAL PERFORMANCE. This duplicator is unique in that the process allows several colours to be printed simultaneously, by using several carbons at the master preparation stage. For example, a map of a country might be prepared by drawing the outline with black carbon behind the master sheet, changing to blue when drawing in the rivers, and changing again to a green carbon sheet to shade in jungle areas. Equally, a master on one colour heat copied from a document can have annotations added by hand (or with a typewriter) in another colour using an appropriate carbon sheet.

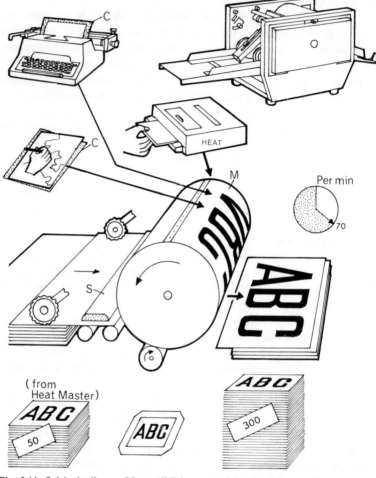

Fig. 2.11. Spirit duplicator. Master (M) is prepared by drawing or typing on master paper backed with a (face up) hecto carbon, or by heat copying. Gloss-surfaced paper is drawn into machine under spirit-soaked pad and so picks up some pigment from back of master.

At any time (even halfway through a duplicating run) unwanted matter can be erased by rubbing the master locally with a spirit-soaked cloth, or, as a temporary expedient, the unwanted area on the master can be masked off with a flap of paper.

Less than a minute is needed to attach a master and prepare the machine ready for printing. However, this can be a rather messy operation.

Most machines will produce up to 300 copies from a typed or drawn master, or about 50 from the more fragile heat-copied masters. The latter will not in any case give good reproduction of intricate detail, or coarse-screened photographs. Electric-powered copiers turn out about 70 copies per minute. Once used, masters deteriorate over a short period of time and are generally not worth storing.

An OHP transparency can be printed off the same master as is used say, for student hand-outs, simply by running a sheet of Cellofilm through the duplicator. This provides a valuable link between group discussion work and take-away notes.

A simple hand-operated spirit machine (by far the most robust type) is the least expensive of the three forms of duplicator to buy.

Ink stencil duplicators

HOW THE PROCESS WORKS. This type of duplicator (Fig. 2.12) uses a form of silk screen printing. A thin, waxy paper stencil is used, on which the wax has been destroyed (cut) wherever text or drawing is to appear. This is attached to a drum, over an already inked-up absorbent pad. Each sheet of paper passing through the duplicator is made to come into contact with the drum, and so receives ink only where the wax-free parts of the stencil allow ink to pass. Stencils are usually cut by:

1. A typewriter (set for stencils, so that the normal ribbon is not used).

2. A metal stylus or fine ball-pen, using a hard surface under the stencil. Lines and diagrams can be cut this way.

3. Using a heat copier to copy an original document on to a thermographic stencil.

4. Using an electrical stencil cutter (see Fig. 2.13).

PRACTICAL PERFORMANCE. As the ink is provided by the machine itself (rather than wearing from carbon on a master as in spirit duplicating) a good ink stencil can be expected to print up to 1000 copies.

By the same token the ink method does not allow simultaneous printing in various colours. Multicolours can be achieved by running each sheet through the machine once for each colour, changing the stencil, cleaning and changing the ink for each pass. As arrangements must also be made to register each successive image this procedure is barely practical.

With care ink stencils can be stored for use again later, although they are messy items to file.

The paper on which duplicates are printed is necessarily rather thick and absorbent, giving a utilitarian quality result and taking up a great deal of space in students' files. Drawing by stylus is awkward and

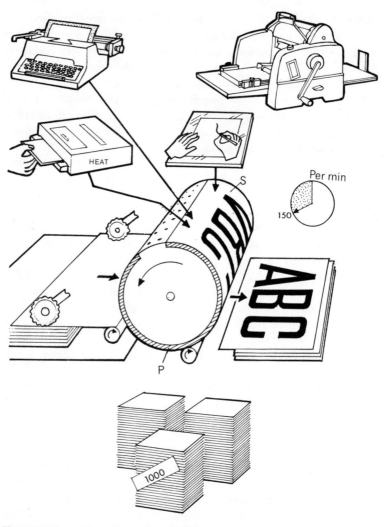

Fig. 2.12. Ink stencil duplicator. Stencil (S) is 'cut' by heat copier, typewriter, or hand-held stylus. On the machine, ink pad (P) squeezes ink through cut stencil to print on to absorbent paper.

inconvenient, and unless a heat copier is available ink stencil duplication is best suited to typescript—outline notes, question papers, etc.

Offset litho duplicators

HOW THE PROCESS WORKS. The principle of lithographic printing centres on the fact that greasy ink will adhere to a greasy (or waxy)

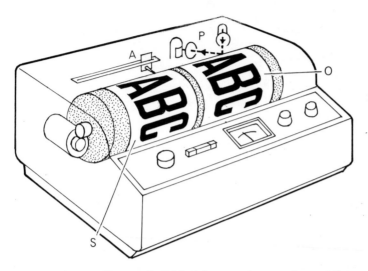

Fig. 2.13. Electrical stencil cutter. O, Original document is wrapped around the same rotating drum as stencil (S). Light/photocell system (P) tracks across original, monitoring stylus (A) which cuts image in stencil by spark discharge. Thus a complete facsimile copy is built up, ready for ink stencil duplicating.

image but is repelled by a surface moistened with water. A litho plate (or foil) of thin aluminium or thick paper has to be prepared so that it carries the printing matter as a waxy image. The plate is attached to the outside of a drum (Fig. 2.14). During printing it is first damped by a water roller so that moisture is absorbed by non-printing areas (the paper fibres themselves in the case of a paper plate, or pores in the metal plate) so that when another roller carrying greasy ink is applied, ink adheres only to the printing areas of the plate. Virtually all mechanical lithography offsets the inked image on to the paper via a rubber blanket roller. Only this intermediate actually comes into contact with the paper, greatly reducing wear in the plate and allowing fast printing speeds. Note how the image on an offset litho plate must be right reading, unlike the mirror images required for spirit or ink stencil duplicating. Offset litho plates can be prepared by:

1. A typewriter, typing direct on a paper plate using a special litho ribbon.

2. Copying a document on a photocopier (chemical diffusion transfer or dye diffusion transfer processes) and using offset metal foil as the final receiving material.

3. Document copying with an electrostatic copier on to a paper plate.

4. Enlarging or contact printing from a photographic (film) negative

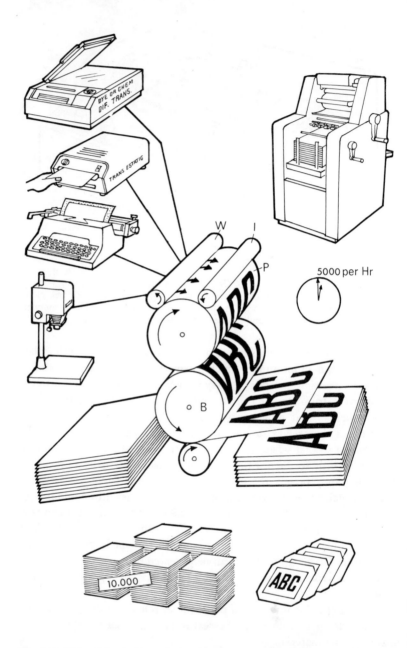

Fig. 2.14. Offset litho duplicator/printer. Plate (P) is prepared by photographic, typewritten, photocopy or electrostatic means. On machine rollers apply water (W), then greasy ink (I). Plate transfers each ink impression to large blanket roller (B) and thence to paper (or a suitable film base).

of line or screened continuous-tone images, direct on to projection speed chemical diffusion transfer material in a darkroom (see page 185). PRACTICAL PERFORMANCE. The office offset litho machine is much more expensive and requires more experience to use than the two other types of duplicator. Runs of up to 10,000 copies from metal plates or 1000 from paper plates at rates of 5000–7000 per hour are usual.

Using metal plates very high-quality, professional-looking results are possible, printed on a variety of paper surfaces. Good-quality photographic illustrations can be included in among the text and diagrams, provided they are prepared from screened negatives (practical procedure, page 186). In fact modest-circulation house magazines, instruction manuals, and other complete publications can be produced.

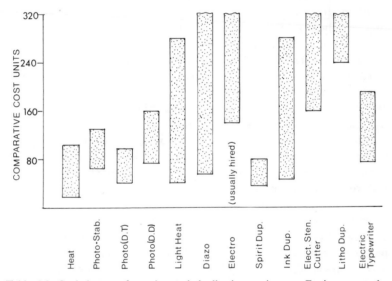

Table 2.2. Capital cost of copying and duplicating equipment. Equipment at the cheaper end of each scale may give poorer quality results, have minimal electrical safety, no thermostat etc (extra wastage of materials). The costlier machines are usually fully automatic. Electric typewriter is included here for comparative purposes (cost units can also be directly compared with units in other tables).

Cleaning, changing ink colour or plates involves the same time and messiness as for an ink stencil duplicator. Paper litho plates are cheaper than ink stencils. Plates can be stored without as much mess or image deterioration as ink stencils or spirit masters.

This duplicator is in many ways a professional printing press in miniature. Providing the capital outlay can be justified by usage, it is a very flexible machine, offering better quality and lower cost per copy for its products than other duplicators. Additionally it is of special value to schools interested in producing their own publications.

EQUIPMENT FOR STILL PHOTOGRAPHY

Most of the bits and pieces of equipment for still and cine photography have much wider-ranging image-making applications than machines such as the document copier or duplicator. They have to be considered as visual communications tools for the learner as much as the teacher's means of producing visual aids.

The principal advantage of the camera is its versatility—able to record all manner of real-life subjects, down to and including the copying of documents. Immense changes in image scale, clarity of detail, the freezing of moments in time and full recording of colour (or alternatively rich black and clean white line images) are all character-istics of photography. A good camera should be quick and simple to use, yet carry sufficient controls (whether automatically or manually moni-tored) to enable pictures to be taken under a usefully wide range of conditions and subject distances. Its lens should give impeccable definition, and both the camera and the films it requires should be realistically priced. Needless to say, this paragon does not yet exist.

With such a multiplicity of cameras now available the aim here will be simply to evaluate the educational potential of the main types and sizes. Their use as tools will emerge in more detail when we come to the production of specific aids, in Chapters 4, 6 and 9.

Cameras using 35-mm film

Cameras of this size are probably the most important of all for teaching purposes, because they enable us to shoot direct colour and black-and-white slides as well as making black-and-white and colour negatives for subsequent enlargement on paper. Although each camera uses film 35 mm wide, Fig. 2.15 shows how the actual picture format can vary. The most common picture size is 36×24 mm with 28×28 mm a close second. Obviously the smaller the format the more pictures may be recorded per film. However, bear in mind the size of the projector to be used for slides and also the degree of enlargement needed when making prints.

Most projectors are made to illuminate and project a transparency 5×5 cm overall, which means in practice a smaller transparency in a masked down mount of this size. The greater the width of mask the more light is unused and the smaller the image appears on the screen. This may mean increasing the projector-screen distance to regain size,

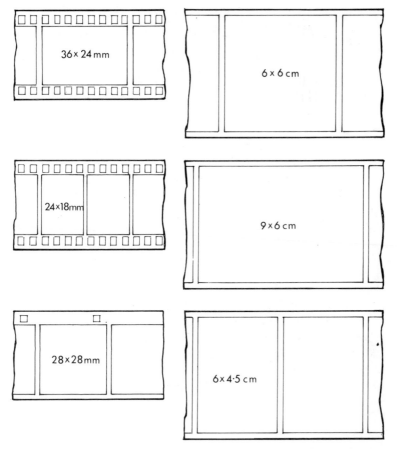

Fig. 2.15. Popular camera picture formats, using (*left*) 35-mm film and (*right*) 120 or 620 rollfilm. The usual picture size for cartridge-loading cameras is 28 × 28 mm, giving 12 or 20 images per film. Compare with slide dimensions, Fig. 1.2.

but in doing so the picture becomes dimmer (twice the distance = one-quarter the illumination). On the other hand cameras shooting 'half-frame' images give appropriate size transparencies for single-frame filmstrips.

These smaller format images must always be extra sharp if detail is to survive the additional enlargement when projecting or making enlargements. Camera lens quality is therefore particularly important.

Current 35-mm cameras can be divided into direct vision and single lens reflex designs.

DIRECT VISION CAMERAS. This type of camera has an optical view-finder quite separate from the lens, usually near the top of the body

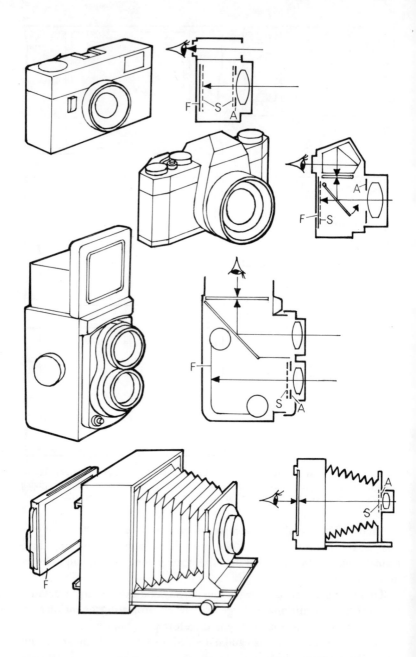

Fig. 2.16. The main still camera designs. *Top to bottom:* Direct vision finder type; single lens reflex; twin lens reflex; sheet film camera. A, Lens aperture. S, Shutter (two alternative designs for direct vision camera.) F, Film.

(Fig. 2.16). Focusing is by scale engraved around the lens—on more expensive models a rangefinder in or next to the viewfinder enables subject distances to be accurately measured.

Some direct vision cameras use 35-mm film in conventional 20- or 36-exposure cassettes. Others accept 12- or 20-exposure cartridges—drop-in plastic units containing feed and take-up spools, which avoid the need to thread film over sprockets, etc. (see Fig. 2.17).

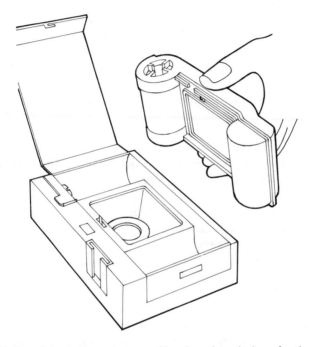

Fig. 2.17. 'Drop in' cartridge and camera. Claw drops into single perforation in film, locking film transport until next picture is exposed.

Most of the cheaper 35-mm cameras are of the direct vision cartridge-loading kind and so are the most likely to be used by children. Often a small flashbulb gun is built in. Exposure controls may simply be a 'sunny–hazy' lever which widens the aperture in the lens, the shutter speed being fixed.

Further up the price scale (Table 2.3) the shutter might have eight or ten speeds with the lens variable between $f16$ and $f2·8$ or $f2$. These cameras may also have built-in exposure meters which show the required f number setting in the viewfinder, or set the lens directly. More expensive direct vision cameras usually enable lenses to be interchanged, allowing the photographer to shoot a wider scene (using a short-focus lens) or enlarge-up distant detail (with a telephoto or long-focus lens).

ADVANTAGES AND DISADVANTAGES. The direct vision camera is simple to use and load, particularly if cartridge loading. The function of the camera is easily explained and in its cheaper forms it is a good starting point for class photography. The finder is particularly convenient for following moving subject matter, and used at eye level the camera quickly becomes accepted as an extension to the eye. It is an easily portable camera for shooting visual aids material on location.

The main disadvantage is that when subjects closer than about 2 metres are approached the physical displacement between viewfinder and camera lens gives what are known as 'parallax errors' in framing and viewpoint. Accurate focusing by scale also becomes inconvenient under critical close-up conditions. It is not possible to *observe* how the closing down of the lens aperture and focusing actually affect the appearance of the image.

SINGLE LENS REFLEX CAMERAS. The SLR camera uses a mirror to deflect the image formed by the lens up on to a focusing screen the same size as the picture format, observed through an eyepiece (Fig. 2.16). On pressing the release the mirror flies out of the way and a blind exposes the film to the lens image. Such mechanism increases the cost of the camera but does away with all parallax problems.

Almost all SLR cameras allow interchangeable lenses; most use cassettes of film but some accept film in cartridges. The effects of focusing, stopping down and using the camera with other devices such as microscopes, telescopes, etc., can all be observed knowing that precisely what appears on the screen will also be imaged on the film. By using extension rings or bellows attachments to extend the lens further from the film it is possible for the camera to photograph sharply very close subjects, and even to magnify them. Lens apertures, shutter speeds and the incidence of built-in exposure meters equal the best direct vision cameras. Often a meter is built-in behind the lens to measure from the actual image—automatically taking into account close-up working conditions, filters, etc.

ADVANTAGES AND DISADVANTAGES. The single lens reflex is very versatile, capable of tackling virtually any subject for colour and black and white visual aids, from distant views to small objects and artwork. The optical effects of lens controls can be observed and there are no parallax errors. Through-the-lens metering can be an advantage.

On the other hand, such cameras are expensive, internally complex (more to go wrong) and the loss of the image on the focusing screen at the moment of exposure can be inconvenient.

Cameras using rollfilm

Cameras using 120 and 620 rollfilm usually give twelve 6 × 6-cm pictures per film. A few give other formats, as shown in Fig. 2.15. We can therefore produce 7 × 7-cm mounted colour transparencies (which have excellent quality but hardly justify the extra cost over 35-mm slides) and large negatives for subsequent printing on paper. Quality and relative freedom from grain pattern when enlarged are the main attractions of negatives in this size format.

Rollfilm cameras today are made in direct vision, single lens reflex and twin lens reflex designs. Single lens reflexes offer most of the design advantages of the 35-mm SLR types, plus the ability to be masked down to 35-mm image size when desired. Unfortunately the scaling up of complex internal mechanism and limited demand brings them into the highest price bracket (Table 2.3).

Twin lens reflexes have two separate sections—a lens-mirror-focusing screen top half, and a lens-shutter-rollfilm bottom half (Fig. 2.16). Both lenses have the same focal length and focus backward and forward on the same panel. The camera is designed so that when the image on the focusing screen is sharp a sharp image will also be formed on the film by the lower lens, when the shutter is fired. The camera is therefore mechanically simpler than a SLR, but the cost of a *pair* of lenses puts it in the medium–high price range.

Generally, the twin lens reflex has fixed lenses with no wide-angle or long-focus capability and, of course, no provision for extension tubes or bellows. There is, however, one model that allows lenses to be interchanged (in pairs).

Fig. 2.18. The twin lens reflex camera is handy for very low or high viewpoints.

ADVANTAGES AND DISADVANTAGES. Twin lens reflex cameras have the advantage of being quick and fairly easy to use and they can allow very low or high viewpoints (Fig. 2.18). The large negative size allows high-quality enlargements.

Disadvantages include parallax error and, in most cameras, inability to focus subjects closer than one metre. The image is reversed left to right on the focusing screen. The cameras are generally expensive.

Cameras using sheet film

The most frequently used size of sheet (or plate) camera takes pictures 5 × 4 in. It is basically a simple device with a movable lens and shutter at one end and a glass focusing screen at the other (Fig. 2.16). The camera is set up on a tripod and the lens moved backwards and forwards until the image is seen to be sharp. The shutter is then closed, lens stopped down and a sheet of film in a holder (previously loaded in the dark) inserted in place of the focusing screen. The exposure is made, and the film holder removed and taken to the darkroom for unloading and processing. Sheet films are bought in boxes of 10 or 25 sheets; it is still possible to buy glass plates.

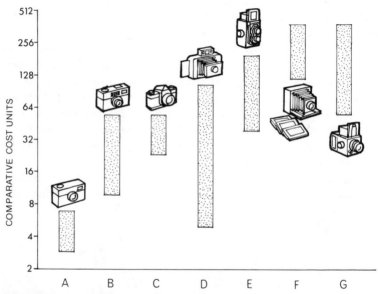

Table 2.3. Approximate (new) price range for various types of camera. A, Direct vision, fixed focus, two shutter speeds, cartridge, or rollfilm size. B, As A but zone focusing, variety of shutter speeds, built-in meter, 35-mm. C, Simplest single lens reflex, or direct vision with rangefinder. D, Polaroid cameras. E, Twin lens rollfilm reflex. F, Sheet film 5 × 4-in. camera with one lens, three film holders. G, Precision single lens reflex with provision for interchangeable lenses, or similar precision direct vision camera.

The sheet film camera is therefore a somewhat limited, slow and specialised tool requiring a little extra knowledge of the photographic process. It offers several unique advantages which at least justify its inclusion in a pool of visual aids equipment. If a simple camera of this type can be picked up cheaply secondhand it can also be well worth acquiring as a teaching tool.

ADVANTAGES AND DISADVANTAGES. The advantage of such a camera is that several special purpose films are available in sheet form only. Pictures can be processed individually. The camera has interchangeable lenses, and allows very close working. It also allows some camera movements. The large focusing screen offers an interesting teaching medium for demonstrating optics and making images (building up compositions, lighting, etc.) even without the taking of photographs. A Polaroid back can be fitted allowing pictures in 15 sec. With the addition of a temporary lamphouse the camera can also be used as an enlarger (see Fig. 2.23, left).

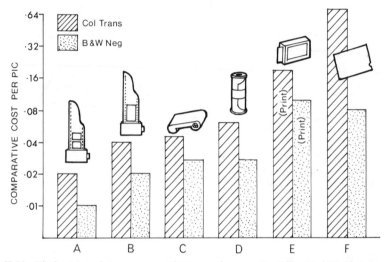

Table 2.4 Cost per picture assumes that an entire cassette, roll, etc., is used at one time, and includes processing (colour by manufacturer or laboratory, black and white negatives by user). A, Half-frame (72 on 36 exposure 35 mm). B, Full frame, 36 exposure. C, Cartridge, 20 exposure. D, 120 rollfilm. E, Polaroid pack film, 8 exposures giving immediate prints. F, Sheet film 5 × 4 in. (35-mm black and white reversal film, including manufacturer's processing, costs the same as black and white negatives.)

The camera is, however, slow to use and really only suitable for inanimate subject matter. The image on the focusing screen is upside down. A darkroom is needed for loading and processing. Materials are expensive per exposure (Table 2.4) owing to their large size.

This type of camera complements the work of the cameras described earlier. It is most useful to a teacher needing to copy documents involving a size change, which are therefore beyond the scope of most document copiers. It has distinct advantages for the photographer of architecture and still life subjects where highest-quality reproduction is required.

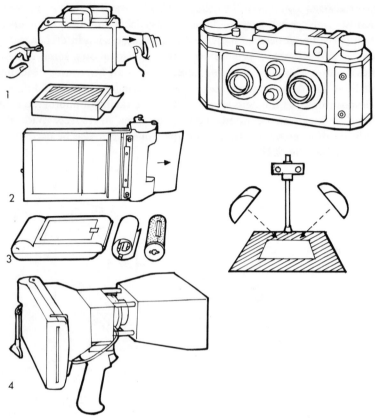

Fig. 2.19. *Left half:* Polaroid cameras and backs. 1, Camera taking 'pack film'—print is removed as a neg/pos sandwich, peeled apart after a few seconds. 2, Polaroid back for 5 × 4-in. sheet film cameras. Separate film envelope inserted for each exposure. (Widest range of films made for this size, see page 313.) 3, Rollfilm back for 5 × 4-in. cameras, oscilloscope attachments, etc. Requires positive and negative rolls. 4, Polaroid oscilloscope recording camera with pack back and lens prefocused for any 'scope pressed against front of plastic hood. *Right half top:* 35-mm stereoscopic camera. *Bottom:* Microcamera for semi-automatic recording of documents.

Special-purpose cameras

Polaroid cameras, or cameras accepting Polaroid backs are mechanically designed to accept a special film and a receiving paper with pods of jellied chemical attached. The image is exposed on the film in the normal way but rollers then break the pod and spread chemical between film and paper. After 10–15 sec a permanent positive paper print can be pulled from the back of the camera. Other Polaroid materials include films giving a continuous tone or line black-and-white transparency for projection, and film which produces an immediate colour print. Table App.3.1 shows the physical forms these films take. Polaroid pictures are ideal for demonstrating image making and giving immediate records (e.g. oscilloscope traces, flash shots of movement, photomicrography). The relatively high cost per exposure (Table 2.3) however remains the most serious handicap to what would otherwise be an ideal medium for much class photography.

Stereo cameras are essentially two cameras working side-by-side (Fig. 2.19) and synchronised to fire together. The two photographs (transparencies or prints) are then examined in a viewer or projected and viewed through spectacles, giving a three-dimensional reproduction. Alternatively a normal camera can be fitted with a beam splitter to give two images side-by-side, or two separate pictures can be taken, moving the camera 6·5 cm (equivalent to eye separation) between exposures. Stereoscopic photography has limited but interesting applications in archaeology, metallurgy and survey work of various kinds. See page 283.

Microfilm cameras are designed to photograph documents and plans on narrow-gauge recording film (usually 35 mm and 16 mm wide). This is processed, stored and retrieved as required—usually enlarged up in a special projector for direct viewing. Most micro cameras are fully automatic and form part of data storage systems often found in central libraries. Prints—run off on document copying type machines—can be purchased from many such sources, notably the British Museum and the Public Records Office.

Useful camera accessories

EXPOSURE METER. If one is only concerned with photographing general subjects under one or two set lighting conditions sufficient exposure information may be contained in the film-packing slip. For accurate calculation under all sorts of conditions, however, an exposure meter can be considered essential. It is simply a device for converting light reflected from or incident to the subject, into camera exposure terms (Fig. 2.20). A meter may conveniently be built into the camera, but is most versatile when a separate unit. One meter will then serve a whole class. Modern meters using tiny long-life batteries are sensitive enough to read down to moonlight level. Often a well-known brand of meter (Weston, Gossen, etc.) can be safely purchased secondhand.

CLOSE-UP DEVICES. The nearer the lens is placed to the subject, the greater the distance needed between lens and film to form a sharp image. Unless the camera is particularly well endowed with lens focusing movement the purchase of rings (or better still adjustable bellows (Fig. 2.21) to fit between camera body and lens greatly extend the range

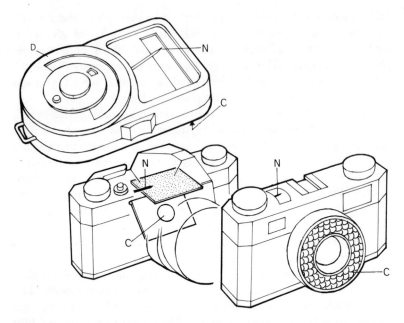

Fig. 2.20. Some exposure meter arrangements. *Top:* Separate meter. *Bottom:* Two forms of built-in meter. C, Light-sensitive cell. N, Moving needle. D, Dial converting reading into *f*-number and shutter speed terms. Built-in meters use match-the-needle system in which aperture or shutter speed is changed until needle moves to a set position. Through-the-lens system (*left*) offers greatest accuracy. See also Fig. 6.2.

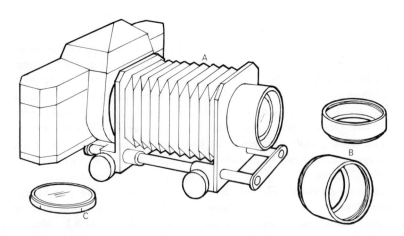

Fig. 2.21. Methods of extending the film-to-lens distance, to focus extreme closeups. A, Bellows attachment. B, Extension rings of various lengths. C, Supplementary lens.

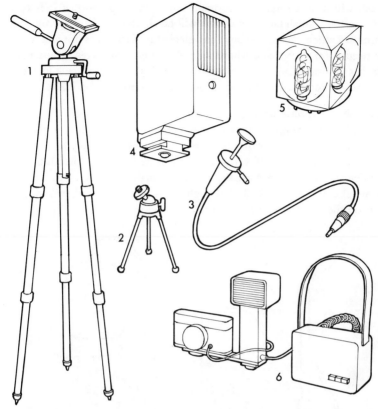

Fig. 2.22. Camera accessories. 1, Extending tripod with centre column and tilting head. 2, A table standing tripod for copying and close-up work. 3, Cable release—note locking screw near top for long exposures on B. 4, Low power one-unit electronic flash. Firing contact with the camera shutter is made through the base or 'hot shoe'. 5, Flashbulb cube. 6, Electronic flash unit with shoulder slung power pack.

of close-up work which can be tackled. These extension devices fit only cameras designed for interchangeable lenses; for fixed lens cameras supplementary clip-on lenses of various powers can be purchased instead.

TRIPOD AND CABLE RELEASE. A firm, portable tripod fitted with a tilting (ball and socket) head combats camera shake when giving long exposure times. It is also a great aid when carefully framing up copies, close-up detail, etc. Tripods with a centre column are the easiest to adjust. A cable release screws into the camera shutter and enables the shutter to be fired without the risk of jogging.

FLASHGUN. Most pictures can be taken with existing lighting, or some modified domestic illumination. A flashgun (Fig. 2.22), however, makes the camera an independent recording unit able to be used anywhere. If flash will only be used occasionally buy a flash*bulb* gun; if it is to be used often a small electronic flash will be cheaper in the long run. Bulb guns are much cheaper to buy than electronic flash units but a new bulb is needed for each flash, whereas an electronic unit gives thousands of flashes at almost no cost. Electronic flash units are also made in special forms, i.e. for the copying of colour transparencies (Fig. 4.23).

The photographic enlarger
An enlarger is simply a projector for photographic negatives. By positioning it near or far from photographic paper and sharply focusing the image, enlargements of various sizes can be made. For handling convenience the enlarger is usually mounted vertically, moving up or down a metal column (Fig. 2.23). The light-sensitive paper is then laid down flat on the baseboard for exposure.

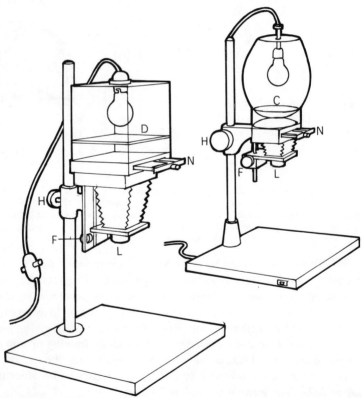

Fig. 2.23. Photographic enlargers for 5 × 4 in. (*left*) and 6 × 6 cm and 34 mm (*right*). This particular 5 × 4-in. enlarger has a diffuse lamphouse which gives lower contrast prints but minimises scratches and spots. D, Diffusing screen. C, Condenser lenses. N, Negative carrier. L, Lens. H, Height-adjustment. F, Focusing knob.

Enlargers are made to accept 35-mm negatives, and others 6-cm square negatives (adaptors also allow 35 mm). A much more substantial and expensive enlarger is required for 5 × 4-in. negatives, but with adaptors and changes of lens this too may adapt down to 6 × 6 cm and 35 mm.

The ability to take negatives at one image size and enlarge (or reduce them) to another, means that enlargers are useful intermediaries for making OHP transparencies, display prints, diazo masters for hand-outs, slides and filmstrips—all on photographic materials.

The similarity between slide projector and enlarger is such that a 5 × 5- or 7 × 7-cm projector can be modified for use as an enlarger. The main requirement is for the projector lamp to have its brightness, heat output and general light spill reduced, perhaps by housing the projector in a (ventilated) box with a hole for the lens and reducing the voltage of the supply.

In experienced hands a photographic enlarger may occasionally be used as a copying camera for documents. The item to be copied is positioned on the baseboard and illuminated by two (desk) lights. Photographic film is loaded into the negative carrier, see page 149.

Equipment for photographic processing

All processing and printing could be sent out via the nearest photographic dealer (colour printing is usually better handled this way because of its complexity and the consistency demanded). But a good deal of student interest is denied if all film processing is sent out, to say nothing of the frustrating delay between photography and its results. Routines for processing camera film and black-and-white prints and enlargements are not difficult to master. Methods of organising students in these tasks are discussed on page 268.

All the basic items required for processing black-and-white negatives and black-and-white prints and transparencies are shown in Fig. 2.24. The function of most items is self-explanatory, but the film tank deserves special mention. In the dark, film from the camera is removed from its cassette, or from the cartridge or rollfilm backing paper, and wound into a plastic or stainless steel spiral. The function of the spiral is simply to convert a long length of unmanageable film to a compact unit which still allows chemical solutions to act evenly on every part of the film surface. Having loaded the spiral (either from the centre outwards, or guiding in film from the outside) it is placed in the tank body, the lid locked and lights switched on. Light traps in the tank allow all subsequent pouring in and out of chemicals and wash water to take place in ordinary white light. Really, spiral loading is the only stage of

Fig. 2.24. Basic equipment for processing black and white negatives. Tank shown side view at top right allows up to three spirals to be processed at once.

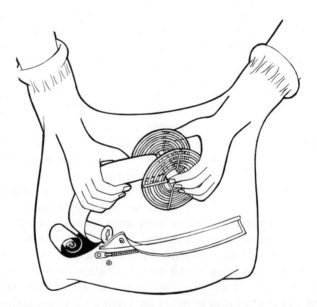

Fig. 2.25. A large light-tight changing bag, showing the loading of a rollfilm into a (stainless steel type) spiral.

processing which requires manual dexterity. After some practice loading with a scrap film it is soon mastered—in fact hands can just be plunged under bedclothes or into a photographic changing bag (Fig. 2.25) and spirals loaded there.

The sequence of solutions for processing black-and-white negatives is:

1. Brief water rinse or 'pre-soak' (this stage is optional).
2. Developer at evenly controlled temperature.
3. Intermediate water rinse.
4. Fixing solution (hypo).
5. Final washing in water.

Typical timings are shown in Fig. 2.26. A similar but extended series of solutions is required for processing colour negatives and colour transparencies—details and kits of chemicals are available from the manufacturers.

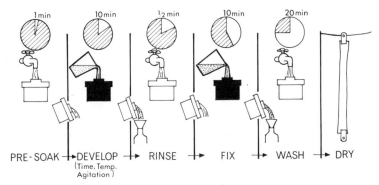

Fig. 2.26. Sequence of stages for processing black and white negatives showing typical accumulated timings. Kodak D.76 developer and acid fixing powder are suggested chemicals.

Equipment for processing black-and-white paper prints and sheet film in dishes is shown in Fig. 2.27. The same type of processing sequence (less pre-soak) is required, handled in three or four dishes of suitable size. Dishes should be plastic or stainless steel—not tinned metal. Black-and-white printing paper and most film made for use under the enlarger is insensitive to orange and red light, so that it is usual to print in a darkroom lit with an orange safelight. Thus we are able to see the image on the printing material actually appearing in the developer—one of the great fascinations of photography. The disadvantage of this conventional arrangement is the need to organise a darkened room big enough for the row of dishes, and water supplies for washing and control of temperature. (Darkroom layout, page 326.)

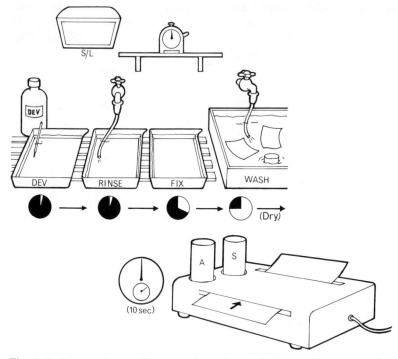

Fig. 2.27. Basic equipment for processing prints. Safelight would be orange for bromide paper, red for lith materials. Ilford PQ developer and acid fixer powder are suggested. *Bottom:* Alternative photostabilisation roller processing machine, giving damp–dry results in 10 seconds.

An alternative is to purchase a roller processing machine of the same type as used for photo-stabilisation copiers. This obviates the need for dishes, water supplies and drainage, so that as long as the sensitive material can still be exposed under the enlarger and fed into the processor without fogging to white light any makeshift enclosed area such as a large cupboard can be used for printing. The processor contains two solutions in small troughs—an activator solution and a stabiliser—sometimes controlled in temperature by a built-in heater. When the exposed paper or printing film is fed in through an entry slot in the machine, motor-driven rollers apply activator to develop the light-sensitive emulsion, then briefly dip it through stabiliser and return it as a finished damp–dry print a few seconds after entry. Its advantages for processing photographs are:

Speed in processing single prints.

Absence of open dishes, water supply and drainage; no contamination of hands (and thereby paper, enlarger, etc.) by wet chemicals.

The machine is simple enough for even infant school children to use safely.

Excellent quality results.

There are, nevertheless, some disadvantages:

Capital cost. The machine is about twice the price of a modest single lens reflex camera (Tables 2.2 and 2.3).

Prints tend to fade after 6–12 weeks unless conventionally fixed and washed.

Special stabilisation printing papers and film must be used. A comprehensive range is available, but cost is about 25% more than conventional materials of equivalent size.

The machine contains liquid chemicals which must be renewed frequently (every day or so).

Despite its cost, a roller processing machine is well worth serious consideration in a teaching situation, as it is seldom possible to wash and dry students' prints conventionally in a brief class period. Also of course the school may already possess a photocopier with a roller processing section.

Drying machines
Rollfilm, sheet films and (conventionally) processed prints all go through a final washing stage and thereafter have to be dried. One

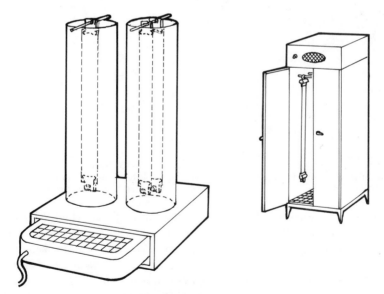

Fig. 2.28. Forced air film dryers. *Right:* Commercially made metal cabinet. *Left:* Homemade unit using domestic fan heater, box and plastic drainpipes.

simple, if slow, method of drying is to peg the material on a nylon line and leave it to dry naturally in a dust-free room, preferably overnight. (Pegs should also be attached to the bottom of the film or paper, to prevent curling.) A film-drying cabinet containing heater and fan will reduce drying time to about 15 min. Cabinets are sold commercially but can also be cheaply and simply made up, using a large diameter plastic pipe and a space heater (Fig. 2.28).

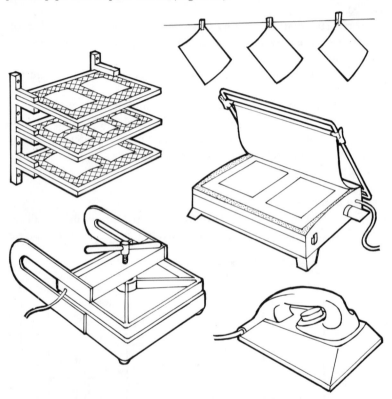

Fig. 2.29. *Top:* Methods of drying prints, using muslin racks or a clothes-line for ordinary room drying, or (right) a glazer showing prints face down on chromium sheet. *Bottom:* Print dry-mounters, mounting press (*left*) and iron (*right*).

To dry prints rapidly electric flatbed drier/glazers (Fig. 2.29) are made commercially in various sizes. They are little more than internally heated metal boxes on which prints are left face up, kept flat under a stretched canvas cover. If the prints have been made on glossy paper they can alternatively be *glazed*. Glazing entails squeezing the wet paper face down on to a polished chromium-plated sheet which is then put into the flatbed drier. Glazing gives the glossy surface usually associated with prints made via a photographic shop. Unglazed (both heat dried and naturally dried) prints have a semi-matt or matt surface, depending upon the printing paper used (see note on page 305). When a photographic print is intended later to receive annotations in pencil or ink, use matt rather than glossy-surfaced paper, because it is easier to write on.

Dry mounter

A small heated press or iron (Fig. 2.29) is a very useful accessory for mounting prints (using dry mounting tissue between print and card). It will also close heat-sealed slide mounts and laminate wallcharts. Pictures much larger than the press can be mounted, provided the machine is open-sided and therefore allows mounting a section at a time.

EQUIPMENT FOR CINE PHOTOGRAPHY

The movie camera

We have already seen (page 33) how the projector capitalises on the eye's persistence of vision, blending a rapid sequence of still pictures into an appearance of continuous motion. The job of the cine camera is therefore to produce sharp, correctly exposed still photographs along a length of film at rates of 18 or 24 per sec.

Most of the space inside a cine camera is taken up with compartments for unexposed and exposed film, a motor (usually electric with batteries, but sometimes clockwork) and a mechanism to hold the film perfectly still behind the lens, one frame at a time. Between film and lens a spinning metal disc with a cut out sector allows light from the lens to reach the film while the latter is held stationary, then blocks light as the film is shifted to the next frame position.

The subject being filmed is sighted through a direct vision viewfinder built into the camera or (on more expensive models) via a reflex system through the actual taking lens (see Fig. 2.30). The camera lens has the usual f-numbered aperture control; shutter speed is usually fixed ($\frac{1}{36}$ at 18 * fps or $\frac{1}{48}$ at 24 fps). Consequently one is really only concerned with three technical operations when filming—focusing, setting the f-number and framing up the scene.

Some movie cameras have interchangeable lenses of various focal lengths—often mounted on a turret (Fig. 2.30) to speed up lens changing. Most cameras today are fitted with zoom lenses (q.v.). Some may

---

* The old standard of 16 fps gives a shutter speed of $\frac{1}{32}$ sec, which for all practical purposes results in the same level of exposure.

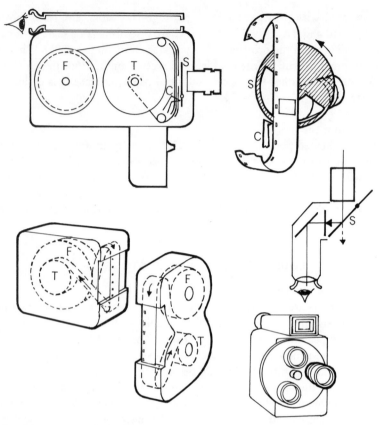

Fig. 2.30. Movie camera mechanisms. F, Feed spool. T, Takeup spool. S, Rotating shutter. C, Claw. *Top left:* Spool-loading double-run 8-mm camera (film, see Fig. 1.14). *Bottom left:* Two types of magazine for single run 8-mm film. Used in their appropriate cameras only a few frames are fogged when loading or changing in mid-film. *Top right:* Shutter, claw and film relationship during exposure of one frame. *Centre right:* Top view of reflex viewfinder type. Shutter is set at 45° and mirrored at front to direct light to a focusing screen when blocking film. *Bottom right:* Camera with lens turret. Right-hand lens is in use.

have built-in exposure meters, and variable speed motors to give high-speed and time-lapse effects.

Motion picture cameras are made for 8-mm-, 9·5-mm-, 16-mm-, 35-mm- and 70-mm-wide film. The last two sizes are used in the cinema industry, and cost and complexity place them outside the scope of this book. The 9·5-mm gauge has been almost wholly overtaken by 8 mm and 16 mm; very little 9·5-mm equipment is now made. As in the case of projectors, 8-mm-wide film can be further subdivided for the present into the old Standard-8 and its eventual successor Super-8 (Fig. 1.14).

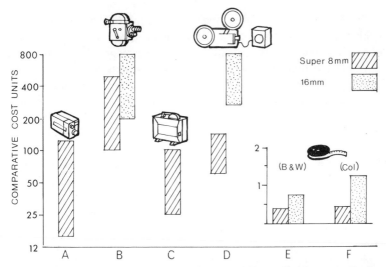

Table 2.5. Cost of (new) movie cameras, projectors and film. A, Simple cassette-loading camera. B, Camera with reflex finder, variable speeds, dissolves, etc. C, Mute projector. D, Sound projector. E, Film cost (per minute running time 18 fps) for black and white reversal. F, Film cost for colour reversal. Note similarity between 8-mm black and white and colour. Cost increases by 30 per cent when shooting at 25 fps.

The comparative capital and running costs of 16-mm and 8-mm camera equipment is shown in Table 2.5.

ADVANTAGES OF 16-MM CAMERAS. Image quality is excellent. The more expensive cameras offer facilities such as long-run magazines, and built-in sound synchronisation, fully comparable with professional film-making. A wide range of film types in colour and black and white are made in 16 mm, and processing laboratories are able to offer services which include special effects and reduction printing down on to 8-mm formats. Film shot on 16 mm can be shown on any 16-mm projector—and many schools already have easy access to this equipment. Almost all professionally made loop films are shot on 16 mm and reduction printed down on 8-mm film.

ADVANTAGES OF 8-MM CAMERAS. Cheaper to buy, much cheaper to run and smaller in size, 8-mm cameras provide image quality perfectly satisfactory for classroom requirements (screens up to about 2 m wide with Super-8). Several cameras are cartridge loading and some have built-in exposure meters—both greatly simplifying technicalities. Cartridge loading is particularly useful when several teachers—or learners— are sharing the camera. Each user keeps his own cassette, slipping it in and out of the camera for each period of use. Only a few frames are fogged each time.

The better cameras offer the more useful refinements for film-making such as single picture device, multi-speed motors and zoom lenses. Sound of excellent quality can now be recorded on a magnetic stripe on the film. Films can be made for cassette loading loop projectors as well as for conventional projection. Several low-cost simple 8-mm cameras with non-interchangeable fixed focus lenses are excellent tools for students to start their own film-making. See Chapter 9.

MAKING THE CHOICE. In recent years manufacturers of 8-mm equipment and materials have been specially developing the gauge for education and industrial training applications. The stimulus of these markets has wrought such technical improvements that the teacher intending to shoot film *for small audiences* need have no hesitation in opting for 8 mm. Again looking to a future in which Super-8 will be the universal 8-mm format he can really only justify investment in a Standard-8 camera if forced by circumstances to use old format 8-mm projection equipment (see page 37). Even here it might be wiser to try to obtain a dual 8-mm projector or conversion kit. Most loop projectors are already designed for Super-8.

If the intention is to make far more ambitious films (e.g. industrial films for duplication and issue to schools in 16-mm, 8-mm or 8-mm loop form) the extra cost of 16 mm is justified on grounds of the scope offered by 16-mm hardware and materials, easier handling in editing and addition of sound, and better image quality when copies are printed off.

Supporting equipment for cine photography

Somewhere in the chain of hardware for cinematography there must of course be some form of projector, but as projectors have been

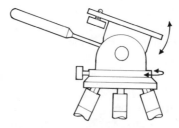

Fig. 2.31. Pan and tilt head for tripod.

discussed on page 33, we should concentrate here on other supporting items—tripod, meter, additional lenses, editor and sound synchroniser.

TRIPOD. A tripod is more important in motion picture work than still photography. Even slight wobble during a shot becomes noticeable and often irritating on the screen. Any stable photographic tripod will do, but it should have a pan and tilt head (Fig. 2.31); this must allow smooth yet controlled horizontal and vertical sweeps of a scene when required to follow action.

METER. The same meter used for still photography can be used for movie work—readings are taken in the same way and the lens f-number shown opposite the camera shutter speed (usually $\frac{1}{36}$ sec) is set on the lens. Several cameras have built-in meters which either open and close the lens aperture automatically (useful when panning from light to dark areas in the same shot), or show the f-number required in the viewfinder.

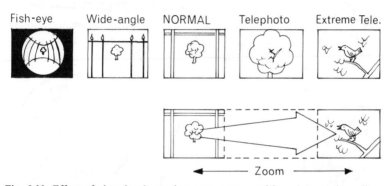

Fig. 2.32. Effect of changing lenses but not camera position. A zoom lens allows infinitely variable image size, usually between limits shown.

EXTRA LENSES. One advantage of a still camera—the ability to enlarge up just part of the image after shooting—is impractical in motion picture work. Lenses of different focal lengths become valuable as a means of including more or less of a scene without having to move the camera (see Fig. 2.32). Zoom lenses, now available for most 8-mm and 16-mm cameras, allow even greater flexibility, as well as allowing image size change during actual shooting—giving the appearance of moving in or out of a scene. Most cine lenses allow focusing down to quite close range, particularly if designed for a reflex focusing camera where parallax differences between viewfinder and lens do not limit the usefulness of close-up facilities. It is also possible to buy close-up lens attachments for fixed lens cameras and special macro lenses focusing down to subjects an inch or so away.

SPLICER. We will be very lucky if we can shoot a scene without wanting to cut out some of it later—or are able to shoot a series of scenes all in correct order and length. Hence a splicer (Fig. 2.33) for cutting and joining film becomes important once the film is returned

101

from processing. (The splicer also has a vital first aid function should any film be torn or broken in projection.) There are two types of machine—one using cement and the other adhesive tape. Both are discussed further on page 229.

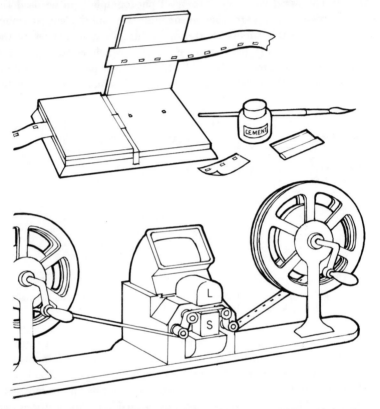

Fig. 2.33. Editing tools. *Top:* Splicing block using film cement and razor blade scraper. Alternatively the short piece of perforated tape could be·used. *Bottom:* Editing machine, or animated viewer. L, Lamphouse. S, Internal shutter, lens, etc., projecting via mirror up to top viewing screen.

EDITING MACHINE. A film editor is a simple type of projector which allows film to be viewed frame-by-frame so that decisions can easily be made on the exact positioning of cuts and joins. Film is usually wound through the machine by hand, giving complete control—fast film travel produces an animated image, slower winding flicks individual frames one at a time on to the screen. Often an editing machine has its own splicer attached.

TAPE SYNCHRONISER. Some sound projectors have built-in magnetic recording as well as playback facilities. They are intended for use with film which has been given a magnetic tape coating along one edge, usually after editing and titling has been completed. Alternatively it is possible to connect up a synchroniser (Fig. 2.34) between a mute projector and an ordinary tape recorder so that each runs exactly in unison. Commentary, music, etc., is then recorded on tape, knowing

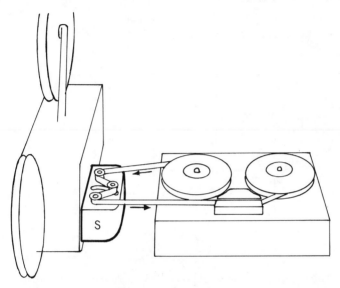

Fig. 2.34. Tape synchroniser (S) for movie projector attaches to side of machine and controls its motor speed.

that every time the two machines are operated through the synchroniser the audio content of the presentation will keep pace with the visuals. A synchroniser system used with an 8-mm projector is usually the cheapest method for teachers and students to make sound films.

From hardware to software
The aim of these opening chapters has been to establish names and functions of the main items of equipment used for visual aids purposes in teaching. The inter-relationship between various items discussed are indicated in Fig. 2.35. Note particularly the cost relationships of equipment and materials shown in Tables 2.3–5. Thanks to what is now fortunately a competitive and growing market many variations in equipment design are appearing every year, and the best way to see what is currently available is to seek the advice of one of the visual aids foundations (addresses on page 321). Comprehensive reviews of new

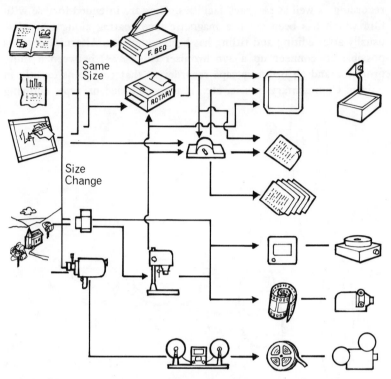

Fig. 2.35. The general interrelationship of copiers, duplicators and photographic equipment for the preparation of visual aids.

items appear regularly in *The Times Educational Supplement* and *Visual Education*, and regional and national exhibitions such as NAVEX also give an opportunity to compare items working side by side.

Hardware certainly has its own intrinsic appeal and one can admire the manufacturers' ingenuity (or deplore the lack of it). However the planning, choice and production of software are the areas where the teacher's own professional skill and experience of those he has to teach comes into its own. Most of the rest of the book will be devoted to this.

3. Software to suit teaching needs

WHAT IS the 'right' visual aid to use for a particular teaching task? Choice is naturally influenced by the availability of appropriate equipment but is really governed by the teaching plan for a particular group at a particular point in the curriculum. Decisions between slide or filmstrip are much less important than what goes on to that slide or filmstrip. The teacher's ability to plan, to select, to *make* the right visual aids software is essentially an extension of his professional skill in class preparation—and often a good deal more stimulating. But resisting the temptation to dazzle bewildered pupils with visual parlour tricks for their own sake, visual aids have to be well integrated with talking, writing, reading and other methods of communication.

Effective use of aids begins with understanding their potentialities. The aim of this chapter is to outline the practical teaching potential of various types of image and forms of software, and the premises upon which appropriate selection might be based. Commercially made software is also assessed, and compared against the possibilities of do-it-yourself aids—the subject of following chapters.

The wrong software

It is a well-known fact that well-meaning teachers who organise a film as a treat but fail to organise time to preview its contents often come to a sticky end. Even when the subject is right, the material can be found to be inappropriate in emphasis and level. Yet the same teacher would regard the issue of totally unknown textbooks to his or her students as highly irresponsible. A few unfortunate experiences can quire irrationally turn us against the use of film as such.

Again, most of us at one time or another have had to suffer a lecturer shuttling a filmstrip backward and forward through the projector trying to find the one frame relevant to his theme. Or the teacher turning from chalk-and-talk to slides, who has first to organise drawing of blinds, then set up the machine and uncertainly load in the transparencies. By the time the first image jerks its way on to the screen continuity has been shattered. The presentation is a giggle for the students and, amid his toppling piles of colour slides, a nerve-racking experience for the teacher.

Nor should we forget the enthusiast determined to put maximum information into his slides and OHP transparencies. Tables and formulae, graphs and histograms fill the screen with data from corner to corner. Even if the students have time to make notes only those sitting in the front row of the class can read the tiny, closely packed information. Sympathise too with the student expected to appreciate the significance of photographs of objects so mixed in with irrelevant foreground and background details that nothing has prominence.

Care in choice as well as planning is therefore advisable if we are not to waste our time and handicap rather than aid our teaching. Bear in mind too that each type of image and form of software—film, film loops, slides, filmstrips, OHP transparencies, hand-outs and display materials—can do only certain jobs well, some rather less effectively and for others are actively disruptive.

General considerations in planning
Visual aids work most effectively if used to supplement what is being taught, as illustrations supplement the text of a book. They should therefore be planned relative to a lecture or class plan, and not as a substitute. Fortunately students are now visually sophisticated, and less prone to think of the use of aids in the classroom as a special occasion. This is helpful because with good organisation learners will experience a smooth transition from talk to projected image, to chalk-board, to talk again—with no conscious break in the continuity of ideas.

Resist the temptation to build a quick-teaching programme around software which happens to be available. A film or filmstrip arrives for a colleague—how tempting to use it for one's own group too, even if it is not quite applicable to today's work. Look at other people's visual aids for preview purposes, but plan and obtain your own in response to the predicted educational needs of students.

The best aids are always the simplest. If an idea in simple mechanics can be clearly expressed using a coin and a stick on an overhead projector, don't make a loop film about it. As a very new teacher I once spent eight days and £10 in materials making a light box with twelve separately illuminated compartments. By manipulating switches photographic transparencies lit up in various combinations. The joinery and electrical wiring were exemplary. It was also heavy, bulky and used only once a year, when the points it made could equally well be conveyed on half a dozen slides. The whole exercise was really protective because

I was nervous of teaching and over-enthusiastic about aids. The box has become a constant reminder to temper enthusiasm with sensible pre-planning. Time in preparing an aid has to be related to its purpose.

Don't overwhelm the student with information. Each projected or displayed image should be planned to make a particular point, legibly and directly. If the information is complex, break it down into several simpler stages, and remember that legibility is determined by local conditions such as screen size, distance of viewer and degree of black-out as well as design of artwork.

Work towards a systematic library of visual aids. This is not of course practical for the more expensive software such as films, but filmstrips and slides (including one's own photographs) can be built up into collections like books and charts. With an efficient school or college filing system (page 262) these can be made available for any individual teaching or learning need.

The actual medium used for the visual aid imposes influences—some liberating and some restrictive. These are discussed below. Any planning of software must take such influences into account so that as far as possible the most effective medium of presentation is chosen. In practice this means knowing in advance what works best on the school's limited VA equipment.

Characteristics of various types of software

SOUND FILMS, VIDEOCASSETTES. 'Package deal' aids which may temporarily take over the teacher's role. Despite freedom to use a section only, sound film is inflexible in content and must therefore be chosen with care if it is to link in well with other material. The original producer may be aiming at a different age group, a more (or less) specialised audience, or gives emphasis in the wrong places. Even when we make our own sound film to use at a particular point in the curriculum it may prove more successful on some occasions than others. Teaching is a two-way business, with ideas, pace and emphasis varying from day to day and group to group. When making a sound film or strip keep the commentary factual, not tailored to any one set of viewing conditions. Alternatively stick to silent material and ad lib a commentary.* Above all, if choosing commercially made material *always preview it first.* A list of the small number of really useful film titles is soon built up in this way.

Films compel attention through their combined influence of movement, sounds and a great range of visual effects. Suitable presentation

* Several modern sound film projectors have a microphone socket or an independent volume control to permit the teacher to 'overtalk' the soundtrack.

of the subject of study on film often stimulates an indifferent student, because he can identify with events on the screen. Another most important characteristic of this medium is its ability to alter time scales—slowing down events normally too fast for the eye to perceive (high-speed cinematography), and speeding up slow changes occurring over a long period of time (time lapse). The former technique allows visual analysis of the behaviour of fast-moving machinery, animal movement and human athletics, and rapid physical and chemical changes. Time lapse is of particular value for botanical subjects—revealing the germination of seed and growth of plants and flowers. Practical details are discussed in Chapter 7.

Films can be good stimulators of discussion, create understanding of situations, explain abstract principles and teach operative skills. Probably their most useful function in the classroom is to consolidate what has already been taught, and to establish background. Technical instruction films (e.g. the setting up of complex experiments) which have to be projected several times to assimilate fully may be more effective in loop film or videocassette form.

At first sight videocassettes seem to offer the same characteristics as sound films, and indeed many programmes are merely transcripts from this form. However the mechanics of the medium (page 40) make it very much easier to select particular sequences, run forward and backward at various speeds, and hold single frames. In the case of EVR, which carries two rows of images (Fig. 1.17) one can switch from track to track where these present related aspects of the same subject, allowing 'do-it-yourself' cross cutting. (Similarly as a simple linear programme individual teaching machine.) Videocassettes are therefore potentially resource materials—more accessible and manipulative than film—but to be fully utilised they need to be originally planned and produced with the potential of the new medium in mind. Sciences and similar subjects which often need to be stopped and studied in detail are a natural for this type of software. Videocassette prices on the whole compare favourably with equivalent film; they can also be hired.

SOUND-LINKED FILMSTRIPS AND SLIDES. Sound filmstrips obviously lack many of the effects possible with film, including the facility to portray movement as such, but by varying the frequency with which frames are projected a surprising degree of apparent animation is possible. A sound filmstrip or sound-linked slide set can very effectively do jobs such as teach the simpler operative skills, give safety propaganda, help with languages and encourage reading by telling childrens' stories. They are very much cheaper to make or purchase than equivalent material on motion picture film.

LOOP FILMS. Loops are excellent for demonstrating to small groups cyclic actions—for example, the function of the internal combustion engine, or movement in animals. Silent loops can be left running to illustrate what the teacher is saying; they can also be used for revision purposes by individual students. Ideally one should be able to start the machine at any point in the loop and immediately have a useful image. The longer and more complex the cycle (e.g. pupa to butterfly) the less easy it is to maintain this start/stop flexibility.

Loops are easy to integrate smoothly into a teaching session because they are usually devoted to single concepts. Using daylight projection equipment one can switch on the moving image at the most appropriate moment in an exposition, continue talking over the picture and switch it off again when going on to the next point.

FILMSTRIPS. Filmstrips contain any subject (whether real or drawn) which can be photographed. They are particularly useful where sequences or images must not be disturbed (e.g. narrative illustrations for language learning) or where the occasional picture might otherwise be projected upside down by a hurried teacher.

Students can use the strips themselves for revision purposes, drawing them like library books from a resources room; alternatively they can be used for quite large group audiences. More educational visual aid software is sold as filmstrips than any other form. Incidentally they are also extremely compact and light—one 36-frame strip weighs about 14 g.

SLIDES. As single units of illustration slides can present tables, graphs, maps, diagrams and sketches, and photographs of outstanding quality. Each individual picture can be repositioned in a sequence (or discarded) to suit the needs of a particular group of students. Slides in a magazine projector can be shown as rapidly as a filmstrip, either to form a short detailed sequence covering a process or skill, or to give background, or may act as the visual structure throughout a complete lecture.

Equally, slides can be used singly or in groups of two or three to provide factual data which would take too long to write up on a chalkboard. (They cannot however be built up or modified while on the screen as in the case of the OHP transparency.) The excellent quality and detail obtainable from modern colour slides give considerable visual impact in presenting natural history, geography, fine art subjects, etc.

Obviously the larger the library of slides available the more permutations are possible in preparing for a particular group. A further important advantage is that commercial slides or 36 × 24-mm frames dismembered from a filmstrip can be mixed in with user-produced transparencies. Thanks to slide magazines, selection and sequence can be finalised at home and the material brought into the classroom all ready for the projector.

If possible try to standardise on 5 × 5-cm slides (Fig. 1.2). Larger slides offer only slight advantages in image quality, which, for classroom use, are outweighed by very limited equipment, extra cost of materials, and almost non-availability of modern commercial slides. Good 5 × 5-cm slides can be projected as images 2 m high and are therefore suitable for large audiences as well as small groups.

OVERHEAD PROJECTOR TRANSPARENCIES. These big (up to 25 × 25 cm) transparencies offer the greatest scope for improvisation and invention—both by teachers and learners. Summaries and notes arising from discussion can be presented; answers to questions can be illustrated on the spot; demonstrations (e.g. with models) can be given. At the same time, prepared transparent images can also be used, the machine allowing visual comparisons to be made between objects—often so difficult with a single slide or filmstrip projector. Equally a degree of animation can be achieved by means of overwriting by hand, overlays and polarising filter techniques (page 241).

The fact that the OHP will serve small groups or audiences of hundreds, functions well in competition with daylight, and (unlike the chalkboard) produces no dust, makes it almost universally useful—even in laboratories, hospitals and clean areas in factories. Smaller (7 cm) slides can be shown by masking down the light box, but they then of course appear small and dim. (A few machines such as Ofrex Fordigraph have special adaptors which allow more efficient projection of slides.)

The overhead projector works best with bold line images (preferably black line on clean film). Map outlines, graphs and schemic diagrams of all kinds are ideal, and further data can be added in grease pencil or quick-drying ink on an overlaying sheet of acetate. This facility makes them exceedingly flexible in terms of the level and structure of the lessons with which they are used. The same base transparency may be used for City and Guilds, C.S.E., O and A level groups, probably with different overlay material or information added by hand during the presentation. Similarly transparencies used in a formal lecture can equally be used in an entirely differently structured session, say in the laboratory.

Excellent commercially produced OHP transparencies are now generally available, particularly for subjects such as geography, biology and modern mathematics (page 117). Thanks to the development of heat-sensitive film and document copying machines able to give immediately usable transparencies the teacher can even copy material on the spot. (For example, an illustration in a book or a magazine article referred to by a student can be enlarged for the whole group to discuss.) Owing to their large *area* the cost of preparing or purchasing a commercial OHP transparency is much greater than a 5 × 5-cm slide.

EPISCOPE MATERIALS. As the episcope works direct from books and other opaque-based materials, preparation of software would seem unnecessary. However, bearing in mind the weak, contrast-flattened image projected by this machine, try to select or make bold diagrams and use glossy photographs which have plenty of tone contrast. They should be as big as possible within the dimensions of the episcope window.

HAND-OUTS. Illustrated notes can be prepared with a document copier or run off a stencil in a duplicating machine. The hand-out, which might be A4 size, may simply be a table of figures or set of graphs to save students time if no suitable textbooks exists. More often it will be a series of headings with gaps between pointedly awaiting students' own notes; or it can be a complete illustrated summary of the lecture. Similarly, the material might be an examination question paper containing diagrams and photographs.

Experiment with the use of line diagrams and even photographs in hand-outs—good illustrations here greatly assist comprehension. (Methods of preparing screened photographs for printing off on a duplicator appear on page 186.) Incidentally if hand-out material is to go into students' notebooks clarity of layout and illustration will be taken as a standard. Smudgy, poorly presented data encourages slovenly note-taking. Worse still, badly presented examination question papers make an already tensed-up student nervous and unsure.

DISPLAY MATERIAL. Students have extensive access to both board and wallchart displays, which are useful media for following up and sustaining interest in subjects under study and providing ready reference, in addition to their general interest value. The software is therefore usually designed to attract, interest and invoke discussion. Photographs, with their detail and invitation to identify are most valuable in this context.

Good progress pictures of archaeological digs and building projects and striking photo-journalistic sequences built around original or locally newsworthy themes will usually attract attention. The best sequences from photographic projects undertaken by students themselves (Chapter 9) could be a regular source of fresh material. Equally pictures showing stage-by-stage progression of processes, assembly operations, etc., have great technical instruction value for learners. Roller-processed stabilised enlargements (pages 94 and 328) are perfectly suitable for a few weeks' display, and quick and convenient to make. Vary the sizes of the prints—like a magazine layout make most forceful pictures as large as possible.

Wallcharts differ from posters in that they justifiably contain more detail and explanatory captions than something to be glanced at in a crowded corridor. They have a useful mnemonic role.

Pictures used on magnetic, plastograph, hook and loop and flannelgraph boards often have a narrower function, namely to directly aid classroom teaching. As such, illustrative material should make visual statements which are simple, bold and limited to the points the teacher wishes to make (Fig. 1.20). It does not have to stand on its own feet, and inessential detail is only likely to reduce legibility. Such material is often most effective when *drawn*, using black or coloured spirit ink.

Analysis of particular teaching tasks

Assessing the visual aid requirements of a particular teaching situation in detail is naturally a job for the teacher on the spot. The following are offered as criteria against which a visual aids requirement might be analysed:

1. What are the important elements of the subjects to be communicated?

2. Will visual images substantially aid this communication? (Abstract concepts, for example, are often conveyed more effectively by verbal than by visual statements.)

3. What is the academic level of the group, how many students are there, and where will teaching take place?

4. At what points in the teaching plan might aids be introduced— e.g. To introduce and give relevance to the subject; to establish a key concept or illustrate important relationships; to consolidate facts and figures; to summarise or revise.

WHAT THE IMAGE MUST DO. Having decided the points at which visual aids would be useful, think around the type of image which will communicate the particular information most effectively.

Images teaching skills such as woodwork and pottery should concentrate on the key stages of production. All inessential oddments should be eliminated from the picture contents and the main subject rendered with extreme detail and clarity. Try to give an 'operative's eye view' for easy learner identification; if necessary some recognisable object can be included to convey scale.

Images showing the characteristic features of objects (e.g. architectural and geological details) must emphasise these chosen features strongly through means such as viewpoint, colour, lighting and composition.

Images presenting statistical data should preferably use pictorial means (block diagrams, graphs,* shaded areas of maps) rather than tables of figures.

Break down data into easily digestible modules (Fig. 4.16). Tables are more satisfactory in hand-outs for later reference.

Images making comparisons (e.g. growth or decay, changing tastes) should do so by arranging as far as possible that all elements except those which are changing remain the same in each picture. Hence picture series should all be recorded from the same viewpoint, using the same background, lighting, etc.

Images conveying technical information are often clearest when prepared in the form of line drawings. Relevant parts (e.g. the water-cooling system of a car engine) can then be drawn in detail, but with surrounding elements rendered in broad outline only (see Fig. 4.18).

Images to provoke discussion, or provide background, or explain attitudes and generally give context to the subject of study usually call for realism, in which case photographs of actual situations are often more effective than drawings. Motion pictures are particularly valuable here (Chapter 7).

Images which allow analysis of phenomena (i.e objective records of rapidly moving or transient events) might include scales against which direct measurement can be made. These could be a grid background, and/or the inclusion of a clock face.

In every type of image, simplicity and aesthetic quality both help to put over the informational content of the aid but neither can act as its substitute. Deciding the most appropriate type of image for the job also brings us back inevitably to media and we must consider:

1. Does the material really require moving images, as offered by loops and films?

2. Will it be helpful to modify and add to the material during display, using an overhead projector?

3. If necessary will students be able to copy or abstract sufficient material for note purposes, or are supporting wallcharts or hand-outs required?

4. Will individuals or small groups of students need to use the material on their own as a form of teaching machine? Loops and filmstrips lend themselves particularly well to this form of use.

PRODUCING THE IMAGE. Images prepared for visual aids purposes can be split into two main illustrative forms—drawings and photographs.

* Assuming that the students are trained to read information in graph form.

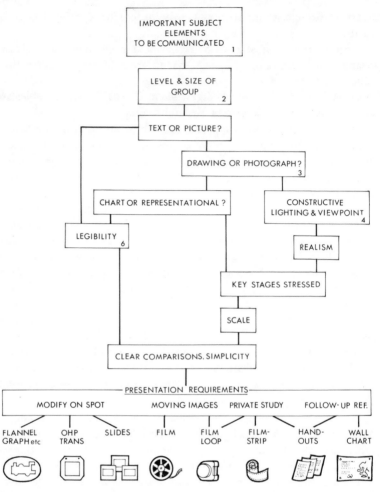

Fig. 3.1. Systems approach to the planning and selection of a particular teaching aid.

Both may be in monochrome or colour, and might be in still or animated picture forms. Drawn images include:

1. Lettering—hand-drawn or printed, stencilled or transferred.

2. Technical illustrations such as cutaway diagrams (Fig. 4.17) and graphs and block diagrams (Fig. 4.2–3); flow diagrams (Fig. 4.5); and including pictorial symbols and shading tints.

3. Sketches and painting, designs and patterns—realistic and interpretative.

4. Complete documents—pages from newspapers, brochures, books and magazines, containing text and illustrations.

Photographed images include:

1. Factual records of actual objects and events—ranging from aerial views of geographical terrain, to biological specimens photographed through a microscope.

2. Analytical records outside the experience of the human eye—frozen images of split-second events; or the tracks formed by movement of stars and satellites over long periods of time.

3. Interpretative images of people and situations—including evocative pictures of other times.

4. Reproductions of paintings, drawn artwork of all kinds, documents and other photographs.

Photographic images have an air of authenticity, can contain a great amount of detail (wanted *and* unwanted), and are often easier for a student to identify with than drawings—particularly within the context of human relations. Drawings allow great clarity of wanted detail, are excellent for simplifying concepts, and link most easily with graphs and written data. It is often easier to reproduce line drawings well when preparing visual aids software.

Sources of software

Having decided the software most likely to be useful, we can acquire it from two main sources: commercial producers from whom ready-to-use software may be bought or hired; and aids made by the teacher himself. To this can be added local authority libraries, teachers' centres, industrial organisations and other sources of free loan material. The remainder of this chapter is concerned with commercial software; preparation of the teacher's own aids is discussed in practical terms in the three chapters following.

COMMERCIAL SOFTWARE. Most of the firms marketing visual aids software today have a background of either book and magazine publishing, or photographic or motion picture production. Some firms produce and distribute sound films and loops; others slides, filmstrips, OHP transparencies and wallcharts; still others market 'multi media' kits centred on tape linked filmstrips or slides. A few specialise in custom-made software and skeleton material (e.g. grid or line ruled acetate for OHPs) for do-it-yourself aids. All these items are for sale, although it is more usual to hire sound films because of their high cost. Loops may be bought or hired. The names and addresses of some of the major suppliers of software are listed on page 317.

The main advantages of commercially produced aids are:

1. Specialised and physically remote subject matter, to which the teacher himself is unlikely to have access, is made available. Some

(regrettably not all) of the material has been thoroughly field tested and modified, or at least vetted by teacher advisors. Most producers welcome and act on ideas from teachers to extend their range.

2. Subjects which are technically difficult to light and photograph are handled by skilled professional photographers.

3. Multimedia kits or packages of linked materials—e.g. strip, sound recording, wallchart and teaching notes and hand-outs—are produced around a particular subject (see Fig. 3.5). This integration is helpful when, say, a wallchart is left as a follow-up to a technical session, or loops used to follow-up and amplify particular sequences in a sound film. They also provide whole-class activities.

4. The price can compare favourably with the cost in time and materials of preparing the aid oneself—particularly filmstrips and loops.

On the other hand the commercial products have inherent limitations too, of which the following are the most notable:

1. With the possible exception of simple factual principles, 'off the peg' aids may treat a subject at the wrong level or with the wrong emphasis for particular group needs.

2. The more subjective and specialised the material the more limited its application. Understandably, commercial producers show most interest in the predictable mass market of fundamental physics, chemistry, biology, geology, etc. More specialist requirements usually have to wait on the success of these best-sellers or a build-up of demand.

3. Some publishers cannot resist the temptation to put more detail into an aid than can be absorbed visually, compromising content in order to widen the market.

4. One is tempted to go on using bought software beyond the point at which it becomes outdated.

COMMERCIAL FILMSTRIPS AND SLIDES. The great majority of 35-mm filmstrips are in colour, contain about 50 single-frame 24 × 18-mm pictures, including title and credits, and have accompanying teaching notes. (Approximate cost is shown in Table 3.1.) Some strips are produced in an alternative form having 24 × 36-mm double-frame picture formats—the point being that such pictures are particularly cheap and convenient to cut up and mount as individual 5-cm lantern slides, because they match standard 35-mm colour transparencies. It is usual to find that a subject is covered by a *series* of strips (e.g. on the basis of one per lesson). A typical series might comprise five filmstrips, although an extended subject such as The Human Body might run to twelve or more strips.

Sound strips have a recorded commentary on separate tape or disc. Usually the cues for picture changing are audible 'pips', but may also be inaudible signals recorded on the second track of a two-track tape for use in an automatic projector arrangement.

The filmstrip is the most prolific form of visual aid used in education and the catalogues list almost every type of subject and level. The following give some indication of their diversity:

Experiments in chemistry, secondary school level.

Use of the micrometer, for industrial apprentice training.

Fairy Tales, for infant schools.

Art History, for adult further education centres.

Plants, junior school level.

Regional Geography, for secondary schools.

Basic Design, for Art Colleges.

English Literature (*Shakespeare*), to accompany class reading in secondary schools.

There are also narrative picture stories forming a key accompaniment to language tuition, for class or individual (language laboratory) work.

The BBC 'Radio Vision' productions combine a high-quality radio broadcast (drawing on the Corporation's vast resources) plus one or more filmstrips, and pupils' notes. The broadcast is intended to be tape-recorded, so that the result is a low cost 'package' capable of use independently of the radio broadcast time and suitable for class, small group or individual study appreciation. This concept is being further explored by local radio and the Open University.

Commercially published slides usually take the form of 24 × 36-mm transparencies mounted in captioned 5 × 5-cm card frames. They are sold singly or in sets of a dozen or so. Although the catalogues apparently contain far fewer slides than strips every filmstrip is a potential (and cheap) set of slides.

A great majority of published slides are in colour, and some of the finest examples are sold by public institutions such as art galleries and museums. This is because they are often photographed direct from exhibits. Discretion should be used when buying slides of the tourist souvenir variety, however, because they can be second- or third-generation copies with degraded detail and colours. Some excellent slides and filmstrips covering general interest and current affairs subjects are sold by magazines such as *Paris Match* and the British weekend colour supplements.

COMMERCIAL OHP TRANSPARENCIES. A typical prepared overhead projector transparency consists of a base transparency (250 × 250 mm

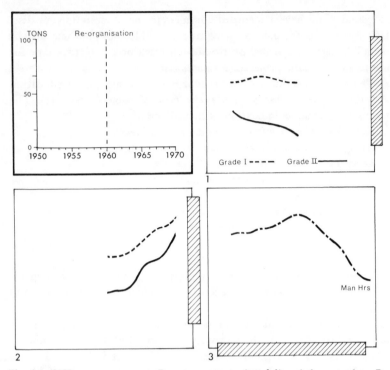

Fig. 3.2. OHP transparency set. Base transparency (*top left*) and three overlays. By mounting overlay 2 with its hinge superimposed on the hinge of overlay 1, overlays cannot be introduced in wrong order. Overlay 3 can be used at any point with or without 1 and 2.

maximum image area) on acetate film mounted in a card surround, plus three or so coloured overlays (or 'flips') also on film, and teaching notes. Each acetate overlay carries some detail, wording or block of colour, and may be hinged to the base transparency as shown in Fig. 3.2. For subjects such as geography as many as eight or ten overlays on separate sheets may be provided. As a typical example, the base transparency might be a black on white outline map of the British Isles. The first overlay then carries blue lines denoting rivers, the second county boundaries in red, and the third shows the names of major towns printed in black. Other overlays may cover crops, natural resources and population density.

One producer* of OHP transparencies publishes them in a spiral-bound book together with teachers' guide text. This is so arranged (Fig. 3.3) that any wanted transparency can be flipped direct on to the OHP

* For brand names see Appendix IV.

light box, leaving the facing text page lying on a desk top attachment where it can be referred to by the teacher.

The most popular subjects chosen for commercial transparencies are basic concepts which lend themselves to sequenced presentation. These include:

Physical Chemistry, structure and molecular shape.

Geology, erosion and landscape formation.

Technical drawing.

Geometry, loci, and lines, arcs and circles.

Biology, human anatomy.

Hymn texts for general assembly.

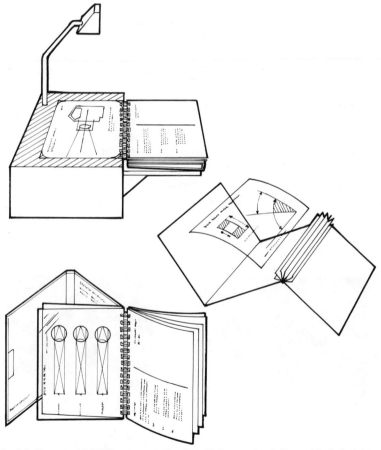

Fig. 3.3. Commercial OHP transparencies. Spiral Flipatran book (*bottom*) is designed to allow projection of transparency without removal from book. Teachers notes can be checked during exposition. Skeleton book (*right*) has self-adhesive strips for similar storage (removable) of bought and self-made transparencies.

As Table 3.1 shows, commercial transparencies for the overhead projector each cost about half as much as a filmstrip of fifty or so frames. This, plus their extra bulk, must be considered when a great deal of visual material is to be presented.

WALLCHARTS. Wallcharts, wall pictures and posters are published commercially by the makers of filmstrips, OHP transparencies and loop films; many are issued free or at low cost by industry, trade associations and government departments. They are almost always printed in colour. Wallcharts may be faced with a plasticised material, allowing the teacher to overwrite in grease pencil, which can be wiped clean again afterwards. The most common wallchart sizes are 20 × 30 in. and 30 × 40 in.

Typical examples of the type of summarised factual information contained in commercial wallcharts include:

Handicrafts—such as 'how to do it' needlework picture sequences.

Geology—reference information and detailed pictures of rock specimens.

Chemistry—periodic tables.

General topics—flow charts showing industrial processes such as steel manufacture or the preparation of foods.

Wall pictures may also be detailed, but often devoid of text. They provide discussion points for:

Language teaching—narrative pictures.

History, Geography, Sociology—scenes in village or town, homes, battles, etc.

FLANNELGRAPHS. Simple pictures printed on flannel (or plastic) are marketed commercially or issued free by manufacturers. They may for

Fig. 3.4. Acetate overlay sheet used with time-saving outline map, either printed commercially or self prepared (see Fig. 4.15). Details are overdrawn on acetate with grease pencil.

example portray a range of foods, each with names and prices, and attach to a background felt showing a market stall or shop interior. Initially each item has to be cut out from one sheet, which is rather laborious. Subjects include:

Nutrition—children's shopping and storage games.

Road safety—symbols and situations.

LOOP FILMS. Super-8 film loops, encapsulated in cassettes, are published by producers of both filmstrips and films. The material is almost always in colour, usually mute and varies in length (typical length being about 3–5 min). Most sound loops use magnetic stripe on the film, although the longer mass-produced film loops (page 43) may carry an optical track instead.

A small collection of loops for introduction, recapitulation and revision purposes either by groups or individuals costs little more than an equivalent number of textbooks (Table 3.1). Popular loop subjects include manufacturing processes, experiments which are too time-consuming for schools, and animated diagrams explaining biological functions. Loops also function as teaching machines for individuals to revise or learn manipulative skills and procedures.

Other typical commercial loop subjects are:

Modern mathematics—transformation geometry.

General science—types of wave motion.

Foundry practice—milling, for industrial training.

Handicrafts—pottery and metalwork, for adult education.

Narrative stories—for language teaching (often accompanied by a specimen teacher commentary in separate tape or note form).

Physical training—swimming and tennis strokes.

FILMS. The sources of 16-mm educational films include the entertainment film industry and its offshoots; also the television companies and independent production companies working for sponsors such as large industrial organisations and government departments. Because of their cost, sound films are hired rather than bought; this side of the business is usually handled by distributing companies and film libraries. Films sponsored by industry are often available free, and constitute a particularly valuable source of material. County education authorities maintain small libraries of well-tried teaching films; another useful source is the National Audio Visual Aids Library (page 321). Material is also becoming available in the form of videocassettes, for replay through the school's television receivers.

The first step is therefore to obtain catalogues and lists from most of the sources of film (addresses on page 318) and to watch out for the film reviews appearing in publications such as *Film User, Visual*

Education and *The Times Educational Supplement*. Popular films often have to be booked weeks ahead, and even then alternative dates may have to be given. Sixteen-millimetre films come from the library on 400-ft, 800-ft or 1200-ft capacity spools (for running times see Fig. 1.16) and usually they arrive about twenty-four hours before the specified showing date. Film *must* be returned promptly or an additional day's rent becomes chargeable.

The range of subjects and levels covered by 16-mm sound films during the past decade is so comprehensive that any summary can be deceptive owing to its omissions. The following titles, all booked during the same month in 1972, illustrate the diversity of film material available:

The Chemistry and Physics of Water—animated colour film produced for Unilever (free loan).

At the Wicket—black and white instructional sound film with teacher's notes from EFVA library.

A House is not a Home—black and white BBC TV social documentary.

Flame of the Future—documentary on natural gas from Gas Council (free loan).

The Solar System—colour sound film with teacher's notes from Colour Film Services.

Silent motion picture films are mostly issued in the form of short cassetted loops, described above.

VIDEOCASSETTES. Part film, part unipurpose resource material, videocassetes do not yet offer the same range of subjects specially prepared for the medium. Subjects include:

Principles of Nuclear Fission.

The Function of DNA.

Chromatography.

RESOURCE MATERIALS AND MULTI MEDIA KITS. Teaching kits can provide stimulating material for group study, projects, etc., particularly in primary and lower secondary education. Some—for example Jonathan Cape's *Jackdaw* series—are packages of printed source materials. These include facsimile-reproduced newspaper extracts, contemporary drawings, photographs ... even cardboard models for assembly. Other kits use a wider range of media and might be centred on a filmstrip or slide set with a tape or EP record, teacher's notes and wallchart. Typical kit subjects include:

The Party—teeth hygiene propaganda. Flannelgraphs of animals to cut out, printed pictures, teachers' notes. British Dental Council, for infant school use.

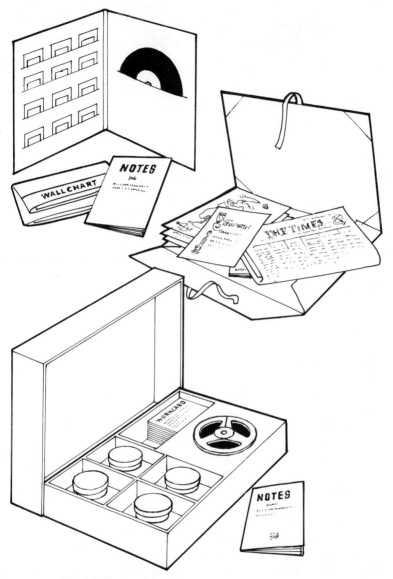

Fig. 3.5. Commercial multi-media kits and resource material.

The Sea Shore—sixteen colour slides, 7-in. record, teacher's notes, all packed in an album. CI Audio-Visual, for lower secondary schools.

Peterloo 1819—a folder of facsimile newspaper cuttings, songs, plans, drawings, etc., and an explanatory text. Manchester Libraries Committee, for fifth-formers.

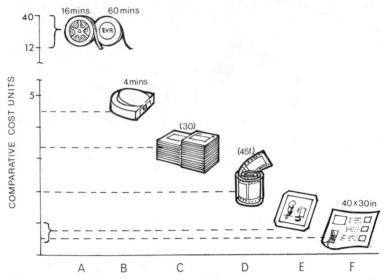

Table 3.1. Approximate cost of commercially produced material. A, 16-mm sound film or (much longer playing) EVR. This can be hired from about 1 unit a day. B, 8-mm mute loop film. C, Set of 30—5 × 5-cm slides. D, One 45 frame filmstrip. E, One OHP transparency. F, Wallchart.

Photo-packs—sets of fifty or so 9-in. sq. laminated aerial photo-graphs* grouped in terms of locality or terrain, and marked with map reference and compass rose—are also very versatile as re-sources material.

Far more ambitious multi-media packages using a complete systems approach are produced by large organisations such as the BBC. One example, the BBC Mathematics series, offered:

1. Key lessons by TV (teachers were able to preview programmes each week).

2. Sixteen-millimetre films.

3. Eight-millimetre film loops.

4. Printed materials for statistics, etc.

5. Student's textbook and comprehensive teacher's notes.

PREVIEWING. From the foregoing it can be appreciated that, whatever the form of visual aid, some opportunity to preview before purchase is highly desirable. Publishers and distributors vary in the facilities offered to teachers to examine their wares. Many have London show-rooms where projection material, charts, etc., can be examined. Or-ganisations such as Encyclopaedia Britannica offer a previewing pack-age delivered to the teacher's own school, a projector and a case of

---

* 'Britain From the Air' series. Macmillan Educational Ltd.

software being provided free for up to three days. Most publishers will supply OHP transparencies, loop films and wallcharts on 10 days free trial. Sound films may have to be hired for previewing—this can be a job for the evenings or vacations. Previews and reviews are also published regularly in the journals listed on page 299.

Do-it-yourself softwear

There are two alternatives to off-the-peg software—aids made to our requirements by a visual aids technician or commercial photographic studio specialising in VA work (Appendix IV), or aids prepared ourselves. The former is an ideal situation where staffing and money allow. However, many of the preparation techniques used by professionals can be handled by teachers too, as described in Chapters 4–8.

The educational advantages of making aids rather than buying off-the-peg products are:

1. Often commercial material cannot be found which is *exactly* right for the teaching task. The teacher is obviously in the best position to tailor software to his own treatment of the subject, to know the current academic needs of his students, and predict how they will most easily identify (e.g. local subject matter raises strong associations).

2. Material can be modified and kept up to date without having to wait for new software to be published.

3. Effective aids made by the teacher himself invite co-operation— students are often interested in material made specially on their behalf, particularly when the teacher can add relevant items of information about the original subject matter.

4. A high-quality original transparency gives a much more vivid projected image than the duplicated material that results from commercial distribution.

5. Provided they are not too ambitious, aids are often easier to make than one might imagine; they are also an enjoyable means of self-expression and an incentive to keep up to date in one's subject. Students themselves are often eager to provide material and this can form the basis of educationally valuable projects.

Summing up choice of software

Software to supplement and enrich teaching should integrate smoothly with other traditional communications media.

Like all teaching material software must be planned. Keep it simple, strictly to the point, legible and tailored to the needs of the group, yet flexible enough to help deal with additional points raised during presentation.

First analyse the need. Will visual images convey the important elements of the subject? What is the level and size of the group and at what point in the teaching session will aids prove most effective?

Consider what images can do; emphasise important stages, present statistics graphically, make comparisons, provide general background, convey technical details, effect realism, make measurement. Drawn illustrations allow great clarity of wanted detail; photographs give authority and encourage audience identification.

Consider the characteristics of various forms of aid: sound films and sound filmstrips tend to be complete in themselves, excellent in establishing background, stimulating discussion and teaching operative skills. The teacher must preview and introduce this material. Loop films are useful for demonstrating single concepts including cyclic material. They are of a few minutes' duration, and designed for small groups or individual study. Videocassettes combine most of the advantages of films and film loops, provided a TV readout is available.

Filmstrips, the cheapest form of software, cover a very wide range of subjects and levels. Sequences are fixed unless frames are cut up as separate slides. Slides prearranged by the teacher in magazines are as quick to use as a filmstrip but selection and sequence can be modified for each class situation.

OHP transparencies allow most improvisation. During presentation basic prepared drawings can be overwritten by hand, overlaid with colour or additional detail.

Hand-out material is expedient when classtime would be wasted in unnecessary drawing, listing of data, etc. Hand-outs should set standards of note presentation. Where possible encourage the addition of students' own material, e.g. supply note headings with gaps.

Wall display materials should attract and interest, and can contain more detailed information than other aids if intended for prolonged display. Illustrations for flannelgraph and similar presentation should be bold, and make very simple visual statements.

Commercial software can be bought or hired, often in packages or mixed media kits. Cost is comparable with teacher-produced software.

Technically difficult subjects are competently translated into visual aid form, but designed to suit a norm for which there is commercial demand. Software prepared by the teacher can be designed for his own particular way of handling his subject and to suit known group needs. Often it will invite co-operation by its local origins, and is stimulating and challenging to devise.

Finally, don't fall into the trap of building a teaching programme around aids which happen to be available (or have been prepared with more sweat than thought). Aids are deployed in response to actual needs as observed and anticipated by the teacher.

The chapters following are devoted to practical ways and means of making visual aids software, with particular reference to the use of equipment described in the earlier part of the book.

4. Getting started—artwork preparation and basic photography

IN GENERAL the basic subject matter for aids is of two main types:

1. Drawn, assembled, or printed two-dimensional flat copy such as hand prepared artwork, posters, magazine clippings, books and documents of all kinds.

2. Actual three-dimensional animate and inanimate objects.

The translation of flat copy into still forms of visual aids is discussed here and in Chapter 5, three-dimensional subjects in Chapter 6, and production of moving picture aids from all kinds of subjects is covered in Chapter 7.

The most common requirement when tackling visual aid subjects is the reproduction of diagrams, tables, text and drawings of various kinds. These may be specially prepared by the teacher or (more often) are illustrations in books, newspapers and periodicals. They are needed either as projectable images, or hand-outs, or display material. We should look particularly at the planning and preparation of any specially drawn material because care at these stages can add greatly to its visual effectiveness. Most artwork is only an intermediary in that it is intended to go to the camera or document copier for conversion into various forms of software, but the skills required for its preparation are equally applicable to wallcharts and display material which are ends in themselves.

If the flat copy is to be photographed we also need to consider the practical skills of setting up, lighting, imaging and exposing with the camera.

Artwork preparation

Most people feel unnecessarily inhibited about preparing drawings and other artwork for visual aids. However, provided we are clear about what we want to convey and choose a clear and simple layout there are now plenty of materials to help give a quick and professional-looking result.

DRAFTING CONTENT. First of all decide firmly what information is to

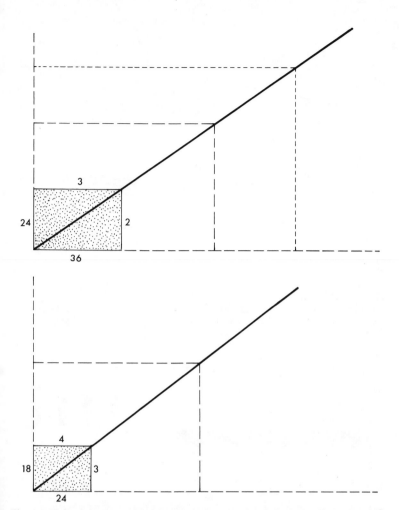

Fig. 4.1. Maintaining correct height-to-width proportions when preparing artwork for an aid to be reduced or enlarged to known final dimensions. An extended diagonal drawn through a scale drawing of the final format will show the correct width for any height and vice versa.

be conveyed (perhaps jot it down as a descriptive paragraph). Remember the age and sophistication of the teaching group—for young people particularly the main theme must be clearly distinguished from a mass of detail. Gather and *check* any figures and other factual data to be presented, e.g. statistics for graphs and tables; the order and names of processes for flow charts, accuracy of detail for diagrams. Begin to sketch out possible alternative forms of presentation, remembering always to plan within the height-to-width proportions of the final aid

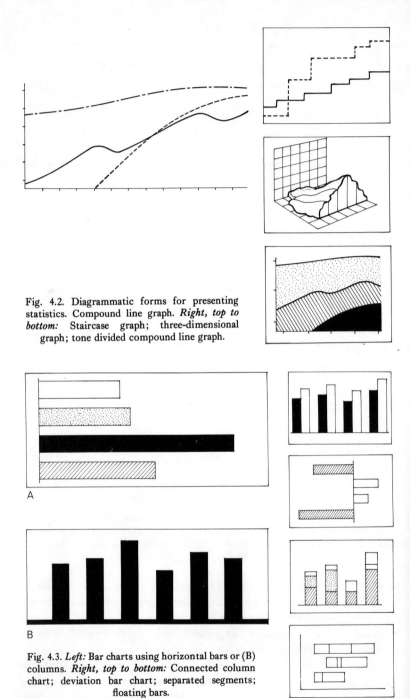

Fig. 4.2. Diagrammatic forms for presenting statistics. Compound line graph. *Right, top to bottom:* Staircase graph; three-dimensional graph; tone divided compound line graph.

A

B

Fig. 4.3. *Left:* Bar charts using horizontal bars or (B) columns. *Right, top to bottom:* Connected column chart; deviation bar chart; separated segments; floating bars.

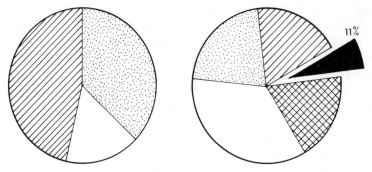

Fig. 4.4. Pie charts.

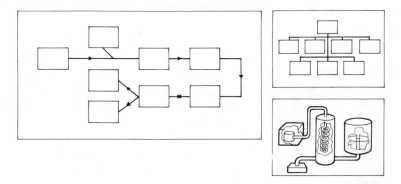

Fig. 4.5. Flow chart with (*right*) variations. *Top:* Organisation chart. *Bottom:* Cutaway flow.

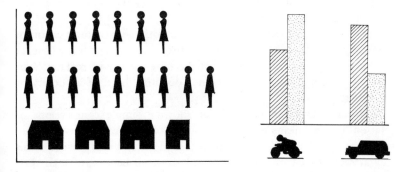

Fig. 4.6. Pictorial chart and (*right*) pictorial additions to charts of other kinds.

(see Fig. 4.1). Strip away irrelevancies until the bare bones of the information are left—whether they be hard statistics or the pictorial representation of a situation (as in language teaching). Imaginative thinking at this stage not only improves clarity (Fig. 4.16) but can result in aids with very effective impact as in Fig. 4.19.

PRESENTING STATISTICS. Even when teaching adult students, tables and statistical data are much more easily assimilated and made more interesting when presented in chart forms. As Figs 4.2–4.6 illustrate, there are five useful ways of graphically displaying statistics—line graphs; bar charts; pie charts; flow charts; and pictorial charts.

Line graphs show a range of relationships between any two scales of measurement, usually drawn at right angles. Aspects of this relationship can be emphasised by adjusting relative scales, e.g. compressing only the time scale axis of a growth/time graph exaggerates growth rate and makes minor fluctuations more obvious. Three-dimensional line graphs (Fig. 4.2) offer interesting possibilities for relating three streams of information in a concise form. They are not too easy to draw, however, and require a degree of graph-reading sophistication on the part of the students.

Bar charts are useful for comparing different items within any one time period (horizontal bars) or the statistical relationship of similar items at different times (vertical bars or columns). It is one of the simplest and easiest charts to make and understand. Although the predominant impression is of blocks, mentally joining the tops of the bars (or tones or colours within the bars) allows graph curves to be visualised.

Pie charts show divisions of a whole, in a direct non-statistical type of presentation. Where one segment is of particular importance it can be shown as a slice slightly withdrawn from the whole (Fig. 4.4). Unfortunately it is often difficult for the eye to measure the relative sizes of segments accurately and very small segments become almost too cramped to appear at all.

Flow charts are good for showing organisational structure: chains of command, the stages in manufacturing processes, or hereditary descent of the family-tree variety. Data might be enclosed in rectangles or other shapes, and connected by lines denoting lines of authority or other ties.

Pictorial charts can be used for showing simple comparisons or relationships by means of symbols—units of men, cars, houses, etc.—representing subject against quantity (see Fig. 4.6). Facts presented this way attract immediate interest and involvement because of their realism, but understandably seldom give as much detailed information as, say, graphs. Image-related symbols may also be used to decorate and attract interest in other forms of chart.

Legibility considerations

We have to ensure that when an aid is presented in its final form it will be immediately legible to all learners in the group. This involves considerations not only of artwork itself but also the physical method of final presentation, brightness of image relative to surroundings, time for viewing and the visual acuity of the individual student. Several of these factors are difficult to forecast but are discussed further on page 250. The following general legibility guides are worth considering at the artwork preparation stage.

Minimise the amount of lettering and figures needed in any one image. Where possible use a pictorial structure to present data. When composing legends first write the message in full, then try deleting superfluous content and making the remainder even more concise—but without weakening or altering the intended message. A document copier or copy camera may prove a danger here—it is almost always fatal to try to put a whole page from a book on to a slide or OHP transparency, as the result is too crowded and illegible.

Lettering *Lettering* Lettering
Legibility *Legibility* Legibilty

Lettering **Lettering** Lettering
Legibility **Legibility** LEGIBILITY

Fig. 4.7. Choice of typeface. The top row, generally unsuitable for quick communication, is set in (*left to right*) Old English, Brush script and Grotesque, an extra condensed face. The bottom row is in Univers Medium, Gill (both sans serif faces), and Times New Roman, both in lower case and all upper case. These are recommended, Univers Medium and Times New Roman being available in transfer lettering form.

Where the style of lettering can be chosen (i.e. when purchasing sheets of transfer lettering or stencils) avoid light or fancy faces such as Old English, or extra condensed faces (see Fig. 4.7), which all require more time to read. Use faces with good body—Univers or Times New Roman or Helvetica Medium are excellent—but having made a choice try not to vary it or mix it with other styles. Upper case (capital letters) take up more space than the equivalent in upper and lower case, and a mass of upper case only can be confusing to read. Notice how lower case is used effectively for motorway signs. Bearing in mind that

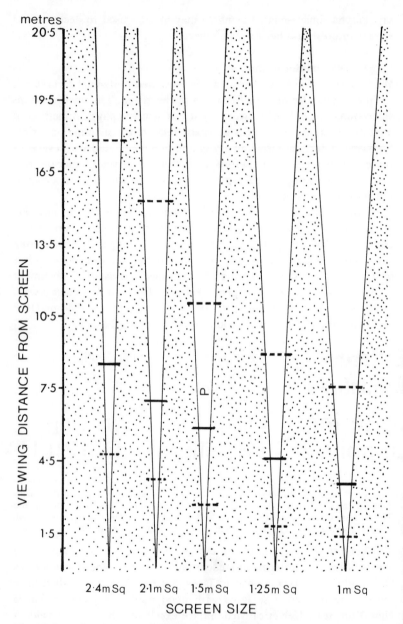

Fig. 4.8. Lettering size on an OHP transparency, related to projected image size and viewing distance. Try to make lettering on the OHP transparency no smaller than will fit between the lines for its screen size and expected audience viewing distance. Filling a 1·5-m screen for a 7·5-m distant viewer, for example, lettering should not be smaller than letter P. The thick vertical line denotes smallest advisable lettering.

typeface in books or typewritten text is seldom the clearest for projection purposes, properly prepared artwork is often more legible than document-copied material.

A good minimum standard for the height of lettering on artwork destined to become overhead transparencies is about one thirty-sixth of the size it should ultimately appear on the screen. Aim to make lettering on an OHP transparency at least 3 mm high, see Fig. 4.8. Remember that if one examines artwork from six artwork widths away this will preview its appearance when projected and viewed from six screen widths away—a good average distance. Be particularly careful to use large simple lettering when preparing artwork for 8-mm loop films (titles, formulae, etc.) owing to the small final screen size.

The tone and colour of background relative to the main subject has an important influence on legibility. Research has shown * that where the nature of the subject allows free choice (e.g. graphs and line charts) black on white background or black on yellow are the combinations

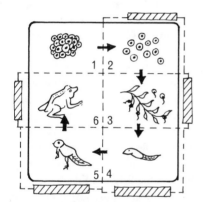 

Fig. 4.9. Designing an OHP transparency. *Left:* One way of planning a cycle to be presented one stage at a time with the aid of revelation masks. *Right:* The same images rearranged and spaced to be presented all at one time and individually captioned while on the screen.

most easily read. However, they are also often the most tiring. Guides must not be slavishly applied, as conditions of presentation and individual variations in eyesight have a much greater influence. White lines on black can be quite acceptable, are certainly less tiring, and are very easy to produce, using a black-and-white negative. Such a predominantly black image minimises the appearance of dust. Similarly, when colour is used throughout, try to choose pastel lettering against a darker-coloured background to show least dust and debris.

* R. Morton, Westminster Medical School, London.

If the final aid is an OHP transparency which will be given handwritten annotations during presentation, make sure the design allows plenty of room for these additions. It is not easy to write very small on an OHP acetate under teaching conditions. Similarly, if information is to be revealed bit by bit by means of an opaque card (Fig. 4.9), design the grouping of items on the transparency to make this form of presentation possible.

If the artwork is finally to be shown via the medium of television, remember the very poor image resolution resulting from the horizontal raster lines. Lettering should appear on the TV screen at least 2 cm high for group viewing. Keep graphs and diagrams extremely simple and avoid high contrast—work in light grey and black rather than white and black.

Artwork materials and methods

BASE MATERIALS. Having produced a sketch layout of the artwork the next stage is to begin to prepare it in final form—ready for copying, or direct use as display material. The most common base for drawn artwork is white or coloured cartridge paper. (Try to avoid fluorescent-coloured material if it is to be photographed, because it records as a rather dingy tint on colour film.) Cheaper material such as kitchen paper may be acceptable for direct display but gives too much smudging of ink-drawn lines to use for photo-originals. A clean chalkboard, flannelboard, plastograph or firm card or wooden surface can also be used.

If reproduction is to be by document copier the actual process to be used may impose limitations. For example, most machines cannot successfully reproduce from originals on coloured paper. Heat copiers have additional limitations, as shown in Table 2.1, and Fig. 4.13.

Matt white or black layout cards are sold by most visual aids suppliers (page 318). These are either plain or printed with various grids, e.g. squared, or lined for music scores. Transparent acetate layout sheets, gridded or plain, are also available for either making OHP transparencies direct or by heat copier, or acting as a transparent master for (diazo) printing of hand-outs. Some acetates are also sold ready printed with specialised outlines, e.g. a map of the British Isles; a circle for a pie chart; or the two axes of a graph. Similarly pre-printed maps on spirit master paper allow all or just the required parts of the outline to be traced using a carbon backing sheet, thus forming a master ready for the spirit duplicator (see Fig. 4.10).

MATERIALS FOR LINES, LETTERING AND SHADING. The easiest and quickest way to prepare bold axis and graph lines and shaded blocks is to use pressure-sensitive transfer materials. Follow the manufacturer's suggestions for spacing letter forms. As Fig. 4.11 shows, special narrow (1–2 mm) tape can be used for laying thin curved graph lines and can be arranged in quite tight shapes without creasing. Wide coloured and cross-hatched tapes are excellent for the bars on bar charts. Use either all light or all dark colours (never both) and place darkest colours

Fig. 4.10. Commercially produced base materials for self-prepared visual aids. Images and outlines are printed on acetate for OHP transparencies or as diazo masters, and spirit master paper for overtracing and duplicating. A very wide range of grids, signs, line drawings of trees, cars, people, etc., chemical and electrical symbols, decorative strip and shading, in black or transparent colours is also made in sheet transfer form. These are applied by burnishing, see Fig. 4.11.

nearest the base line. Pie chart shadings are cut from pressure sensitive sheeting.

Rolls of tape and sheets of transfers are expensive, and there are cheaper, slower methods of achieving similar results, using broad-nibbed pens of various widths and Indian ink. Felt- or fibre-tipped pens also give excellent results on good quality paper. Pencils give insufficiently bold results for photography, and are used for layout only. Large blocks of tone can be outlined by pen and filled in with coloured ink or poster colour applied with a brush, or even coloured gummed paper. Unless one's freehand skill is above average it will still be worth while buying a stencil or keeping to transfers for numerals and lettering.

ADHESIVES. When cut-outs are to be glued to backgrounds, either as

137

artwork for photography or wallcharts, or to act as facing for three-dimensional models, take care over the adhesive used. Many office pastes cause wrinkling or soon lose their adhesiveness. Rubber gum gives a clean, relatively flat join. It can be put on with a brush if diluted

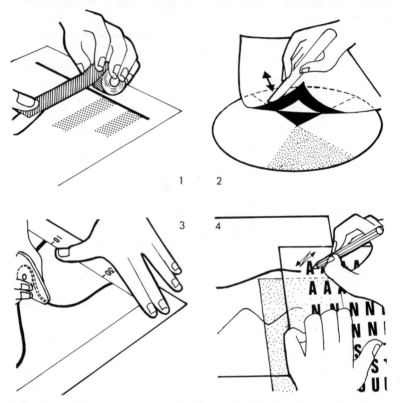

Fig. 4.11. Methods of applying professional-looking line, shading and lettering to artwork. 1, Applying cross-hatched transparent self-adhesive tape. 2, Introducing solid colour or dot shading pattern, by burnishing from transfer sheet. 3, Very narrow adhesive tape (from dispenser) even allows curves to be 'drawn'. 4, Burnishing a wanted letter from a transfer sheet.

with benzine. Surplus rubber gum around the edges just rubs off cleanly when dry. Dry mounting is quick and clean, and gives an excellent finish, see page 97.

CHART DRAWING. Start with a light pencil drawing of the design made on the base material (or in the case of acetate on paper which can be laid under the material). Once again remember the proportions of the final aid. If the artwork is to be copied in a document-copying machine it will probably have to be drawn the same size as the required final form. If it is to be photographed (e.g. turned into slides) the artwork can be prepared at any scale to suit drawing convenience. However, if the drawing is too small, lines and lettering will appear relatively thick and clumsy, and it may be difficult to focus the camera near enough. If it is excessively big, drawing of large-scale lines and lettering becomes laborious and costly. A good average size is 36 × 24 cm (the same proportions as a full 35-mm frame) and by standardising artwork the

Fig. 4.12. Materials and equipment for producing most non-movie visual aids. 1, Home-made light box for direct preparation of large transparencies on acetate or Cellofilm. 2, PVC and tabs for attachment to plastograph drawings. 3, Fibre-tipped coloured pens. 4, Pelikan broad-nibbed pen. 5, Rapidograph ink pen. Heat transparency maker, copy camera and duplicator at top are used for the next stage, converting handwork to final aid.

photographic set-up can be standardised too. As an alternative to drawing, consider using plastograph, flannelgraph, magnetic board, even chalkboard.

If the resulting chart is to be photographed on black-and-white film remember that several dissimilar colours (e.g. reds and greens) may record as similar tones of grey (see Fig. 4.13). To begin with, play safe and try to make up such artwork in terms of black, white and hatching or dot patterns to simulate grey.

When preparing artwork direct on to acetate—for example drawing an overhead projector transparency or a diazo master—use a fibre-tipped pen or pen filled with acetate ink. This ink slightly dissolves the acetate base to key the dye but also tends to attack the pen. Rapidograph make a special version of their pen to cope with this problem.

	PALE BLUE	GREEN	YELLOW	RED
DIAZO	WHITE	DARK		
ELECTROSTATIC	LIGHT	DARK	LIGHT	DARK
PHOTOCOPIER	WHITE	DARK		
HEAT	Usually WHITE, but depends on type of pigment			
PHOTOGRAPHY: LITH FILM	WHITE	BLACK		
PAN FILM	LIGHT	DARK	LIGHT	DARK

Fig. 4.13. How black and white document copying methods record colours. Tones relate to the final *positive* results.

If pressure sensitive tapes and rub-down letter transfers are used for the finished stage of chart artwork on film or card, burnish down thoroughly (Fig. 4.11) making sure no air bubbles remain trapped between these and the base. Bubbles photograph with depressing clarity, particularly as they are greatly enlarged on the screen. If these materials are used for an OHP transparency direct, be prepared to renew them from time to time.

TECHNICAL DRAWINGS. Every effort should be made to simplify technical line drawings by:

1. Showing only the important item in detail and indicating surrounding components as simple outline (Fig. 4.18).

2. Avoiding lettering as much as possible.

3. Using colour to separate important elements.

4. Breaking down complex subject matter into several simpler illustrations (see Fig. 4.16).

5. Using a style of illustration appropriate to the teaching task (Fig. 4.17).

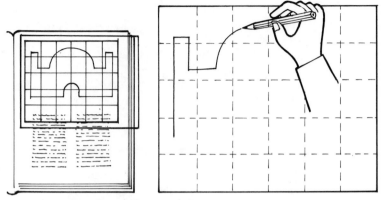

Fig. 4.14. Method of freehand copying from a book, using a series of squares ruled on acetate and another set marked in faint pencil on the artwork. If artwork squares are used larger (or smaller) than those over the original the copy can be enlarged or reduced.

In the case of OHP transparencies remember how various parts of a complex diagram can be built up one at a time, using overlays. For example, the drawing for the base transparency might just show the overall outline of a car engine. A second drawing on acetate is made to show valves. This will become the second overlay. More ambitiously, where an existing drawing must be copied from a publication, it is

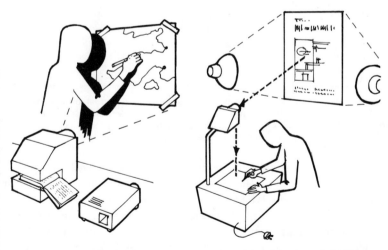

Fig. 4.15. Optical methods of preparing enlarged or reduced tracings. *Left:* Using an episcope or slide/strip projector. *Right:* By brightly illuminating the original and using the head of an OHP to focus a suitably miniaturised image down on to artboard.

141

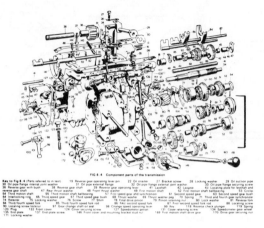

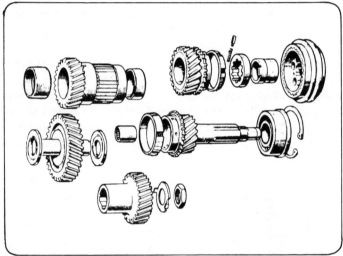

Fig. 4.16. Keeping diagrams simple. *Top:* A straight reproduction from a page in a technical manual, hopelessly complicated for single slide. *Bottom:* A small part of the top illustration copied using a macro lens, and with unwanted numbers, etc., blocked out with red dye on the negative before printing.

possible to photograph this several times, using opaque dye on the negative to black out different details on each, and then enlarge them on to films to form OHP overlays. See also Fig. 5.14.

GENERAL ILLUSTRATIONS. Drawings of people and environments for story illustration, history, religious instruction, etc., can be extracted, an element at a time, from illustrations in books, magazines and wallcharts. Use a system of squares for freehand copying, or project an image at the required size via an episcope and trace each item by hand.

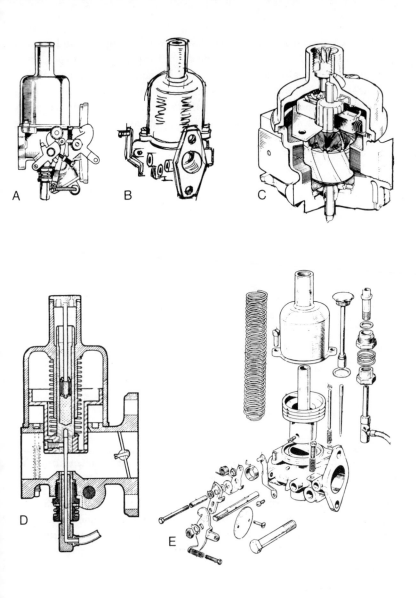

Fig. 4.17. Types of drawn technical illustration. A, External elevation. Factual yet more selective in its detail (and easier to reproduce) than a photograph. B, Freestyle sketch, giving an impression only. C, Cutaway view. Good for showing important internal component without losing relationship to general exterior appearance. D, Sectional drawing. Excellent engineering information but requires more experience to read. E, Exploded view. Realistic, clear relationships—excellent for recognition of parts and for training in methods of assembly. One of the most difficult illustrations to draw accurately, but see also Fig. 6.14.

Sometimes miscellaneous slides and strips can be projected and wanted parts traced, e.g. to give tree shapes, landscapes, figure shapes, cars, buildings. It may also be possible to cut images—drawings and photographs—from publications and if they are the correct relative sizes make up new images by montaging them against a simple drawn background. (Try to make the result all line or all continuous tone—or be

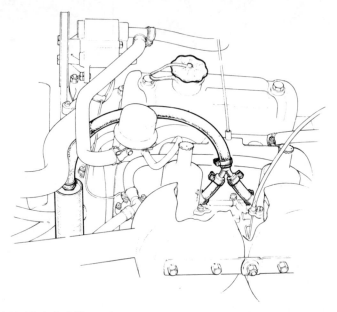

Fig. 4.18. Technical illustration giving emphasis to important components purely by weight of line. For a *photographic method* achieving similar differentiation, see Fig. 4.29.

prepared for the continuous tone elements to become very contrasty or the lines rather weak if the montage is document copied or photographed.) Hence a series of story slides can be made up featuring, for example, a well-loved cartoon figure, using drawings clipped from cartoon strips, rearranged and against new backgrounds.

Photographic arrangements for copying
A great deal of repetition can be avoided if some general, practical points concerning the photography of artwork can be discussed before getting down to procedures for handling specific jobs. These points concern lighting, imaging at the correct size, film and exposure calculations.
LIGHTING THE ARTWORK. The prepared artwork can most easily be

144

taped to a board, taken outside and illuminated by daylight. Flat, even lighting is usually desirable, and hazy diffuse sunlight is ideal (for black-and-white and daylight colour film). Watch out for shadows from the camera or any other cause of uneven lighting across the drawing.

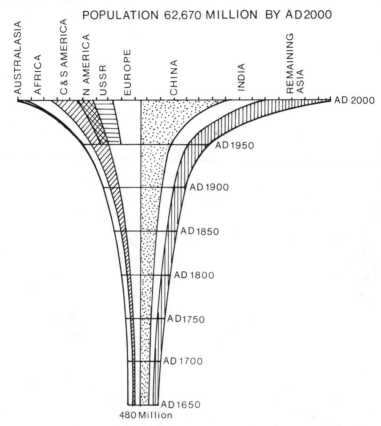

Fig. 4.19. Imaginative graph design. The population explosion presented in a form more dramatic than a table of statistics or conventional graph. Suitable for progressive revelation on an OHP, provided that names of countries are first re-set to a key adjacent to bottom part of drawing. *Readers' Digest Atlas.*

Unevenness must be avoided when using daylight through a window— a white reflector may be needed (Fig. 4.21).

If photography is taking place indoors two floodlamps each about 45° to the artwork surface will give even lighting of document size originals—large canvases may need four light sources. Table or desk units with bowl reflectors containing pearl lamps (say 100 W) are sufficient for small originals. If shooting in colour be sure to use the

145

type of lamp specified for the film, e.g. photoflood lamps for Kodachrome II Type A. Alternatively a correction filter may be available to match film to light source (see Fig. 4.27).

Try not to bring lamps too close to the artwork or it will be overlit at the edges—and may also curl in the heat. One simple test for evenness is to hold a pencil or ruler at right angles to the centre of the

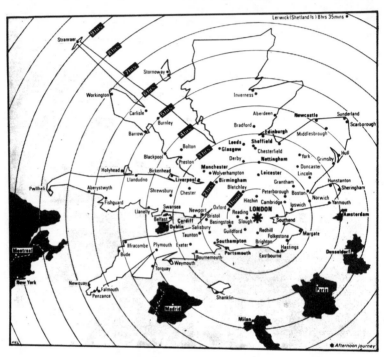

Fig. 4.20. Imaginative map design. Redrawing a map in terms of time travelled— locating towns in terms of their time distance by fastest-moving public service from London. Facts presented in this original way provoke discussion and interest. Perhaps other data could be given a similar freshness of approach at the artwork stage? *New Society*.

artwork and compare the length, direction and above all tone of the shadows it casts (Fig. 4.21). Lights can then be adjusted until these shadows are of equal depth. Watch meticulously for glare spots from shiny chart tape or paint—a good reason for using matt rather than glossy surfaced artwork materials.

Be careful not to record the camera, tripod (and photographer!) when shooting originals such as low key paintings behind glass. Shield as much light as possible from these reflected objects. It may even prove necessary to shoot through a hole in a large black card.

146

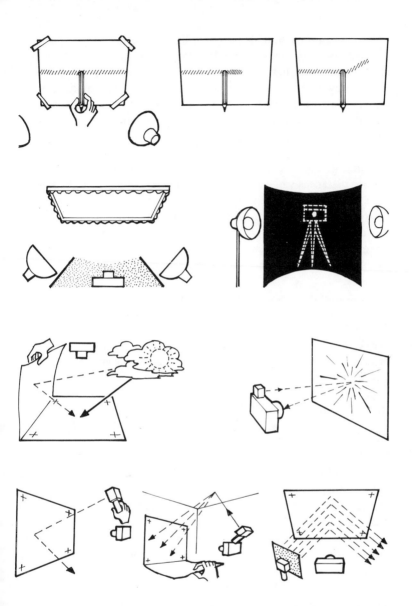

Fig. 4.21. Lighting for copying. *Top row:* Evenness test. When one lamp is too near front (*centre*) or set too low (*right*) shadows formed by pencil are no longer symmetrical. *Upper centre:* Avoiding reflection of camera in a glossy surfaced original (*left*) by screening camera from light or (*right*) shooting through hole in black screen. *Lower centre:* Balancing-up daylight with white reflector. *Right:* The danger of glare reflection when using flash is eliminated by (*bottom row*) angling flash, or bouncing, or diffusing with tracing paper. If flash must be used close to original, try to arrange a white reflector on the shadow side (*bottom centre*).

Flash is another suitable source of lighting but may reflect back flare spots if used on the camera. Where possible position the flashgun further away and slightly to one side, diffusing it with tracing paper. If much copying is to be done some form of permanent lighting and camera support arrangements will speed up the work and give consistent results. As shown in Fig. 4.22, the copy stand can be organised either horizontally or vertically with artwork secured by tape, pins or (if backed by a steel sheet) by magnets. Lamps are supported in fixed positions giving even illumination, and the camera can be positioned at various distances while always remaining centred and at right angles to the subject. An enlarger stand adapted to carry a camera instead of the enlarger head makes an excellent vertical copy bench.

Not all copy originals are on opaque bases. Sometimes it is necessary to copy transparencies such as slides, filmstrip frames and OHP transparencies. These can be set up in front of an evenly lit white area such as:

1. An evenly overcast sky. Tape the transparency to the glass of a window and photograph it against the white sky.

2. A piece of diffusing material such as opal glass or white Perspex. White tracing paper is also satisfactory but must be several centimetres behind the slide so that any pattern is rendered unsharp (Fig. 4.23). The sandwich is rear-illuminated by daylight, flash or a suitable lamp.

3. A sheet of matt white paper some distance behind the slide and front illuminated by one of the sources above.

4. A specially made slide copying attachment. This may contain its own light source.

In all cases it is advisable to arrange a strip of black paper about 5 cm wide on all four sides of the transparency, in order to prevent direct light spilling into the lens.

IMAGING THE ARTWORK. The main requirements in photographing artwork are that it should be evenly lit, sharply focused, square-on and centred in the picture area. There are several ways in which an ordinary camera will sharply focus a small piece of artwork so that it fills the frame:

1. Using a simple supplementary (or close-up) lens over the camera lens. The strength of supplementary lenses needed for particular conditions is shown in Appendix VII.

2. If the camera has a removable lens, extension rings or bellows can be fitted between the camera body and lens, so effectively focusing out the lens to image very close subjects.

3. If the camera accepts interchangeable lenses, hire or buy a macro lens specially designed to focus on copy close to the camera.

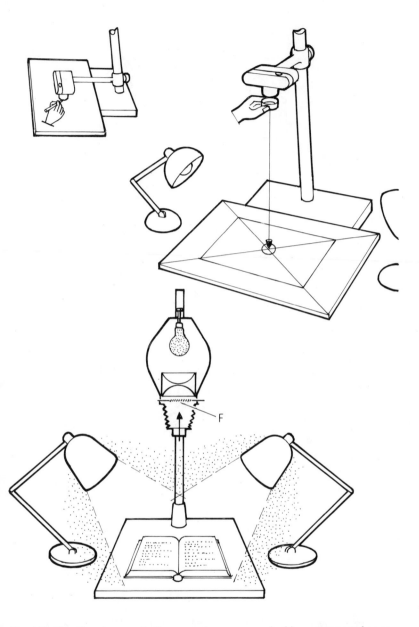

Fig. 4.22. *Top:* Centring a vertically arranged copy camera, in this case supported on an old enlarger column. *Bottom:* Using an enlarger for copying. Enlarger is first set up with old negative in carrier sharply projected on to face of book. Negative is exchanged for light-sensitive film (F) and with enlarger lamp *off* exposure made by switching on desk lamps. (Enlarger head may need wrapping with black cloth to prevent entry of light.)

149

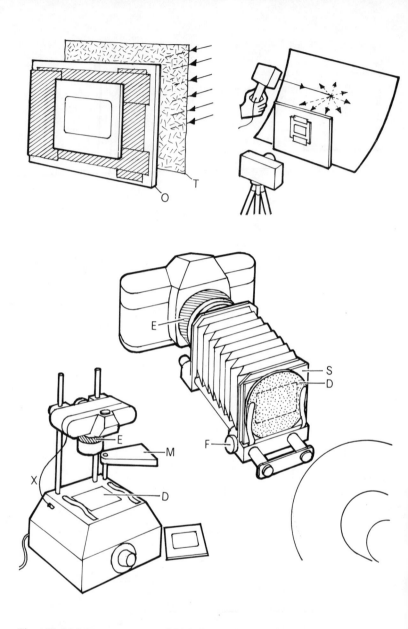

Fig. 4.23. Lighting transparent originals for copying. *Top left:* Light diffused by either tracing paper (T) or opal Perspex (O), or (*right*) reflected from matt white paper. *Bottom left:* Commercially made slide copying device with built-in electronic flash and swing over exposure meter (M). *Bottom right:* Copier which attaches in front of camera lens and carries slide (S) backed by diffuser (D). Combined unit is then pointed towards any convenient light source. E, Extension ring for camera lens. X, Flash triggering lead. F, Focusing.

Some cameras do allow quite close focusing even with their normal lens, and the situation is of course helped if the artwork is prepared fairly large in the first place.

The most common requirement is to produce 36 × 24-mm images, the universally used size for 5 × 5-cm slides. If a camera for a larger size of film has to be used (i.e. rollfilm or 5 × 4-in. sheet) it may be possible to image several originals at a time, making each one no bigger than 36 × 24 mm (see Fig. 4.24). After processing, the individual images can be cut from the film and mounted.

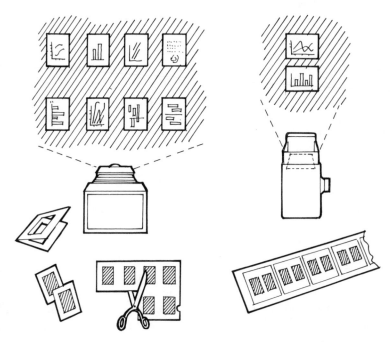

Fig. 4.24. Making several slide images by a single exposure on a larger format camera. Sufficient spacing between the copy originals is essential. Individual images are later cut from film.

Always take care to see that the camera is exactly square-on to the artwork—the back of the camera parallel to its surface and the lens opposite its centre. Even slightly oblique viewpoints result in images with obvious converging lines, parallelogram distorted rectangles, etc., when the results are projected. Centre the lens by setting up the camera on its tripod an inch or so from the exact centre of the artwork, and then pull camera and tripod back along a straight path at right angles until all the artwork is included in the finder (Fig. 4.22). Using a piece of string check that the lens is exactly the same distance from all four corners of the artwork. Centring is easier with a single lens reflex or sheet film camera, because the actual image given by the taking lens can be seen. The focusing screens of such cameras sometimes carry a grid of fine black lines—right angles against which the shape of the image of the artwork can be compared.

Accurate close-up focusing is also easier with a reflex or sheet film camera than with a direct vision camera. The latter can be fitted with a supplementary lens or extension ring and focused by scale according to the instructions packed with these close-up devices. More accurate still, it may be possible to take the back off the (unloaded) camera and place a piece of tracing paper across the path normally occupied by the film. If the shutter is set on T (or B and the release held down) the image can be seen and focused on the tracing paper. This also allows checking of centring and squaring up. The shutter is then closed, film loaded in place of the tracing paper and exposure made. Provided that all the artwork has been prepared the same size each piece can now be taped up in turn in the same position relative to the camera.

A steady tripod or camera clamp is obviously valuable for this work. Similarly a permanent set-up arrangement for copying with camera positions and the *areas* imaged by the lens at these positions marked out, greatly speeds up copying.

Another quick method for copying small items of artwork all the same size (e.g. stamps) is to rig a fixed spacer frame (Fig. 4.25) to the front of the camera. The camera lens is focused out or fitted with a supplementary lens so that it sharply images any flat copy positioned in the plane at the far end of the frame and lying within its boundaries. Thus the whole camera unit simply requires to be placed down on the artwork—viewfinding and focusing are unnecessary. Always surround artwork with strips the same colour and tone as the predominant background in the drawing itself—this will minimise the appearance of a slightly off-centre image.

CHOOSING THE FILM FOR COPYING. Table App.3.1 on page 312 shows a range of useful commercial materials; recommendations for specific subjects are made in the reference section beginning on page 159. In general, artwork which is to be photographed in black and white can be recorded on one of three types of film:

1. Continuous tone film, which like everyday camera film yields a good range of grey tones between black and white. However, if the artwork contains only solid black and clean white (including shading dots and hatchlines) these films tend to record the black as very dark grey and white as faint grey, giving a rather flat appearance.

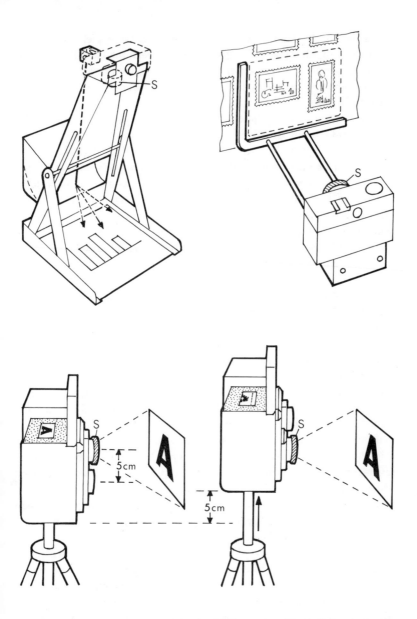

Fig. 4.25. *Top left:* Accessory stand for fixed ratio copying. Simple flash-cube camera attaches at top, looking down through built-in supplementary lens. Light from flash reaches copy via matt white reflector box which spreads and softens beam. *Top right:* Camera with supplementary lens, attached to fixed spacer frame which defines area recorded and distance for sharpness. *Bottom:* Copying with a twin lens reflex. After focusing and framing, supplementary lens (S) is changed to lower lens and the camera is raised by amount equal to lens separation.

2. Line (or lith) films which give high contrast—rich blacks and clean whites with virtually no grey tones between the two. This is ideal for boldly recording line artwork but turns existing continuous tone photographs and drawings, including coloured illustrations, into stark black and white.

3. Colour films, which however give accurate reproduction of subject colours only when the light source used meets the manufacturer's specification. Some films are intended for use with daylight (and electronic flash or blue flashbulbs), some for photoflood lamps, and some for 500-W photopearl lamps. Always try to avoid a situation in which a mixture of these alternative light sources illuminates the subject. Although *line* colour film as such is not available to the general user the general contrast of colour transparency materials (plus the subjective influence of colour itself) is sufficient to give acceptably bold results from line artwork. At the same time they will record continuous tone images without excessive contrast.

All three types of film are made as negative materials and reversal materials. *Negative* films give images reversed in tones (colour film also giving complementary colours). Normally these require subsequent printing on to paper or film. Often a negative image of a line original forms a very successful slide as it stands (see Fig. 5.4). *Reversal* films are designed to be processed in such a way that the original film exposed in the camera is returned bearing a positive image, with correct tones—in other words the familiar transparency, ready for projection. Reversal films call for more care in exposure and composition than negative films, as corrections cannot normally be made later when printing. Most colour films are reversal type, but note the monochrome reversal film Agfa-Gevaert Dia-Direct, App.3.1. This comes back from processing as a series of black-and-white transparencies.

USING COLOUR FILTERS. Colour filters are sometimes helpful when copying, their type and function varying according to whether monochrome or colour film is used.

In *monochrome photography* coloured filters can help the reproduction of various colours in dark or light grey terms when these would otherwise be unsatisfactory. For example, we may be reproducing from a published diagram which has white lines on a pale blue background. All black and white films give rather anaemic results—even using line film the final positive tends to be white on pale grey. But by shooting on panchromatic film with a deep red filter over the lens the final positive appears white on dark grey or strong black.

Again we may be copying a half-tone monochrome photograph from a brochure, but half the illustration is overprinted with a solid area of light green as part of the page design. Unfiltered photography would reproduce one half of the picture darker than the other, but shooting through a green filter (the same tint as the green ink) on to panchromatic film causes the overprinting to vanish.

There are three points to remember when using colour filters with monochrome films:

1. Always use panchromatic black-and-white film.

2. The filter *lightens* part of the subject matching the filter colour, and *darkens* complementary colours. It does not alter black, white or other neutral tones. A red filter, for example, makes red very light, blues and greens very dark (see Fig. 4.26). The filter's effect can be forecast by looking through it at the subject and observing which coloured areas go darker and which lighter.

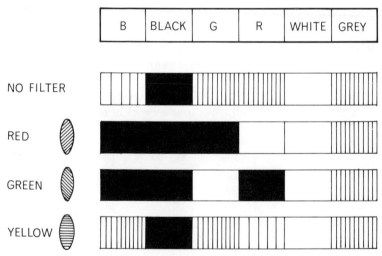

Fig. 4.26. The final reproduction of colours photographed on panchromatic black and white film, showing the effect of strong filters.

3. The filter reduces some of the light entering the lens and more exposure is needed. Filter manufacturers quote the number of times by which normal exposure must be multiplied. Alternatively, putting the filter over the light measuring cell of an exposure meter and comparing filtered and unfiltered readings gives a good guide to the increase required.

In *colour photography* of artwork the chief value of colour filters is to equate different light sources to various types of film. For example, a deep orange filter over the lens enables photoflood-type colour film to give accurate results when the artwork is lit by daylight. A bluish filter

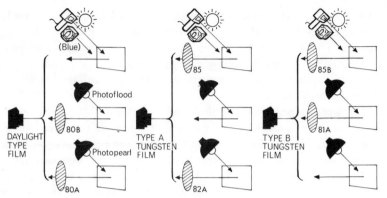

Fig. 4.27. Colour filters used to correct light source to suit type of colour film. Odd filter numbers are orange on colour; even numbers bluish.

allows daylight-type film to be used with photofloods, and so on (Fig. 4.27 quotes actual filter numbers and shows further permutations). In each case a slight increase in exposure is necessary, and this is quoted by the film manufacturers either as a manipulation factor or change in effective film speed.

MEASURING EXPOSURE. The exposure meter can be used normally when measuring from continuous tone artwork of reasonable size—for

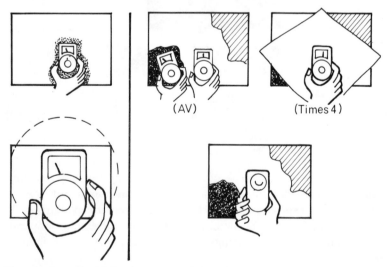

Fig. 4.28. Exposure reading for copying. *Left:* Wrong methods. *Top:* Meter too close, measures own shadow. *Bottom:* Too distant, meter measures from surround too. *Right:* Correct alternatives—average readings from light and dark areas; white card reading with exposure increased fourfold; meter (fitted with incident light attachment) turned to face light source.

example, measuring darkest parts and lightest parts and choosing a reading halfway between the two. With very small originals local readings will not be practical. Use a piece of grey card matching a midtone in the artwork, place this over the artwork and measure exposure for the card. For line work, charts, etc., it is usually easier to cover the artwork with a sheet of white paper, measure off this, and then give 4 times the indicated exposure (Fig. 4.28).

If the camera is being used very close to the subject (i.e. less than 4 focal lengths, or about 20 cm for a 35-mm camera fitted with a standard lens), extra exposure has to be given, irrespective of subject.* The

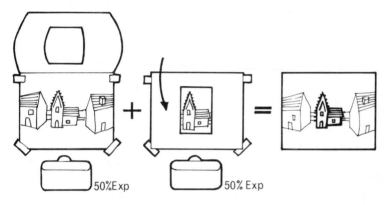

Fig. 4.29. Method of emphasising part of a picture by 'ghosting' remainder. Half correct exposure duration is given to whole image; white paper then covers unwanted parts and second half of exposure is given. Separation is also possible using coloured or black paper.

increase required can be read off the chart on page 335. Some macro lenses and extension bellows have the exposure increase already marked on their focusing mechanism. If a fixed copy set up has been made, the subject illumination is standardised and a list of exposures can be made out for each type of film and subject. Exposure increases for close-up working can also be permanently marked off on the camera support. Appendix VII gives exposures required for an actual set-up—if you can recreate this an exposure meter will be largely unnecessary.

Copying small transparencies sometimes creates difficulties in making exposure readings. An effective through-the-lens internal exposure meter is particularly valuable here. If a separate meter has to be used an overall direct reading from very close to the tiny image will usually

* If the camera has an *internal* meter system measuring from the SLR mirror or focusing screen this will take the close-up conditions into account and no further exposure increase is required.

suffice if it has approximately equal distribution of light and dark areas. Give double the indicated exposure if there are relatively small but important darker areas; give half the exposure if important areas are small but light, e.g. faces against large dark backgrounds. Again remember to give extra exposure for the close working conditions unless exposure is measured through the lens.

PHOTOGRAPHY OF TELEVISION OR PROJECTED IMAGES. The image on a TV screen or an image projected on a screen from a slide or filmstrip projector can be photographed without much difficulty. Switch off all other light sources and have the camera mounted on a tripod. If the photographs are being made on colour film use daylight type film for TV, and type B film for film/slide projectors.

One complete picture is formed on a TV screen every $\frac{1}{25}$ sec.* so choose a lens aperture which calls for an exposure time no faster than $\frac{1}{25}$ sec ($\frac{1}{15}$ second on most modern cameras) or part of the picture will be missing. Turn down the contrast control to give a rather flat image, and shoot when there is least action on the screen. Try taking pictures at various exposure levels because meter readings tend to be inaccurate. The raster pattern on a TV image destroys fine detail, so try to select parts of the programme featuring close-ups.

Slides and filmstrips must be projected on to clean, still, flat materials such as smooth matt white card. Measure exposure by reading from highlight and shadow areas on the screen. The smaller the screen image the brighter it will be, allowing faster shutter speeds and reducing the risk of slight image shake owing to vibration from the blower. Set up the camera as close to the projected beam of light as possible (Fig. 9.11), without of course casting a shadow. Interesting images are made possible if *two* projectors are used to give montage effects on the screen, which is then photographed. This is described further in Chapter 9.

* European TV; American TV is $\frac{1}{30}$ sec.

5. Step-by-step methods
for making aids by copying

THIS CHAPTER takes the form of a methods-of-copying directory, explaining in detail how to get from original flat copy point A to visual aid point B. Each route between the various permutations of original material and VA software is described in terms of equipment, materials and manipulation. Specific brand name recommendations appear at the back of the book, on page 312. While it is intended to keep these as up-to-date as possible, the current availability of such products should be checked. New and improved materials are regularly appearing in this expanding market.

For the most part, the copying of drawn or printed originals calls for the use of a camera for slide and filmstrip making, document copiers for OHP transparencies, and copiers and duplicators for hand-outs on paper. There are, of course, many cross-routes too and, while the methods described are not exhaustive, special attention has been paid to the ones requiring least outlay, time and experience. Simple sketches head each 'to' and 'from' requirement to give a quick visual reference.

Towards the end of the chapter flow chart Fig. 5.23 gives a general idea of how the main methods described relate to type of original, preparation equipment and required result and Fig. 5.24 shows the all-important relative costs of producing these aids. Incidentally, considered in conjunction with Chapter 2, this Methods Directory should provide some insight into the practical usefulness of specific items of visual aids preparation equipment the school may intend to buy—or already possess.

Making slides
Making slides (5 × 5-cm and 7 × 7-cm frames) almost always requires the use of a camera or enlarger because a change of size is involved. Remember that a camera taking 35-mm cassetted or cartridge-loading film can be used for 5 × 5-cm slides. A 120- or 620-rollfilm-size camera giving twelve exposures per film is suitable for 7 × 7-cm slides (see page 79).

As a final check before starting, be certain in your own mind that the teaching material is more effectively presented as slide(s) than, say, the more adaptable overhead transparency (page 110). Ensure, too, that the artwork is suitable in format (Fig. 4.1) and does not carry too much data to be legible (page 133). Check that the camera is suitable for the job (page 78) and key accessories such as exposure meter, tripod, and close-up attachment (page 87) are available. Finally, make the choice between black-and-white or colour reproduction to provide the most effective result. Black-and-white materials give maximum contrast.

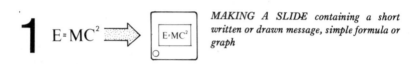

1 $E = MC^2$ ⟹ | $E \cdot MC^2$ |

MAKING A SLIDE containing a short written or drawn message, simple formula or graph

Method 1. Direct writing. Write direct on a 36 × 24-mm area of matt surface film, slipped into a 5 × 5-cm card mount (Fig. 5.1). This is then projected. Ready made write-on slides consist of matt clear film 38 × 38 mm mounted in 5 × 5-cm mounts and accept about 20–50 words if written with a sharp lead pencil or Mars fine overhead projector crayon. A fibre-tipped pen can be used to add areas of colour.

It is also possible to type written material direct on acetate within 36 × 24 mm or 36 mm square. Use a sheet of tri-acetate or cellofilm between two heavily coated carbon papers, coated surfaces inwards. Set the typewriter for stencil cutting so that the ribbon is not used. An

Fig. 5.1. Write-on slides using matt surfaced film, bought either ready-mounted or as lengths of 35-mm stock for cutting up. The latter can also be used for direct drawing of film-strips, see Plate 7. For brand names, see Appendix IV.

elite-faced typewriter gives about 9 lines of 15 spaces within 36 × 36 mm. Finally spray with a fixative varnish (as made for charcoal drawing) and mount in the usual 5 × 5-cm card frame.

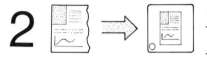

2 *MAKING A MONOCHROME SLIDE from a black-and-white line drawing, text or chart, either prepared as artwork, or from a publication, including reproduced photographs with coarse, clearly defined screen pattern*

Method 2a. Direct photography. Photograph on 35-mm black-and-white reversal film. The manufacturers return the processed film bearing positive monochrome slides, ready for mounting. This film is not strictly designed for line work, but gives adequately contrasty results. Alternatively shoot on a general-purpose fine-grain negative film, giving generous development, and contact print on positive printing film in the darkroom (Fig. 5.2).

Alternatively, photograph the original on reversal colour film appropriate to the light source (page 312). Shooting colour film seems

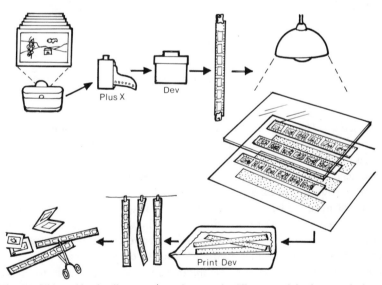

Fig. 5.2. Slide making by direct neg/pos photography. The artwork is photographed on general purpose material and contact printed on to fine grain 'positive' film in the darkroom (orange safelight), using concentrated print developer. When dry individual frames are cut up and mounted. For extreme image contrast shoot or print on 35-mm lith film and use lith developer.

extravagant (double cost) but this is really only a few pence more than when using black-and-white neg/pos methods (see Fig. 5.31). It is also often expedient when shooting a mixed bag of monochrome and colour pictures. Results are acceptably contrasty, although the transparencies may have slight overall greenish or bluish casts when compared with slides on black-and-white film. These colour materials are processed by the manufacturers and returned mounted ready for use, in about a week.

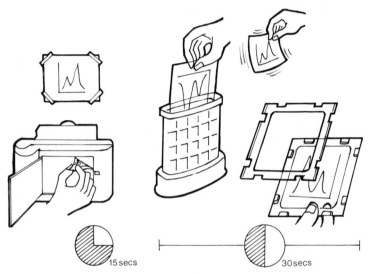

Fig. 5.3. A Polaroid back used with line type projection film for rapid slide production, see text.

Method 2b. Direct photography, negative image. This method is worth considering wherever the projection of a *negative* image (white lines, black background) will enhance appearance. Shoot an appropriate final size negative on film such as lith (35-mm), general-purpose neg film (35-mm or rollfilm), or on a sheet of line film. Process to give a maximum contrast negative by using lith developer for the lith and concentrated print developer for the other film types. Fix, wash, dry, and mount up ready for projection. Advantages of negative slides include ease of colouring individual lines (with phototints or transparent ink), less dust, etc., to show on the screen, and an image better able to stand competition with ambient light when projected.

Method 2c. Direct Polaroid photography. Shoot with a large format camera fitted with a Polaroid rollfilm back (described on page 86). Use Polaroid line-type projection film, which gives a high contrast positive film transparency peeled from the camera 15 sec after exposure. The transparency is briefly dipped in a small container of stabilising solution, waved in the air to complete drying, and may be immediately sealed into a card mount ready for projection (Fig. 5.3). This material gives an image $3\frac{1}{4} \times 4$ in., but as described on page 151, by carefully setting up several pages to be copied at a time and shooting so that each

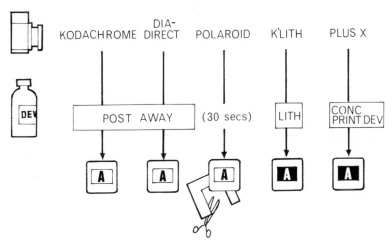

Fig. 5.4. Summary of direct photography single stage routes to the production of a slide (negative or positive). There are also other colour transparency materials, e.g. Ektachrome, Ferraniacolor, which can be user processed as shown in Fig. 9.4.

occupies 24×36 mm or less on the film, up to eight 35-mm images may be cut from each film and mounted in individual 5×5-cm frames. Quality is excellent but the film is rather expensive (Fig. 5.24).

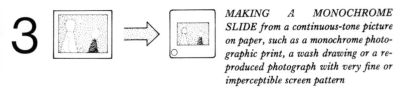

MAKING A MONOCHROME SLIDE from a continuous-tone picture on paper, such as a monochrome photographic print, a wash drawing or a reproduced photograph with very fine or imperceptible screen pattern

Method 3a. Direct photography. Photograph with a 35-mm camera, using reversal black-and-white film or a reversal colour film. Proceed as for Method 2a. Results are excellent in terms of sharpness and quality, and are relatively inexpensive.

Method 3b. Direct Polaroid photography. Shoot with a Polaroid rollfilm back as in Method 2c, but use Polaroid continuous-tone projection

163

film. Results can be peeled from the camera two minutes later and the transparency can be mounted, ready for projection within 5–10 min of exposure.

Method 3c. Neg/pos photography. Copy the illustration on general-purpose 35-mm camera film. Process the negatives normally and contact print them in the darkroom on positive printing film (35 mm) or continuous-tone printing sheet film, as shown in Fig. 5.2. When an equipped darkroom is available this method, although slow, gives excellent results. It is most practical when several slides are required, as whole strips of negatives can be printed at one time.

4   *MAKING A MONOCHROME SLIDE from a line drawing, chart or text in black on coloured paper, or paper which is partly overprinted in solid colour*

Method 4. Direct photography, using a filter. Procedures using non-panchromatic photographic materials will probably result in the coloured area reproducing black or very dark. Shoot direct on panchromatic film, using a colour filter over the lens which closely matches the colour area of the original (see page 155). Remember to increase exposure. Shoot on:

1. Black-and-white reversal film (35 mm), which returns from processing ready for projection.

2. General-purpose (35 mm) negative film or panchromatic line film (sheet film), both of which can be processed in concentrated print developer (in total darkness) to give contrasty line negatives. These can be used as negative slides, or they can be contact printed (Fig. 5.2) to give positive transparencies.

3. Polaroid line-projection rollfilm, giving a high contrast positive transparency ready for trimming down to 5 × 5 cm a minute or so after shooting.

5   *MAKING A MONOCHROME SLIDE from a line drawing, chart, text, etc., in various colours, and on a white or black or coloured base*

Method 5. Direct photography. In general, of course, this type of original is most effectively reproduced by colour transparency material

164

(using Method 2a). If a monochrome result is essential the main point to remember is that only panchromatic films will give tone values approximately equal to brightness or darkness of colours as seen by the eye. The more contrasty the film (and the more development it receives) the more brightness differences are exaggerated. It may therefore be wise to aim for a moderately contrasty image in order to avoid the reproduction of light colours simplifying into white, and dark colours becoming black. Pay special attention to the background colour—a colour filter may help to separate coloured lines from background. Shoot on the films specified for Method 4.

6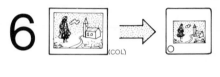

MAKING A MONOCHROME SLIDE from a colour photograph, colour-wash drawing or other continuous-tone original including fine-screened photographic reproductions in colour magazines, etc.

Method 6. Direct photography. For reasonably accurate representation of colours in monochrome terms a panchromatic film is essential. Shoot on 35-mm monochrome reversal film, as in Method 2a. Alternatively, use Method 3b for direct Polaroid photography or Method 3c for neg/pos photography.

7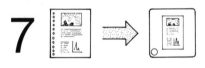

MAKING A MONOCHROME SLIDE from a combination of line and continuous-tone images such as a typewritten report illustrated with actual monochrome photographs, or a page from a publication containing text and fine screen reproduced photographs

Method 7. Direct photography. First decide which parts of the original should reproduce with maximum quality. If it is approached as a line image (using Methods 2a or b) any continuous-tone photographic content will reproduce as 'soot and whitewash'. Conversely, if the original is treated as continuous tone (using Methods 3a, b or c) the text and other line content may reproduce flat, with off-white whites and/or grey blacks. In most cases treatment as a continuous-tone original will at least reproduce all the informational content of the original, even if the text and line parts then appear rather flat. To re-

165

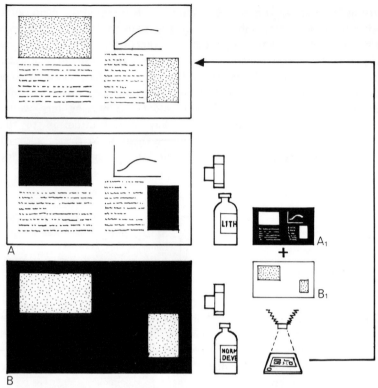

Fig. 5.5. Photography of an original having line and continuous-tone elements. *Top:* Original material. A, Original with black card covering illustrations—this is photographed on lith film, giving neg A_1. B, Original with *text* covered by black card, photographed on general purpose film to give continuous tone neg B_1. The two negatives, sandwiched in the enlarger, thus give a print on continuous tone material which reproduces original. (Negatives could be printed on fine grain positive film to make a slide.)

produce both line and tone content with minimum loss of quality and assuming that the job justifies the extra time, proceed as shown in Fig. 5.5.

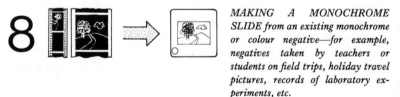

8   *MAKING A MONOCHROME SLIDE from an existing monochrome or colour negative—for example, negatives taken by teachers or students on field trips, holiday travel pictures, records of laboratory experiments, etc.*

Method 8a. Same-size printing. If the negative is 35 mm (or an equivalent area on a rollfilm negative) it can be contact printed in the dark-

166

room, under glass, direct on 35-mm positive printing film (see Fig. 5.3). This is handled and processed just like printing paper. If a *colour* negative is being printed on these films some distortions in the monochrome representations of colours will occur—red parts of the original subject appear nearly black, and blues very light grey. If this is unacceptable it will be worth printing instead on general-purpose panchromatic film, but unlike the films above, these have to be handled and processed in total darkness.

One convenient method of working is to arrange the enlarger to form an image the same size as the negative. Load film into the body of

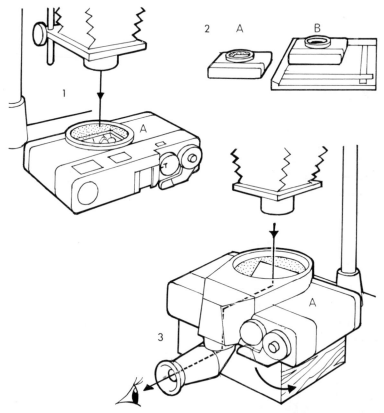

Fig. 5.6. Camera bodies used as film holders under enlarger when printing slides. 1, Camera A with shutter locked open on T and white card in place of film. This is used only for focusing and composing projected image. 2, Body B (loaded with sensitive material) exactly replaced body A on baseboard and shutter opened to receive exposure. By continuing sequence many negatives can be printed on to film (giving each several bracketed exposures) before processing. 3, Alternative, using one single lens reflex with 45° viewfinder attachment and lens removed. Image can be seen for focusing, etc., through finder. Wooden block allows easier wind-on.

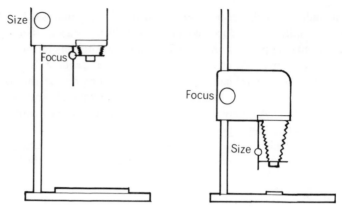

Fig. 5.7. Reduction printing. *Right:* Using the enlarger to make images same-size or *smaller* than the negative it is easier to move the lens alone to adjust size, and move the whole head to focus, i.e. reversing normal procedure (*left*).

a camera with a focal plane shutter, placed on the enlarger easel, as shown in Fig. 5.6. An enlarging exposure meter is very useful under these conditions—but if the camera has an internal meter this can be used instead. As a rough exposure guide, test on bromide paper which can be processed on the spot, then give an exposure time based on the relative speeds of the two materials (grade 3 paper is about ASA 2). Following exposure the film is processed (in a developing tank) but using print developer to give the slightly enhanced contrast needed for projection positives.

Method 8b. Direct enlargement or reduction. Often the negative size differs from the image size required on the final slide—being larger (rollfilm) or smaller (half-frame). Frequently the negative may be of the same format but require cropping of unwanted parts of this image. In all these cases project the negative through the enlarger. If the negative is much larger than 36 × 24 mm the enlarger lens will have to be focused well forward of its usual position (see Fig. 5.7). Expose on to the same film stock as suggested for Method 8a.

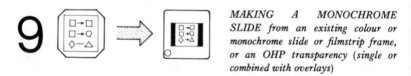

MAKING A MONOCHROME SLIDE from an existing colour or monochrome slide or filmstrip frame, or an OHP transparency (single or combined with overlays)

Method 9. Direct photography. Providing the original transparency can be evenly lit from behind it may be photographed on a 35-mm

168

camera, using similar materials to those required for shooting equivalent artwork on paper. The slide first needs a backing of light-diffusing but patternless material. Various lighting arrangements are discussed on page 150.

The camera must, of course, be capable of giving a sharp image when very close to this small subject. Remember that extra exposure is required when working so close. Figure App.7.2 shows these increases. Exposure calculation is discussed on page 157.

For type of film and processing, see recommendations contained in Method 3a or b if the original is a monochrome continuous-tone transparency, Method 6 if it is in colour continuous tone, Method 2a, b or c if it is a monochrome line image and Method 6 if a line image in colour.

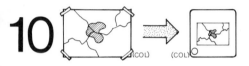

10 MAKING A COLOUR SLIDE *from coloured line artwork and published material—maps, graphs, technical illustrations, etc.*

Method 10a. Direct colour photography. Shoot on 35-mm reversal colour film. If a larger size camera has to be used, shoot on roll or sheet film, and arrange that the image is small enough to suit the final slide (see Fig. 4.24). In each case the film should be of the correct type for the light source in use, or be filtered to give the same effect (see Fig. 4.27 and page 312). Although these colour films are intended for continuous tone work the results will be sufficiently contrasty, provided that the original itself is drawn bodily.*

For meter reading technique, see page 156; lighting arrangements are on page 147.

Method 10b. Direct (black-and-white negative) photography and hand colouring. Shoot on 35-mm high contrast line negative material, which gives a transparency with clear lines against a dense black background. Colour the clear lines by hand, using transparent phototints on an 'O'-size brush (Fig. 5.8) or use a fine-tipped marker or fibre-tipped pen. For photographic technique needed, see Method 2b.

---

* Agfa make a high contrast 35-mm colour film called *Agiphot Color Dupe* which can be reversal processed. However, the material demands extreme exposure accuracy and must be processed by the user. It can be recommended only for experienced colour photographers.

Fig. 5.8. High contrast negative images of graphs, etc., used direct as slides lend themselves to hand colouring of local areas, using transparent dye photo-tints. Overspill of dye will not be noticed on dense black areas.

11 MAKING A COLOUR SLIDE *from continuous-tone colour photographs on paper, paintings, colour-wash drawings and screened reproductions of photographs in magazines and books*

Follow Method 10a, using the same continuous-tone colour film.

12 MAKING A COLOUR SLIDE *from an existing colour transparency, coloured OHP transparency or frame from a colour film strip*

Method 12. Direct colour photography. Follow the same procedure as for Method 9, using reversal colour film, but ensure that the light source behind the transparency suits the film (page 156). For example, use a photoflood (at a reasonable distance to reduce heat) and shoot on Kodachrome Type A. Similarly, electronic flash might be used with daylight colour film. Unfortunately the results from this method of copying are often rather harsh, with bleached highlights and/or heavy image shadows. If the original was a line image or a rather low contrast continuous-tone transparency (i.e. subject flatly lit) this distortion will probably be acceptable and, indeed, may even improve the image.

Method 12b. Using laboratory services. Colour transparencies and filmstrip frames can be sent to a colour laboratory for duplication as colour slides. Special low contrast duplicating colour film is used and the work is often carried out on semi-automatic machines. Some laboratories are run by the film manufacturers themselves such as Kodak and Agfa-Gevaert (Appendix IV). Manufacturers' laboratories are not particularly expensive and the quality of results is often excellent. On the other hand the job takes a week or two, during which time the original transparency is out of our hands. Independent commercial colour laboratories offer a faster service and can often coax an acceptable duplicate from an unpromising slide. These laboratories are very expensive.

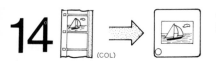

13 *MAKING A COLOUR SLIDE from an existing colour negative—pictures taken on location or in school by teachers and students*

Method 13. Using laboratory services. Although a teacher equipped to do his own colour printing could tackle this job, the time required and cost of colour materials (special colour printing film is needed) make it very impractical unless many negatives are to be printed. Usually the manufacturer of the colour film offers a slide printing service. Alternatively try a commercial laboratory (page 320), although this is rather more expensive. Often the easiest solution is to print off one's own *monochrome* slide (Methods 8a or b).

14 *MAKING A SLIDE from one frame of a (positive) motion picture film*

Method 14. Direct enlargement. Locate the motion picture frame in the negative carrier of a 35-mm enlarger (on almost all models the film slips into the enlarger without requiring cutting). Enlarge the image up to the size required. A 16-mm film frame will require the enlarger close to the top of the column to give a 36 × 24-mm image. An 8-mm frame will probably have to be left smaller than this, even when enlarged from the top of the column (see Fig. 5.9).

If a monochrome slide is required, expose on to black-and-white reversal film, handling the film in a camera body (Fig. 5.6). To produce a slide in colour use the same technique but expose on Kodachrome Type A, using a small photoflood in place of the enlarging lamp. (Warning: These lamps give off considerable heat and will damage enlarger and movie film unless used for very short periods such as the exposure itself. Use the normal lamp for all setting up, focusing, etc.) For a further data, see Method 6, but remember that the films suggested above are sensitive to all colours and must be handled and processed in total darkness.

When working from an 8-mm frame or part of 16 mm, it is usually

171

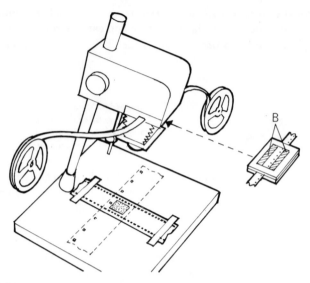

Fig. 5.9. Direct enlargement (on to film) of a frame from a movie film to make a slide. Unused areas of the negative carrier are masked off with black paper (B) to prevent light flare giving a low contrast image. (When exposing on to panchromatic or colour film it may be easier to work as shown in Fig. 5.6, or copy by camera as Fig. 4.23.)

necessary to enlarge in two stages. First the image is magnified as much as possible and exposed on to 35-mm positive printing film (or Plus X if correct tonal rendering of colour is important). After processing in print developer this negative goes back into the enlarger for final magnification to the full 36×24-mm slide format, printing on to positive film.

Making overhead transparencies
These large transparencies are usually made on some form of document copier, or with the aid of a camera and enlarger. Relative to slides the image should be kept light in tone because the projector tends to exaggerate density and contrast. At present a stumbling block exists in the user production of full-colour, single-sheet OHP transparencies. Colour transparency photographic materials this size are prohibitively expensive. Full-colour commercial OHP transparencies are printed mechanically, thousands at a time. At present we can produce only monochrome (single-colour) transparencies, often building up the *appearance* of a full colour image using several overlays, or applying colour locally by hand. Direct picture transfer (see Method 16d) is another, although unreliable, alternative.

172

Before making an overhead transparency consider whether the material would not be more effectively presented as, say, a diagram hand-out, slide series or short film. Is best use being made of the OHP's special features—ability to add on-the-spot connotations, reveal information a bit at a time, add overlays, etc. (page 110)? Ensure that the artwork has an appropriate format (page 129) will be legible (page 133) and is prepared in a form which will reproduce (note particularly heat copies, page 58).

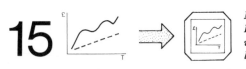

15 MAKING AN OHP TRANS-PARENCY *containing simple written or drawn information in line form*

Method 15. Direct drawn preparation. Use a 25 × 25-cm sheet of clear acetate or a cut from a roll and draw on this direct, using the pens and transfers described on page 140.

Mount the transparency in the usual card frame.

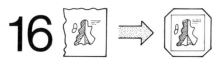

16 MAKING AN OHP TRANS-PARENCY *from a monochrome line drawing, text or chart, either prepared artwork on paper or reproduced in a book or magazine, same size as required for the transparency*

Method 16a. Heat copying. If the original is in sheet rather than bound form it can be fed through a heat copier in contact with a heat-sensitive transparency film material, see page 55. Some of these materials, such as Agfa-Gevaert Transparex film, afterwards require sponging over with water. For working procedure, see page 56, but remember that not all originals will reproduce—Table 2.1. Alternatively, and especially for bound books and coloured or vegetable inks, use a light-heat copier, forming the final image on a film base.

Method 16b. Hand tracing. If the content is simple enough, lay a sheet of acetate over the work and trace it. This gives an advantage in that images can be built up from parts of several originals—a block diagram from one, a symbol from another, and so on. The transparency can be given finishing touches with commercial shading, tint or lettering transfers, using materials described for Method 15.

Method 16c. Episcope or OHP tracing and spirit duplicator printing. If

173

the original will fit within an episcope or can be imaged by reverse use of an OHP (see Method 17a) the projected picture can be traced direct on to a spirit master (see Fig. 5.10). Not all episcopes allow sufficient lens focusing to give small pictures. Use the usual spirit carbon beneath the sheet as when drawing maps free hand. Attach the master to a spirit duplicator, run off a few copies on paper and then run through a sheet of Cellofilm. Check that the transparency has sufficient density. Additions can now be made with shading tints before mounting up.

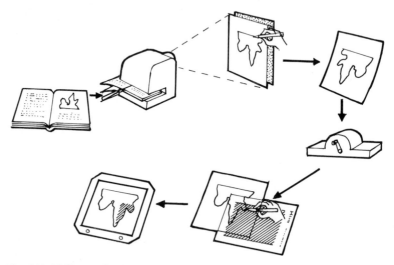

Fig. 5.10. Making an OHP transparency via episcope, hand tracing and spirit duplication, see Method 16c.

Method 16d. Direct picture transfer. This method requires no equipment but it means stripping the image from its paper support. It also has a reputation for unreliability as it will work only with certain types of original—boldly printed reproductions on *glossy art or semi-art paper*, as used in many quality periodicals and specialised journals, e.g. *Visual Education, Mathematical Pie*, etc. The reproduction must also be in new condition. If a moist finger is rubbed over unprinted areas of such paper some faint chalky residue will rub off on the skin. (Parts of this book carrying half-tone photographs are suitable, but not the text and diagram pages.)

Transfer can be made on to a piece of transparent self-adhesive covering material such as shown in Fig. 5.11. Alternatively a proprietary brand of heat tissue allows transfer, using a dry mounting press. At the time of writing, this is available only in the United States. Both forms of transfer are of course equally suitable for coloured originals.

174

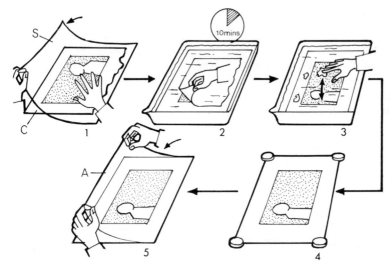

Fig. 5.11. Transferring a printed illustration direct from clipped magazine page on to OHP transparency base. 1, Self-adhesive transparent material (e.g. Fablon) about 1 cm wider all round laid over face of suitable illustration (C). 2, Plastic covered picture having soaked in tepid water for 10 minutes, paper is peeled away. 3, Final scraps gently rubbed away. 4, Transparency left to dry. 5, Sheet acetate (A) laid over face adheres to still adhesive 1-cm border, forming protective backing to transparency.

Method 16e. Photocopying. Use a flatbed photocopier of the chemical diffusion-transfer or dye-diffusion (Verifax) type. Reflex expose and transfer the image on to a final acetate base (page 61).

Method 16f. Electrostatic copying. Using a transfer electrostatic copier (e.g. Xerox) copy on to specially made transparent film, which gives an indelible black image on a clear or coloured base. See page 319.

17 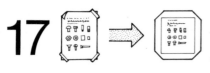   *MAKING AN OHP TRANSPARENCY from a monochrome line drawing, text or coarse screen photo reproduction, on a poster, in a book, etc., involving a change of size between original and transparency. (Note the maximum size of words on an OHP transparency if they are to be legible—Fig. 4.8.)*

Method 17a. Hand tracing with the OHP. If the original material contains simple line images and particularly if it is poster size attach it to a wall where it is brightly illuminated. Use an overhead projector (not switched on) to form an image of the poster on a piece of paper on the projector stage (see Fig. 4.15). Move the projector nearer or further from the poster, focusing the lens until a sharp image of a suitable size is formed. This is then traced. In all cases the tracing could be made direct on to a spirit master, pressing on to carbon tissue (Method 16c). The transparency is then produced in a spirit duplicator printing on to acetate.

Method 17b. Direct photography and enlarging. Photograph the artwork with a camera (35 mm, 6 × 6 cm, 5 × 4 in.) capable of close working. Shoot on 35-mm or 5 × 4-in. lith film (processed in lith developer) or a slow, general-purpose negative film overdeveloped in normal negative developer to give maximum contrast. The resulting line negative is then placed in a photographic enlarger and enlarged up to 10 × 8 in. Expose on lith or ordinary line film which is processed by the conventional sequence of development (in lith or a concentrated print developer), fixing, washing and drying. The double stages of photographing and enlarging mean that this is a relatively slow and expensive method, but gives highest quality results. The negative can of course be stored and used for making other aids. If 35 mm it can even be projected itself as a negative black-and-white slide.

18   *MAKING A MONOCHROME OHP TRANSPARENCY from a monochrome or colour continuous-tone wash drawing, photograph, slide or filmstrip frame, or fine-screen reproduced photograph*

Method 18a. Direct photography and enlarging. Photograph the original with any suitable camera able to work close enough to fill the frame. (Page 144 explains setting-up for shooting a print; page 148 covers photographing a transparency.) Shoot on normal contrast general-purpose film and give normal development in a negative developer. Enlarge the negative up to 10 × 8 in. and expose it on a sheet of line or process film. Process in normal strength print developer. (These films can be handled in the usual orange safe-lighting of a photographic printing room.) The best way to check density and contrast is to compare the transparency with another known to project well. Avoid making the image too dark. After fixing, the film is washed, dried and mounted.

If the original is a fine-screened illustration from the page of a magazine and requires no size change it may be possible to use direct picture transfer, Method 16d.

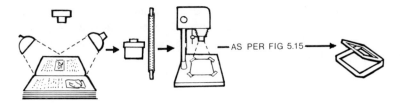

Fig. 5.12. OHP transparency making by photographing and enlarging. *Left-to-right:* Photographing wanted material; developing and drying negative; enlarging 10 in. square and then proceeding as in Fig. 5.15.

Occasionally the content of the image is such that 'soot and white-wash' reproduction would not seriously destroy its information (e.g. the picture content of Plate 16, but not Plate 18). In such a case treat as line, using Methods 16a or e.

Method 18b. Direct photography and photo-copying. Work as in 18a, but enlarge on to projection speed chemical diffusion transfer material, as shown in Figs. 5.12 and 5.15.

19 *MAKING A MONOCHROME OHP TRANSPARENCY from an existing OHP line or coarse-screened transparency*

Method 19a. Diazo copying. Demount the transparency and contact print it on a sheet of gas-processed diazo-coated film. If a diazo machine is not available use sunlight, sandwiching the two layers between curved sheets of clear acetate (see Fig. 2.7). Expose until the yellowish diazo is bleached white in the areas unprotected by the printed parts of the original. This material is then 'developed' by placing it in a jar containing ammonia.

If the original OHP transparency has coloured overlays, they must be copied one at a time, making sure that the printed side always faces the coated surface of the diazo film. (Some pale blue image overlays may not reproduce.) Films giving various image colours can be chosen shown in Figs. 5.12 and 5.15.

Method 19b. Photocopying. Back up the transparency with white paper and using a flatbed chemical diffusion transparency or dye diffusion photocopier contact print the transparency just like a page from a book. Use the processing sections of these machines to transfer the final positive image on to a transparent acetate base (page 61).

177

If a darkroom but no photocopier is available try contact printing (under glass under the enlarger) on a 10 × 8-in. sheet of 3M Direct Copy reversal film. This is developed in concentrated print developer, fixed, washed and dried.

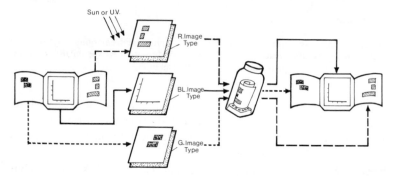

Fig. 5.13. Copying an OHP transparency by diazo. *Left-to-right:* Original, having overlays in red and green. Separated sheets printed on diazo films of appropriate image colour. Ammonia vapour processing. Assembly of copy transparency.

Method 19c. Heat copying. Reproduction is possible only if the original transparency has a photographic image, or has been mechanically printed (like many commercial OHP transparencies) in non-vegetable-based printing inks. Feed the unmounted transparency through the heat copier with its printed surface in contact with heat sensitive transparency material. Results are ready for projection within a few seconds. Alternatively back up the transparency as for Method 19b and reproduce via a light-heat copier.

Method 19d. Hand tracing. Lay a sheet of acetate over the OHP transparency and trace the outlines by hand. Finish off by colouring or applying various shading transfers (see page 138).

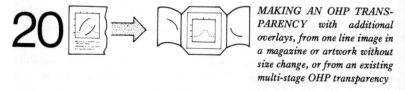

MAKING AN OHP TRANSPARENCY with additional overlays, from one line image in a magazine or artwork without size change, or from an existing multi-stage OHP transparency

To produce a base transparency plus overlays offering pieces of additional information, in contrasting colours—all from a single drawing —we have to mask off areas not required when making each transparency. This can be done in various ways, appropriate to the copying method chosen.

Method 20a. Heat copying. With pieces of thin white paper cover all parts of the original not required to appear on the base transparency (Fig. 5.14). Feed through a heat copier in contact with heat-sensitive film (page 56) designed to give a black-on-clear image. Now remask the original so that only those parts required on the first overlay are revealed. Heat copy again on the same kind of heat-sensitive material but choosing a sheet which gives say, red-on-clear image. Several further overlays in different colours can be made on this way, altering the parts masked off for each one.

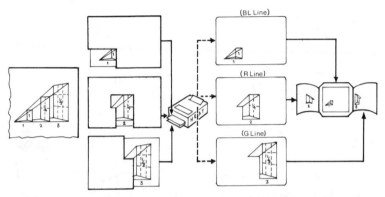

Fig. 5.14. Copying a single diagram clipped from a magazine to give OHP transparency plus overlays. *Left to right:* Original figure; selective masks cut from thin white paper are overlaid in turn; each sandwich copied by heat or light-heat machine on to a film of an appropriate image colour; assembling transparency and overlays. Alternative methods include hand tracing mounted elements on to film, see text.

When working from an existing OHP transparency each layer—base or overlay—is simply printed separately on a heat film of appropriate colour. If the image will not reproduce by heat use a light-heat copier, or Method 19a. Mount up the base transparency and attach overlays in register by tape along one edge.

Method 20b. Photocopying. Using the same masking technique described above, back up the transparency with white paper and reflex print it on a photocopier as for Method 16e. Overlays produced this way are all in black and white only, but if necessary they can in turn be contact printed on diazo film (Method 19a) to form a coloured version. Using a flatbed photocopier allows transparency and overlays to be prepared this way from a drawing in a bound book.

See also electrostatic copying, as in Method 16f.

Method 21a. Hand tracing and heat or diazo copying. Project the transparency on to a sheet of 10 × 10-in. paper by means of an enlarger or slide projector. Using a 2B pencil trace off all the parts required for the base transparency. Change the paper and on this trace only the bits for the first overlay, and so on. Finally feed these 'separations' one by one through a heat copier in contact with heat-sensitive film giving different image colours.

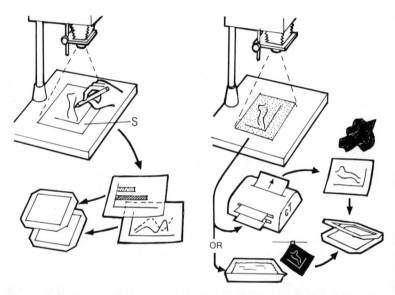

Fig. 5.15. Making an OHP transparency from a line image on filmstrip or slide. *Left:* Enlarging on to acetate or Cellofilm and tracing wanted material by hand. A 10 × 10-in. sheet of paper (S) indicates area of transparency. *Right:* Enlarging on to projection speed chemical transfer paper which during processing is brought into contact with receiving film base. Alternatively use photographic line or lith film conventionally processed and dried. The latter gives negative images relative to image projected by enlarger.

Alternatively use a fibre-tipped pen to trace the projected image direct on to separate pieces of acetate placed in turn over the 10 × 8-in. paper 'screen' (Fig. 5.15). The tracings themselves can then form the final result, or can be printed on diazo films of differing image colours (Method 19a).

Method 21b. Direct photoprinting (giving neg image). Place the original in an enlarger, form an image 10 in. wide and expose on to projection speed chemical diffusion transfer paper (e.g. Instafax CT). This goes into a chemical diffusion copier processor, where it is brought into contact with a sheet of the same maker's film base. Alternatively expose on to a large sheet of line or lith photographic film, processed conventionally and dried. To give overlays, paint over unwanted parts of the original (on the back of the film) with liquid opaque or black poster colour. This can be rubbed off again after exposing the overlay, and more masking then carried out before printing further overlays.

22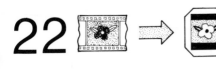

MAKING A MONOCHROME OHP TRANSPARENCY from a black-and-white or colour negative, line or continuous tone, such as pictures taken by students and teachers

Method 22. Direct photoprinting. Use an enlarger to project an image on to 10 × 8-in. photographic film. Lith film, processed in lith developer, or line or process film processed in strong print developer, will give the contrast required for line images. Use continuous-tone printing film in normal strength print developer for continuous tones. Working from colour negatives these materials give distorted monochrome reproductions of original subject colours (reds very dark). To avoid this, print on panchromatic lith or line film, or general-purpose panchromatic film for continuous tones.

Making prints and hand-outs
Hand-outs, in small numbers or moderate quantities, usually call for a copying machine and/or duplicator. In the case of continuous-tone images some photography will be necessary.

Before making prints and hand-outs, consider whether the information is really best used in this form—it is suitable for individual study or ready reference, or more for display. Is the original material suitably laid out, e.g. space left on hand-outs for addition of notes (page 111)? If possible avoid the need for a size change. Ensure, too, that the original material will reproduce on the copier/duplicator available (Chapter 2). Check the total number of copies required, as this greatly influences the cheapest method of production.

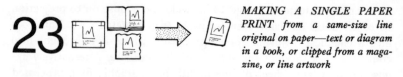

23 *MAKING A SINGLE PAPER PRINT* from a same-size line original on paper—text or diagram in a book, or clipped from a magazine, or line artwork

Method 23a. Photocopying. Reflex print on a flatbed-type photocopier, using diffusion transfer materials as explained on page 61, or dye diffusion (more expensive, see Fig. 5.24) or negative/positive stabilised materials (page 59). The first two give most permanent results.

Method 23b. Light-heat copying. Reproduce using a dual-spectrum type machine.

Method 23c. Reflex copying in the darkroom. Using an enlarger (or just a white ceiling light) as a light source, reflex print the original on grade

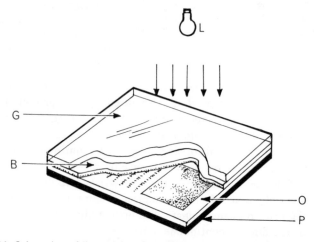

Fig. 5.16. Orientation of line original for simple reflex printing in the darkroom. G, Cover glass under some pressure. B, Bromide paper (grade 4), sensitive side down. O, Original, wanted side up. P, Pad of felt or other soft material. L, Ceiling light bulb, distant to give even illumination. The resulting negative is printed face to face with another sheet of bromide paper, passing light in through the back of the negative.

4 single-weight bromide paper, arranging the material as shown in Fig. 5.16. Use stabilisation bromide paper if a roller processing machine is available—if not develop in concentrated print developer, fix, wash and dry. The resulting negative is printed direct, under a sheet of glass, on another sheet of grade 4 bromide paper. A longish exposure time is needed, to penetrate the paper base of the negative. Process this in the same way.

Method 23d. Electrostatic copying. Reproduce using an electrostatic machine. (N.B. Many of these are rotary and will not accept bound materials.)

24  *MAKING PAPER PRINTS (a dozen or so) from a same-size line original on paper—text, diagrams in a book or clipped from a magazine, or line artwork*

Method 24a. Photocopying. Reflex print on a flatbed-type photocopier use dye diffusion materials or negative/positive stabilised materials—only one negative is required.

Method 24b. Tracing and diazo. If the original is a fairly simple map or diagram, trace it on a sheet of acetate or tracing paper using a fibre-tipped pen. The tracing is then printed direct on diazo paper—page 64.

Method 24c. Heat copying and spirit duplicating or diazo printing. Provided that the written matter is on a single sheet and is suitable for heat copying (page 58) pass it through the copier in contact with a heat-sensitive master. The result is then ready to mount on a spirit duplicator and run off copies. Annotations can be added direct to the master by hand. Alternatively pass the original through the heat copier in contact with a heat-sensitive film which gives a black line transparency. This now becomes a master for contact printing on diazo paper-based material.

Method 24d. Light-heat copying and diazo printing. If the original is bound in a book or otherwise unsuitable for heat copying, use a light-heat flatbed machine (page 63) to give a transparency for diazo printing.

Method 24e. Direct electrostatic copying. See Method 25c.

25 *MAKING PAPER PRINTS (several dozen and upwards) from a same-size line original —book, magazine or artwork*

Method 25a. Heat copying and spirit duplicating. Suitable for up to 50 copies off a single sheet original. Follow Method 24c.

Method 25b. Copying on to a stencil, and ink duplicating. Suitable for up to 1000 copies off a single sheet original (see Fig. 5.17). If the original will reproduce by heat copying pass it through the copier with a thermal stencil. Alternatively attach the sheet to an electronic stencil cutter and prepare the stencil this way. Finally attach the stencil to an ink duplicator and run off the copies required.

183

Method 25c. Direct electrostatic duplicating. Suitable for indefinite numbers of copies from single sheets, or bound material using a flatbed machine. Paper duplicates tumble off an electrostatic machine, working direct from the original which is held inside its exposing section (page 68). This is fairly economic for about 20 copies but for large numbers it is cheaper per copy to use the machine to make a paper litho plate, and proceed as below.

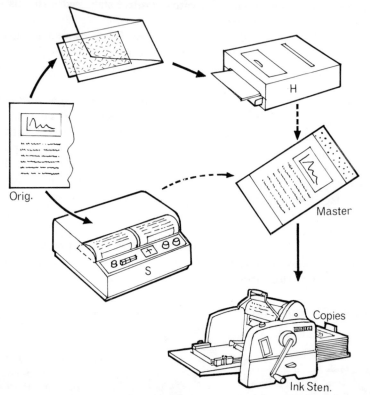

Fig. 5.17. Producing paper print handouts from a single sheet original. Ink stencil master is first prepared via heat (H) or light-heat copier, or electronic stencil cutter (S).

Method 25d. Litho plate preparation via electrostatic or photocopier and offset litho printing. Suitable for up to 10,000 copies from bound or single sheets. Reflex print in a photocopier on to a dye-diffusion paper offset plate, or reflex print on to a chemical diffusion paper, transferring the image on to a litho foil. Alternatively make a paper plate direct on an electrostatic machine. The metal or paper now goes on to an offset litho printer.

184

26

MAKING PAPER PRINTS *from a*
line original requiring a size change

Method 26a. Photography and darkroom preparation of a diazo or photo-copier master. Photograph the original on high contrast lith or similar film. Use panchromatic line film if the original has coloured lines. Enlarge this negative up to the final required size and expose on to hard-grade bromide paper. Proceed then as if this print is the original, and use Methods 24a or 25a. Alternatively, instead of bromide paper, expose the image on to line or lith film. The resulting positive transparency then forms the master for contact printing on to diazo paper.

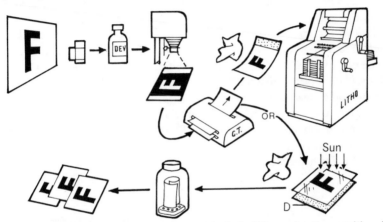

Fig. 5.18. Multiple paper prints from a line original of a different size. Copy positive of the original is enlarged to required size on chemical diffusion transfer (projection speed) paper. In the processor this is brought into contact either with a litho paper plate, or film base. The latter is used to make cheap diazo prints.

Method 26b. Photography and darkroom preparation of a litho plate. Photograph on 35-mm B & W reversal film but at the enlarger stage expose on to projection speed chemical diffusion transfer paper, and transfer on to a litho foil, ready for machine printing. (By transferring instead on to a film base, prints can be made by diazo, see Fig. 5.18.)

27

MAKING PAPER PRINTS *from a continuous-tone photograph, wash drawing, etc., on paper*

Method 27a. Direct negative/positive photography (small numbers off). Photograph the original on to general-purpose negative film, see page

312. Use the enlarger to make enlargements from this negative on to normal grade stabilisation bromide paper which is machine processed, e.g. in the motorised processing compartment of a photo-stabilisation copier (page 94). Each print thus has to be printed individually. See also note at the end of Method 18.

Method 27b. Photography plus diazo/photocopier heat/master preparation (for small or moderate numbers off). Photograph as in Method 27a but place the negative in the enlarger with its dull (emulsion) side *upwards*. Enlarge the image to the required final picture size and expose on to Kodalith Autoscreen film. This is handled just like ordinary lith (red safelight, lith developer, fix and wash) but gives a screened positive image on film. The result can be used as a master for contact printing on diazo paper, or contact printing in any form of photocopier, or heat copier.

Method 27c. Photography and litho plate preparation (large numbers off). Proceed as for 27b but position the negative in the enlarger dull side downwards. Having produced the final-size autoscreen positive on film contact print this on a chemical diffusion transfer or dye diffusion photocopier machine, on to a litho offset paper or metal plate. Attach the plate to an offset litho duplicator and run off prints. N.B. Autoscreen film images can be combined with line images so that picture and text can be reproduced together, see page 166. This is particularly valuable for hand-outs.

28 *MAKING PAPER PRINTS from a line image on a slide, filmstrip frame or OHP transparency*

Method 28a. Direct photoprinting. If a *negative* representation of the original on paper is acceptable, enlarge (slides or filmstrips) or contact print (OHP transparencies) on to roller processed bromide paper (page 94).

Method 28b. Diazo printing. Remove the transparency from its frame and contact print on to diazo paper. This of course gives a same-size image. Enlarge slides and filmstrips on to 10 × 8-in. 3M reversal film processed in print developer, using this film positive for diazo printing.

Method 28c. Reflex printing and duplicating. Working from an OHP transparency remove frames and back the transparency with white paper. It can then be treated as a paper line original using any appropriate technique—for example, Methods 24a or d, or 25c.

Method 28d. Tracing and spirit duplicating. If the line image is fairly simple, project it at the required final size—say A4—and trace over the outlines on to a spirit master. OHP transparency originals can usually be traced direct. Run off copies with a spirit duplicator.

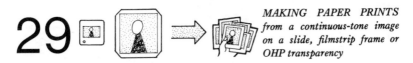

29 MAKING PAPER PRINTS *from a continuous-tone image on a slide, filmstrip frame or OHP transparency*

Method 29. Direct photography and direct printing, or screened master making for the duplicator. Light the transparency and photograph it with a camera as suggested on page 150, or (slides, filmstrips) project it through the enlarger or contact print it on to Kodak Fine Grain positive film and print this on stabilisation bromide paper. To produce larger quantities, using a duplicator, follow Method 27b.

Making filmstrips

The filmstrip, that essentially inexpensive visual aid when produced in quantity, takes time and considerable care in planning when shooting. It involves us in the use of a camera and associated skills of lighting and exposing for copying (pages 144–58) and direct photography of actual subjects (Chapter 6).

Before making a filmstrip, consider whether the information is most effectively presented in this form. Is it better than a slide series for example (page 109)? Ensure that the series of images is thoroughly planned in terms of format (page 129), legibility (page 133) and order of presentation. Check that a suitable camera and accessories are available (page 78), and that you have some idea of the number of copies of the strip which will be needed (see below).

Plan the informational content of each picture relative to the verbal comments which will accompany its presentation. If there is much to be said, additional pictures can be used (e.g. detail) to give visual variety. (This is particularly important in strips for younger students.) Remember to keep the pictures all positioned the same way, preferably horizontally.

Preplanning is best carried out by sketching the visual content and commentary for each frame on a postcard. Cards can then be arranged as a storyboard—changed in sequence and content until the right arrangement has been established. In general, follow the motion picture principle of establishing general views first before moving into medium shot and close-up (Fig. 5.19). Try to plan variation in visual

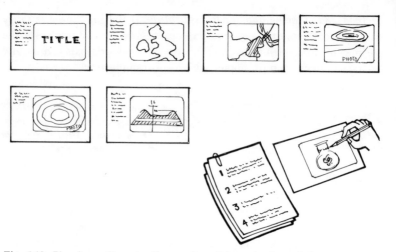

Fig. 5.19. Planning a filmstrip. From a list of frame-by-frame information, rough sketches are prepared on separate cards. Even here try to work to the proportions of the final frames.

composition, viewpoint and camera angle as much as possible, as this gives variety and injects life into a strip.

In all cases try not to place important subject matter too close to the edges of the picture. By allowing a border zone of unimportant 'bleed' (Fig. 5.20) all round there is less risk of accidentally losing information through slight errors in framing when photographing. Line artwork should have bold contrasts of colour and/or tone because (unless the whole strip is line image) copying will take place on continuous tone film.

Fig. 5.20. *Left:* Always keep important content out of the zone near the very edges of the picture. Inaccuracy in copying, masks in the film strip projector, carrier masks etc may all encroach here. *Right:* When a set of 3 : 4 ratio prints is to be copied for (single frame) filmstrips this can be done two at a time on a 36 × 24-mm frame camera, carefully spacing prints on black card of generous size, as shown.

There are four basic methods of making filmstrips:

1. Producing a single filmstrip by the direct photography of each subject in planned order on one length of 35-mm film, then reversal processing it to give a sequence of positive images. By shooting on negative film numbers of strips can be printed off, see below.

2. Assembling material in the form of artwork, photographs and colour transparencies, and then *copying* these in sequence on to reversal or negative (colour or monochrome) 35-mm film. If shot on negative material the resulting master negative can be commercially printed in bulk to give very low cost copies. This is described in Method 32.

3. Producing a single filmstrip by printing in sequence from various existing negatives on to 35-mm film, using an enlarger.

4. Direct hand-drawing of *simple images* on 'write-on' matt-faced 35-mm clear film (page 192).

MARKING FILMSTRIPS *from actual original subjects*

Method 30. Direct photography (*to give one filmstrip*). Use a 35-mm camera—preferably one taking half-frame (24 × 18 mm) images, as this is the most common filmstrip frame format.

Load the camera with reversal black-and-white film, or a reversal colour film balanced for the light source to be used. If some colour frames must be taken by tungsten lighting (e.g. maps, captions, diagrams) and some in daylight, use an appropriate compensating filter (see Fig. 4.27). Pictures must be shot strictly in sequence according to the script, and exposure must be correct each time. There is little room for technical error.

If many of the frames are exterior views on location, try to wait for the best conditions and direction of lighting for each. If natural conditions do not work in favour of the planned sequence this may mean shooting one frame per day. Instruct the processing laboratory to return the film *uncut*. This method of filmstrip production can give excellent quality, as each frame is an original rather than a copy. It is easy to appreciate the difficulties of this method for anything other than a series of similar subjects, all shot in one location and at one time. A more practical solution is to shoot several negatives on each subject, select the best of these, then use Method 33 or make enlargements and use Method 31.

31

MACING FILMSTRIPS *from art-work, books and other assembled flat copy material*

Method 31. Photographic copying (to give single or multi-printed filmstrips). Assembling the content of each filmstrip frame separately and then copying everything takes time, but is a more realistic way of working, as it does not demand superhuman technical control. Having planned content as outlined on page 187 prepare the artwork, photographic prints or transparencies required for each frame. These original photographs can be taken on any size camera, provided that the proportions of the final format are always borne in mind (Fig. 4.1). Correct proportions are important too for artwork and clips from magazines.

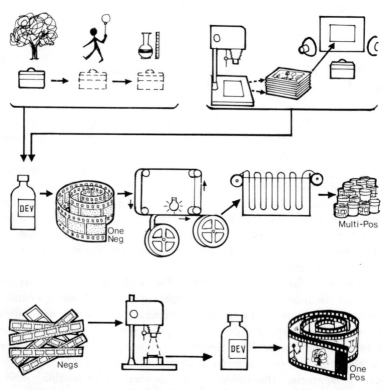

Fig. 5.21. Filmstrip making. *Top row:* Shooting actual locations in sequence, or preparing photographic prints and copying these in sequence, to give (*middle row*) one master negative. This is looped and continuously printed by a commercial laboratory to give multi copies. *Bottom row:* Variety of negatives printed in sequence on film (see Fig. 5.6) to give one filmstrip.

Monochrome prints of black-and-white frames can be made on bromide paper—8 × 6 in. is a useful size. Make prints which match in contrast and density; shade where necessary. In selecting transparencies try to choose similar densities, preferably flat or moderate in contrast.

When everything is organised, copy the material in sequence on a 35-mm camera fitted with close-up facilities. Most 35-mm cameras are full 36 × 24-mm frame, while most filmstrip frames are 24 × 18 mm. To overcome this apparent incompatability make up a mask or print holder containing two pictures at a time (Fig. 5.20). Two half-frames are therefore exposed each time the shutter is fired.

For black-and-white filmstrips, shoot on reversal black-and-white film or (for a master negative) on a fine grain general-purpose negative film. For colour filmstrips shoot on a colour reversal film or (for a master colour negative) Eastmancolor. Illuminate the copy material with the light source recommended for the colour film.

Arrange for reversal films to be processed and returned (uncut of course) ready for projection. The colour or black-and-white negative can be sent to a motion picture laboratory (page 320) where it is spliced into a loop and continuously printed by machine on 35-mm stock. Hundreds of metres of positive images are run off this way and later cut up into individual strips (see Fig. 5.21).

32 *MAKING FILMSTRIPS from slide series or OHP transparencies*

Quite often a slide series is evolved over a period of time, modified and knocked into shape in the light of practical teaching experience, and could then be usefully issued in filmstrip form (e.g. for individual study on a viewer).

Method 32a. Direct photography. Rig up a transparency rear-illumination system using either daylight, photoflood or flash. Better still use a slide copier attachment (pages 148 and 150). Some of these have built-in electronic flash—and can be hired commercially (page 317). Shoot on black-and-white or colour reversal film for single strips, or negative colour film for multi-copy printing.

Method 32b. Laboratory printing. Many colour processing laboratories offer a special service for converting 35-mm slide series into filmstrips. This service is not particularly expensive as methods are standardised, and positive or negative strips can be provided. For addresses, see page 320.

NOTE: The proportions of the 24×18-mm filmstrip frame are slightly squarer than the 36×24-mm format of most 35-mm colour slides. Be prepared to lose parts of the image tight up against the shorter sides of the slide when converting from the larger to the smaller size.

33 *MAKING FILMSTRIPS from existing negatives*

Method 33. Direct printing. Arrange the enlarger to give a constant size of image (preferably 36×24 mm) from the various negatives or parts of negatives. Expose on to positive printing film handled in a camera body for convenience (see Fig. 5.6). Exposure tests for each image can be made on short clips of this film processed in a dish. Finally the exposed film is processed in print developer in a tank (orange safelighting). If the material includes colour negatives expect some tonal distortion of colours.

34 $E = MC^2$ *MAKING FILMSTRIPS by hand*

Method 34. Direct writing. Write direct on matt-faced clear film as shown in Fig. 5.22. Use a fine marker pen as suggested for OHP

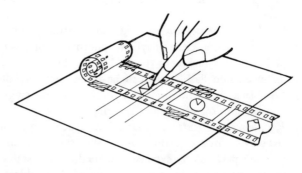

Fig. 5.22. Direct drawing of simple symbols on to matt faced write-on film. Use a fine marker pen.

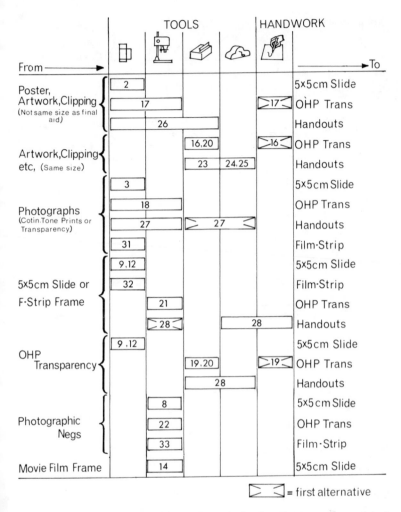

Fig. 5.23. Flow diagram summarising main methods of converting various originals into visual aid form. Figures in boxes refer to Method numbers. NB. Brand names of actual materials appear in Appendix III.

transparency preparation, etc. This method is naturally limited to very simple images or messages—incidentally providing good design discipline. Learners themselves will find that this method offers interesting possibilities (see Plate 7).

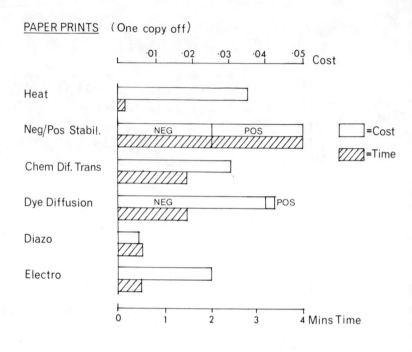

PAPER PRINTS (One copy off)

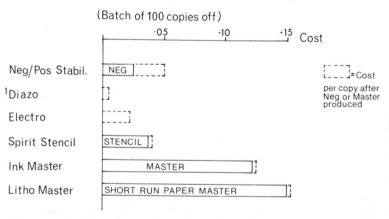

(Batch of 100 copies off)

[1] Assumes original is translucent—if not add cost of intermediate.

Fig. 5.24. Preparing software—relative material costs. Cost figures are used here primarily for comparative purposes, but broadly relate to the units used elsewhere in this book. In each case the image is assumed to be line in character. If the image is

TRANSPARENCIES [2] (One OHP transparency)

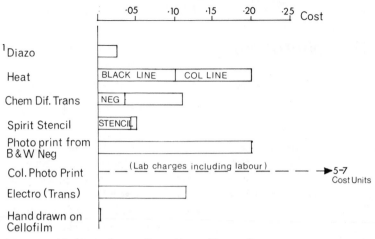

¹ Assumes original is translucent—if not add cost of intermediate.
² Where overlays are prepared, cost each as separate transparencies.

[3] (5×5 cms slides – cost per slide)

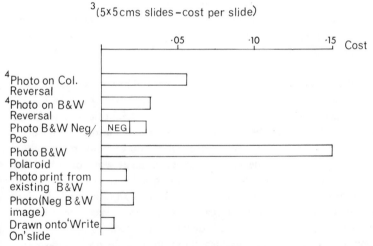

³ Assumes that enough slides are made at one time to absorb a full cassette or pack of film (advise adding 100 per cent for wastage due to wrong exposure, etc).
⁴ Includes costs of processing.

continuous tones and needs conversion to a dot image before reproduction (e.g. as on document copiers, duplicators) extra cost is involved. Autoscreen film (page 186) is about 0.25 cost units per 10×8-in. sheet.

6. Still photography

USING photography only as a means of copying books and drawings leaves its greatest potential untapped. The intelligent recording of situations, scenes, people, specimens and other three-dimensional actuality offers enormously wide educational possibilities.

Photographs to stimulate talking and story-telling in infant schools may simply show domestic pets or local zoo or farm animals, complemented if necessary by library shots of wild animals. In secondary education, illustrations of the workings of local government, local industry, particular trades or the everyday work of local individuals provide good centre points for class work. There is also great value in encouraging students to devise picture series themselves as a creative activity (Chapter 9). In technical training, picture series are of great value for giving individual instruction on methods of assembly, processes, etc.

Local geography, geology, history and natural history are made more worth-while if good transparencies are produced during practical field-work. Local photographs can be used to put scientific and technical principles discussed in the classroom into realistic context—e.g. showing expansion joints in a local bridge, refraction of light in the school swimming pool, or the design of a tower crane at work on a building site. Indoors there is the ability of photography to make permanent records of experiments over a period of time. Examples include plant and animal growth, chemical reactions and any classwork which it would be impractical to preserve for later reference.

Such a wide variety of subject matter means that the problems-solving section which follows cannot be as specific as for flat copy work. The general points covered are based on the sort of problems everyone is likely to encounter when applying their photography for the first time.

Purpose of educational photographs
Apart from specialist requirements inherent in the curriculum and the subject matter itself, objective photographs for teaching purposes

should emphasise the educationally important elements in the picture. This usually means a sharp, accurately exposed, well-designed image in which lighting, viewpoint and timing all work together to the same end. An otherwise perfect geological illustration can be ruined by lighting which fails to emphasise the different textures in exposed rock strata. It is equally important to shoot action pictures at the decisive moment—much of the point of a shot of an athlete crossing the bar in a pole vault is lost if the picture is taken even minutely too early or late. Emphasis is particularly important in 'how to do it' picture series which will be used by individual learners. Such photographs must be largely self-explanatory.

Emphasis is aided by the elimination of extraneous detail—particularly when such items themselves attract attention for the wrong reasons. One of the characteristics of photography is that it can record a great mass of detail yet, unlike the eye, cannot itself differentiate between important and unimportant subjects. We have to discipline ourselves to examine critically every part of the picture seen in the viewfinder. An old 'banger' parked outside an historically important church could receive more attention from the class than the building itself. The headline on a newspaper lying on a workbench could be all that a student remembers of a workshop illustration. A photograph to show the mechanical principle of the escapement or gear train in a clock is confusing if too much irrelevant textural detail of the parts appears. Sometimes these problems can be solved by changing viewpoint; using shallow depth of field (with a wide lens aperture); choosing or arranging lighting to emphasise locally wanted parts; and choosing an exposure level which will reproduce unwanted trivia very light or dark.

Simplicity must not lead to monotony. Variety can be injected by using variations in *viewpoint*—high or low, close or more distant camera positions, the use of underlit or unsharp foreground objects to give framing and depth, use of strong perspective lines and shapes. At the same time avoid eccentric viewpoints with which the student cannot possibly identify.

Like poster images which are designed to be seen and absorbed quickly, most educational pictures should be strong, simple and to the point. If the aid is a photograph of an animal running, emphasise its movement with blurred background, low viewpoint, and expression and leg positions which epitomise determination and effort. This will almost certainly mean taking several pictures and selecting the best.

In short, interesting educational pictures do deserve time and effort.

Fortunately the task is an absorbing and fascinating one which can give great fulfilment.

Choice of film

Which film you use depends upon the type of final aid required and the conditions of shooting. A cross-section of commercial negatives and reversal films with their suggested applications is set out on page 314.

The principal advantage of negative films over reversal films is that any number of positive images can be printed off one shot at various sizes, also allowing alterations to density, image cropping, etc. As discussed on page 154, reversal films give projectible transparencies in one stage, and obviate the need for printing facilities and know-how. Against this, lack of second-stage control necessitates greater care in exposure and framing when shooting.

BLACK-AND-WHITE NEGATIVE FILMS. Monochrome films for continuous tone negatives and intended for general use range in speed from 32 (Panatomic X)–1000 ASA (Agfapan 1000). It is characteristic of photographic materials that the greater their sensitivity to light the more pronounced their grain pattern. Grain tends to obscure fine detail and limit tonal gradation in the image. On the other hand the ultra-fast films do allow hand-held photographs to be taken under poorest lighting conditions, or when depth of field demands a small lens aperture, or fast-moving subjects require briefest shutter speeds. Films within the 125–400 ASA range provide a good compromise and also offer wide exposure latitude—one-quarter or four times 'correct' exposure will still give printable results.

High contrast lith materials such as Kodalith are not normally used for direct photography of general subjects, but, as we saw in Chapter 5, have greatest value for copying artwork or for printing purposes. As an example of the latter, having photographed a tree on continuous tone general-purpose film such as Plus X, the negative might be enlarged on lith film to convert it to a high contrast line image. From this a heat copier will provide a spirit master so that pictures of the tree can be run off on a duplicator—and the lith film itself used as an OHP transparency.

BLACK-AND-WHITE REVERSAL FILMS. It is *possible* to reversal process several types of negative film into direct positive transparencies. However, apart from Kodalith, which responds to this treatment quite successfully, image colour and 'body' are really only acceptable if the film is designed for reversal processing in the first place. In practice, limited demand for monochrome reversal films leaves us with Agfa Dia-Direct for general-purpose continuous-tone work, and an appropriately processed lith film for line. Both types of material are very useful for 35-mm slide production.

COLOUR NEGATIVE FILMS. As Appendix III shows, these range in speed between 40 and 100 ASA. They offer the same practical advantages over reversal films as discussed under monochrome materials, and allow prints to be run off in black and white paper or film as well as colour. It is desirable to expose colour negative films using light sources as specified by the manufacturer (usually daylight), although even here correction can be made in printing as long as light sources are not *mixed* in the same picture. Processing a colour negative is little more complicated than black-and-white negative processing. Unfortunately the cost, time and complexity of making good-quality colour prints on paper or film of any size diminishes the attraction of colour negative films for the user-producer of visual aids.

COLOUR REVERSAL FILMS. Colour reversal films give quicker, cheaper and often higher-quality projection slides than colour negatives. However, like all reversal materials, greater exposure accuracy is necessary when shooting the picture. It is also essential to use the light source specified for the film, or otherwise use a correcting filter over the lens (Fig. 4.27). Acceptable copy transparencies and prints on paper can be made from transparencies by colour laboratories.

Various photographic manufacturers offer reversal colour films ranging from 25 ASA to 500 ASA. The fastest films are usually more expensive and give slightly poorer image detail than slow films, but under difficult conditions any additional speed is usually all-important. Try, however, to keep to one manufacturer's products when shooting a slide series, as each brand uses slightly different dyes, resulting in subtle but noticeable differences in image colours when mixed in together.

Reversal colour films can be subdivided into (a) films such as Kodachrome, which can only be processed by the manufacturer because of the complex stages involved, and (b) films such as Ektachrome and Agfachrome which can either be processed by laboratories (usually through dealers) or by the user himself, see page 272).

Camera technicalities
The three controls on the camera—focusing, aperture and shutter settings—represent something of a barrier between photographer and subject. Everyone has lost good pictures of fleeting situations because of preoccupation with camera adjustments. Maybe we worry too much about these things.

Focusing is most critical when working close-up and/or with the lens at its widest aperture; also when a long-focus lens is being used.

Under each of these conditions the depth of subject which can be rendered sharply at one time (depth of field) is very shallow. However, as Fig. 6.1 shows, if the subject is beyond 3 m and the lens stopped down to ƒ16, focus can be left set at about 6 m and the scene will sharply record from 3 m right through to infinity (35-mm camera with standard lens). Under such conditions, therefore, time need not be taken up critically adjusting focus for each shot. Equally, distance can be guessed approximately and set on the scale when shooting pictures

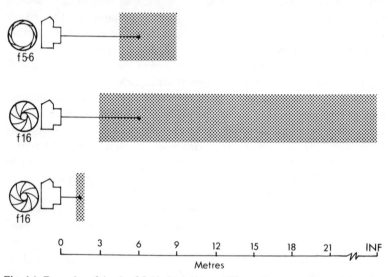

Fig. 6.1. Examples of depth of field obtainable at different lens apertures and focusing distances.

in quick succession, or when working surreptitiously. Notice how one can focus about 'one-third in'—sharpness extending further *behind* the part critically focused than in front of it.

EXPOSURE CALCULATIONS. Exposure recommendations packed with the box of film cover quite a range of popular subjects and typical lighting conditions. (The packing note has value too when students themselves are taking photographs—they have to recognise these conditions for themselves.) Results will be near enough correct for black-and-white negative materials exposed out of doors, but for more ambitious work and when shooting expensive colour film an exposure meter is invaluable.

Exposure readings are not, however, necessary for every shot if the subject's lighting conditions remain unchanged. Instead of using the meter like an electric razor, constantly checking readings from people's

200

embarrassed faces, use substitute subjects. Read off the back of your hand instead of a face; nearby grass or brickwork instead of more distant subjects. (The lighting on these substitutes must of course be the same as on the subject itself.)

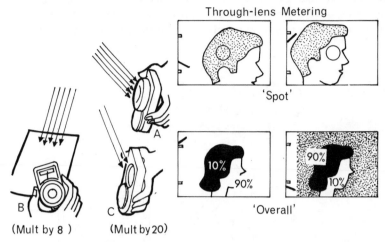

Fig. 6.2. *Left:* Instead of reading direct off the subject, a meter can be used indirectly (from near the subject position). A, Pointed at light source using a plastic incident light attachment over cell. B, Measuring directly off white card and giving 8 times indicated exposure. C, Pointed as A but without diffuser, then giving 20 times the exposure. B is a good way to take readings in poor lighting; C is for emergency use in extremely dim conditions. *Right:* A through-the-lens meter giving spot readings allows separate high-light and shadow measurements (average the two). Systems giving overall readings are deceptive when important parts are small, backgrounds large.

Another time-saver in reading technique is the use of an incident light attachment to the meter. By pointing the meter towards the light source from the subject position, one reading shows exposure required for most subjects. The same result should be obtained from taking a reading direct from a grey card. Only very dark and very light objects call for modifications to this reading.

A meter built into the camera is a convenience, particularly a through-the-lens meter which allows local 'spot' readings, see Fig. 6.2. FAST-MOVING SUBJECTS. Subjects such as figures running, vehicles, aircraft, etc., seldom allow sufficient time for critical image focusing, and we have to rely on estimated-distance or substitute-subject focusing. The former technique simply means intelligent guessing of distance, which is then set on the focusing scale on the lens. Remember that a small aperture and a subject some distance away both increase permissible error in focusing. To use a substitute, find some object estimated to be the same distance from the lens as the subject will be (perhaps in another direction) and accurately focus on this.

Shutter speed is most critical when subject and/or camera are moving, and this includes shakiness on the part of the photographer. Most people can hold a camera sufficiently still while exposing at $\frac{1}{60}$ or $\frac{1}{125}$ second to give sharp results from an inanimate or slow-moving subject. The shutter can therefore be left at one of these settings to serve most

Fig. 6.3. Panning the camera when shooting a moving subject results in a well-separated blurred background. Start a smooth movement of the camera when the subject is still some way off and try shutter speeds of 1/60 and 1/125 sec.

purposes. Even fast-moving subjects can be sharply recorded at such speeds if the camera is panned during shooting (Fig. 6.3). The background blurs under these conditions but usually this gives emphasis and interest.

Cameras with direct vision finders are by far the most convenient to use for panning. Twin lens reflexes are the most difficult, because images on the focusing screen of this camera are reversed left to right, making it extremely inconvenient for following a subject moving rapidly across the field of view. For this reason the front of the hood surrounding the screen normally has a fold-down section to act as a simple direct vision finder.

The brief duration of flash makes it a convenient light source for rendering detail in moving subjects, but this very movement-freezing characteristic (particularly electronic flash) often destroys all impression of speed. At the other end of the scale a long exposure time given to relatively slow-moving images (ships, distant traffic) make them blur and appear to hurtle along.

INTERCHANGEABLE LENSES. Changing the camera lens for a lens of different focal length, has various purposes:

1. Smaller or larger areas of the subject can be imaged from the same camera position. For example, changing to a wide-angle (short-focus) lens allows most of the interior of a room to be imaged from just within its doorway; changing to a long-focus or telephoto lens fills the frame with the image of someone's head seen through the window out in the street.

2. Bigger magnification of close subjects can be obtained. If, despite using extension bellows or rings, the normal lens will not focus out far enough to give a sufficiently large image of a very close subject, change to a lens with a shorter focal length.

3. Compression or expansion of the perspective effect between near and distant objects is possible. Photographing a crowded street with a telephoto lens from a long way away cramps up the appearance of pedestrians, traffic, and shop facades into an almost perspectiveless mass of detail. Photographing a nearby cat on a garden gate with a wide-angle lens makes the tiny garden behind the animal appear to taper away like a vast park, to a distant semi.

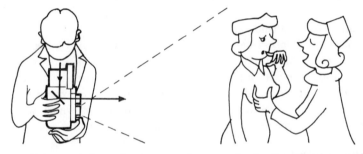

Fig. 6.4. Using a twin lens reflex camera to shoot a nearby situation when (apparently) facing away at right angles.

PHOTOGRAPHING PEOPLE. There are three main lines of approach when photographing strangers in the street or in their own environment. One method is to become 'invisible', i.e. photograph a situation without influencing it. A telephoto lens used from the seclusion of a doorway across the street, shooting from behind shop or car windows, photography of reflections in mirrors, or appearing to shoot in a direction at right angles to the subject (Fig. 6.4) are all possible techniques.

Another approach is to arrange or choose people who are too absorbed in what they are doing to notice the photographer—people in crowds pouring into stations in the rush hour, craftsmen working at a difficult job. Often such subjects can be shot close-up using a wide-angle lens, the steep perspective giving a feeling of closeness missing from distant viewpoints. Again the blatantly posed shot—the shopkeeper standing with folded arms behind his counter looking straight at the camera—can work effectively for objective factual illustrations, particularly when part of a similarly organised series.

Remember the way people steal attention from things. Ideally the action or reaction shown in the expression and position of any person portrayed (even when subsidiary to the main subject) should contribute towards the photograph's educational purpose, never distract. Where the situation can be directed try to omit anything which does not help to make the point, thus simplifying the picture. In close-ups of workpeople remove distracting irrelevant items in top pockets, on bench tops or shelves in the foreground or background. Watch out for clothing—Sunday best gear specially donned for the photograph is as inappropriate as torn and dangerously flapping industrial overalls.

To suppress the human element, arrange lighting to emphasise the machine, job, etc., and dress the operative in clothing of similar tone to the background, or include only the hands. At the same time don't avoid all use of people—figures are particularly valuable for enlivening architectural and landscape photographs.

Where a situation naturally presents itself in front of the camera always shoot first (including any irrelevancies) and, if circumstances allow, follow up with further pictures having more carefully considered viewpoints and other directed improvements. Despite everything you may not be able to better that first spontaneous picture which, with too much concern for detail, would never have been taken.

Influence of lighting

Sympathetic quality and direction of lighting is as important as its quantity. Oblique light from a 'hard' source such as a flashbulb, spotlight, or the direct sun can emphasise the texture of a surface (Fig. 6.5). Diffuse flat lighting—overcast daylight, a large floodlight, or light reflected off white card near the camera—gently reveals form and detail in complex groups of items which would otherwise become a confusion of shadows. In general, black-and-white photography requires somewhat bolder lighting than when shooting on colour film. This is because monochrome film relies on *tone* contrasts instead of colour contrasts.

When the subject is small enough for lighting to be completely under control—a small still life, for example—try to build up the

Fig. 6.5. *Left:* Sources of hard lighting, giving strong hard edged shadows. *Right:* Sources of diffuse lighting. Note the use of matt white paper and tracing paper to effect lighting *quality*, although reducing *intensity*.

lighting one source at a time. Figure 6.6 illustrates the progressive use of key light, fill-in, background lighting, etc.

Photography of large subjects such as buildings and landscapes requires good organisation to make use of the most sympathetic lighting conditions. If hard direct sunlight is needed to emphasise some fold in the ground or one face of a building, use a compass to predict the path of the sun. A pretty accurate estimate can be made of the best time of day to shoot when suitable weather conditions materialise. If the lighting is more appropriate diffused or if the subject faces north wait for light cloudy or overcast conditions. Of course there may not be time for such niceties, but factors such as care over lighting distinguishes the outstanding image from the adequate. As many subjects will be local based we should be in a much better position to pick and choose near perfect conditions than a commercial producer of VA software.

When small, movable subjects are shot out of doors they can of course be moved into the most favourable lighting environment. Place

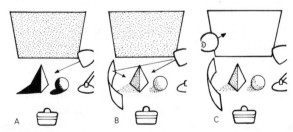

Fig. 6.6. Building up lighting. A, Main or key light alone. B, Addition of fill-in—here simply a white reflector. C, Addition of background light. Placing the background some distance away allows separate lighting and therefore full control of background tone relative to the subject.

205

the subject in a large shadow area for diffuse lighting, and use sunlight as hard lighting; a shadow area plus sunlight reflected from a light surface (Fig. 6.5) gives directional diffuse quality lighting somewhere between the two. (Don't shoot in colour if the subject is in shadow lit only from a blue sky, as this will result in a blue cast. Instead photograph in sunlight but try to diffuse the sun's rays with tracing paper.)

Bear in mind always that the eye can perceive detail in harshly lit highlights and shadows which are beyond the capability of photographic film to record. When using strong lighting a little illumination reflected back into shadow areas (e.g. from a white card) lowers contrast and allows the film to record detail the eye sees. Conversely this limitation in photographic recording can be turned to advantage by arranging that any unwanted or unimportant parts of the picture are in shadow, and judging exposure for the brighter areas only.

Little can be done to modify locally the lighting of whole rows of buildings and other distant subjects, apart from choosing another time of day. The problem is however less acute here as the light scattering effect of atmospheric haze reduces contrast, and shadows are often only a small part of the picture area.

Shooting in poor light

No exposure is photographically impossible, provided there is *some* illumination present to which the film is sensitive. By exposing for hours instead of fractions of a second photographs can be taken even on moonless nights. The best modern built-in or separate meters using a battery * are usually able to give readings in very poor light. However, when conditions are such that a meter seems unable to give a reading in the normal way it may be possible to achieve a weak reading off a sheet of white paper. Give 8 times the exposure shown, Fig. 6.2.

Dim light usually calls for fastest film, widest lens aperture and slowest shutter speed. Wide-angle and telephoto lenses tend not to have such wide maximum apertures as normal types—wide apertures are also related to price. Remember that focusing must always be more accurate when shooting with the lens wide open, as this gives minimum depth of field.

The decision whether to shoot black-and-white pictures on a moderately fast film (125 ASA) and give longish exposure times, or expose ultra-fast (1250 ASA) film for shorter times depends on the subject. Ultra-fast film gives a more grainy, tonally restricted image than the slower stock. Good technical quality is important for clarity

* CdS cell types.

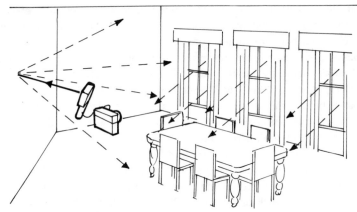

Fig. 6.7. Using flash to fill-in shadow areas. Use the stop recommended if flash were used direct from a total distance of flash (via wall) to picture centre. Measure daylight lit areas (e.g. table) to discover shutter speed needed at this *f* setting.

and often the best course is to shoot on 125 ASA film and if necessary try to support the camera on a tripod, shelf, or the back of a chair.

As Table App.3.1 shows, the average high-speed colour reversal film is 160 ASA and the fastest film made is only 500 ASA. However, in emergencies where slight loss of brilliance and colour accuracy is unimportant most colour processing laboratories (Appendix IV) can give forced development and so allow most films to be exposed at twice or three times its rated speed, e.g. 160 ASA film exposed as if 320 or 480 ASA. Naturally the whole film must be exposed at the chosen uprating, and the laboratory warned how much compensation to make.

Many poorly lit subjects are also unevenly lit and therefore contrasty. Streets at night, the interiors of rooms or basement workshops, are often a patchy mixture of light and shadowy areas. The resulting photographs have burnt out white areas in a sea of featureless grey or black shadow. Additional lighting such as a flash or photoflood lamp reflected off the ceiling is a useful means of adding detail to the darker areas without destroying the character of actual conditions (Fig. 6.7). For colour photography this extra lighting should of course be a close match to the *colour* of the existing light. Where extra lighting is impractical under dim contrasty conditions shoot on black-and-white negative film, giving generous exposure and less than normal development to reduce image contrast.

Lighting difficult subjects
Some subjects are made of materials which present particular lighting problems when pictures having maximum detail are required. Often

good ideas on lighting can be picked up from the way similar objects are displayed in department stores, or photographed for advertising purposes, but here are some suggestions:

GLASSWARE. Transparent or translucent glass looks and photographs well when backlit by either of the following methods:

1. Use a light toned wall or a large sheet of white paper some distance behind the subject and illuminate this background only.

2. Use black material (or the open door into a darkened room) as background and then direct light on to the glassware from the rear, from just outside the picture area (see Fig. 6.8).

Method 1 shows the glass shapes in great clarity as black lines against white, rather like a line drawing. However, thick lumpy glass may appear too dark and clumsy. Method 2 gives white shapes and highlights against black, making much more of the reflective qualities of glass, but at some expense of clarity owing to the many highlights.

Fig. 6.8. Methods of shooting glassware. *Left:* Putting all light on to a well separated white background silhouettes shapes and contents. *Right:* Shooting against a dark cavity with (hidden) side/back-lighting of the glass gives *white* shapes and highlights.

POLISHED METAL. Much depends on the degree of polish. Often if the subject has a satin chrome finish we can use frontal lighting, diffusing the light through sheets of tracing paper. Highly polished mirror finishes are more difficult. We can let relevant surroundings appear as reflections, diffusing the light and removing only items which detract from subject form and detail. Alternatively we can create a detail-less environment by placing a tent of muslin or cylinder of white paper around the subject, just cutting a small hole for the camera lens to peep in. An opal glass sphere (as used for suspended lighting in older schools) is a useful ready made 'tent' for small reflective subjects, as shown in Fig. 6.9.

208

Lighting can either be passed through 'tent' walls or (large sets) reflected off its inside surfaces. Try not to make the elimination of reflections too perfect or the subject will appear as if sprayed white or made of china. If necessary position strips of black paper to give simple reflected lines in the metal, particularly along edges which might otherwise merge with the background.

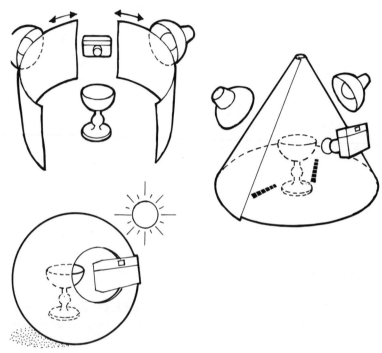

Fig. 6.9. Even lighting of highly reflective subjects. *Top left:* Sheets of tracing paper, kept moving during a time exposure of several seconds. *Bottom:* Subject placed in opal sphere from a lighting fitting. *Right:* Tent of muslin or paper. Black strips are used to reflect into subject and help separate perimeter from background.

PLANTS AND FLOWERS. These are live objects liable to move during long exposure times, and wilt rapidly under hot light sources. Even with cut flowers try to shoot outdoors, because lighting is more natural (and often brighter) than artificial conditions. If indoor shooting is essential use one main light plus white reflector (Fig. 6.10) to simulate daylight. Diffuse the lamp with tracing paper for more gentle (i.e. overcast) conditions. Flash is a very practical light source—freezing movement and avoiding heat. To prevent subject movement try to avoid conditions requiring exposure times longer than 1 sec.

SELF-LUMINOUS SUBJECTS. With candle or gas flames, welding, etc., visual results are much influenced by (*a*) the ratio of light actually emitted from the subject to light illuminating it, and (*b*) the length of exposure time given. If the only light comes from the subject itself (e.g. a flame) and the meter indicated exposure is given, details of the flame may record in a sea of black. More exposure may give some surrounding detail but also records an exaggerated white and featureless flame.

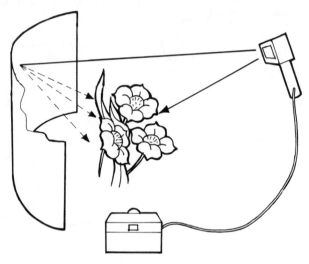

Fig. 6.10. Simulated sunlight conditions when shooting flowers, etc., indoors. Reflector is matt white.

Supplementary lighting is therefore often needed. Check its effect on surrounding detail visually—make lighting seem to originate from the general direction of the flame. For colour photography this lighting should be of similar colour to the flame (e.g. use lamps rather than electronic flash).

When deciding which *f*-number and shutter combination to choose remember that the appearance of flame movement is exaggerated by long exposure time. Sparks falling from a welding job record as trails— their length varying with the duration of exposure. Each white trail will be sixteen times as long at $\frac{1}{8}$ sec as at $\frac{1}{125}$ sec. A speed of $\frac{1}{15}$ sec gives a fairly objective record but try others faster and slower (with appropriate adjustment of diaphragm).

Dealing with unwanted backgrounds

A method already mentioned of subduing the effect of a background is to over or under light the background relative to the subject, so that when correct exposure for the subject is given these areas record as very light or very dark. This is even easier if a roll of white or black paper is carried around for background use. If the background material improvised for a static subject is dirty or marked put the camera on a tripod, stop the lens down well and use a slow film. This allows us to give as long an exposure time as possible, during which the background can be moved up and down to blur its unwanted detail. Another method is to shoot at a wide lens aperture, checking that depth of field just extends through the subject itself.

Fig. 6.11. Simplifying backgrounds. A, White paper sheet placed between subject and unwanted background, and moved during time exposure. B and C, Methods of producing solid white or black backgrounds. *Bottom:* Straight shot with background detail bleached white on print, or cut out and mounted on white ground. Bleacher, 1·5 gm potassium iodide plus 0·5 gm iodine in 100 ccs water, is followed by fixing.

Small objects can be laid out on opal plastic or glass lit from below, or shot horizontally against the void of a doorway into a darkened room. In extreme cases, where nothing can be done at the time of shooting, a photographic enlargement on paper can be prepared from which the background is either bleached (Fig. 6.11) or cut away with a sharp blade. The print of the subject alone can then be mounted on a card of suitable tone and rephotographed.

Shooting extreme close-ups (macrophotography)

Close-up photographs—taken with the camera direct rather than through a microscope—are usually possible down to images about twice subject size. This is a visually rewarding field to explore. Results offer great educational scope by allowing group viewing of detail, and are particularly effective in colour. Bear in mind the following practical points:

1. Any differences between the viewpoint of viewfinder and camera lens is very apparent. Use a single lens reflex if possible.

2. The lens has to be more distant from the film than usual and extension tubes or bellows (page 87) will probably be essential.

3. The small subject may be difficult to read with an exposure meter and unless the camera has a built-in through-the-lens meter a substitute subject (page 200) will probably have to be used. Some extra exposure is needed owing to close-up working conditions (page 335).

4. There will be minimal depth of field, so we must close the lens diaphragm well down to produce even modest front-to-back sharpness.

5. Some indication of scale is usually advisable. This might be simply a graph-paper background. Better still, if much macro work is to be done, design a miniature ruler.

6. If the subject is a scale model try to work to the same scale, viz.: an 'eye level' viewpoint for a $\frac{1}{36}$-scale model building might be 150 cm (average eye level) multiplied by this scale. The centre of the camera lens should be 4 cm above the model's 'ground level'. See Fig. 6.12.

Fig. 6.12. Shooting from a (scaled) eye-level viewpoint inside an architectural model. Sometimes this may mean shooting downwards on to a 45° front silvered mirror.

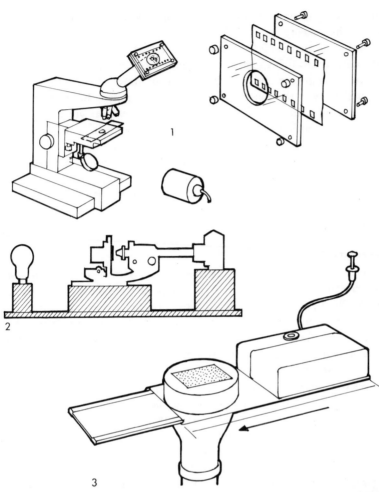

Fig. 6.13. Photographing through a simple microscope. 1, By attaching a piece of (FG Positive) film to the top of the draw tube (with eyepiece removed). Film is sandwiched between two sheets of thick clear Perspex, the front one drilled through to grip tube and present film surface direct to image. (Image can be focused through back of a spare piece of film.) Work is carried out in printing darkroom. 2, By pointing SLR camera down draw tube. 3, By using attachment with sliding focusing screen. Sliding unit shifts film into exact plane occupied by screen.

Photography through a microscope

This is not as difficult as it sounds if we are not too ambitious. Any type of camera can be used—simply focus its lens as for infinity and place it up close to the microscope, which has been focused visually for the specimen and had its eyepiece removed. The easiest arrangement is to line up the camera, microscope and light source (e.g. a photoflood)

213

horizontally using an absolutely rigid base. Vibration during exposure is the chief enemy.

A better method of positioning the camera is to use a microscope adaptor. This allows a 35-mm camera (minus lens) to be screwed on to the end of the microscope draw tube. If the camera is a SLR type the image can be focused through the usual camera eyepiece; for direct vision cameras the attachment will either have a sliding focusing screen (Fig. 6.13) or a built-in reflex focusing system.

If the camera has a sensitive built-in meter, readings can be made with this; otherwise estimation will have to be by trial and error. Very high-quality eyepiece cameras with semi automatic exposure control are made by microscope manufacturers, but are usually expensive.

Special techniques

EXPLODED VIEWS. Often it is valuable to be able to show in one informational picture how an item is assembled from various separate parts. By laying out each part adjacent to, but spaced apart from its neighbour, students can see how the various bits and pieces fit together (Fig. 4.17E). Laying out the subject requires much patience, in order to line everything up. If the camera focusing screen is accessible draw one or more straight lines in grease pencil to act as centre lines for each series of component (Fig. 6.14).

If the subject is a simple one it may be practical to lay everything out on white plastic or glass lit partly from beneath, and photograph it straight. For more elaborate exploded views ignore background and prop up each item on blocks, or suspend them from cotton. A large black-and-white print is then made, the whole background painted out with process white poster colour, and the result rephotographed.

SUPERIMPOSITION. Sometimes superimposing the image of one subject within or beside another is the best way to show how two items relate to each other. Both pictures are exposed on the same piece of film. For example, imagine that we wish to show how two simple batteries fit within a torch body (Fig. 6.15). First the torch itself is photographed, lit so that the main part of the body is in shadow, e.g. rim lit from the sides or rear. The position of the body within the frame is carefully noted (marked on the focusing screen if possible). Now the two batteries, one on top of the other, are placed in front of a *black* background, and lit to show their detail. Checking through the camera their image is made to fit within the marked outline of the torch body, and

Fig. 6.14. Exploded view photographs. *Top:* Components meticulously laid out along common centre lines. (Main axis can be drawn on camera focusing screen.) Print from negative is retouched—using Process White or bleacher, or cutting out and remounting. The print is finally re-photographed if several copies are required.

then exposed on to the film too. In both cases normal exposure is given.*

Another method of superimposition is to expose separate negatives of the components (the 'inner' component at least against a black background). The two negatives are then sandwiched and printed together. Similarly they can be shot on two frames of colour reversal film

* Most, but not all, cameras allow two pictures to be exposed on the same frame. On many 35-mm cameras a button has to be depressed to disengage film transport when winding to cock the shutter.

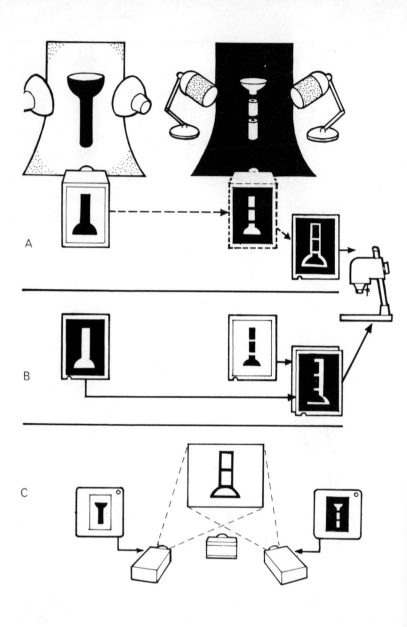

Fig. 6.15. Techniques for superimposing internal detail within external view. Outside casing is set up as semi-silhouette against white ground. Conversely, contents are double side lit against black. A, Both images are exposed on to one common sheet of film, then printed straight. B, Two separate negatives are made, and sandwiched together for printing. C, Two transparencies are made, separately projected to superimpose on a screen and the image rephotographed (see also Fig. 9.11).

and the resulting transparencies projected in separate projectors to superimpose and combine on one screen. This is an interesting method of presentation in itself—furthermore, the combined image on the screen can be photographed, using a camera loaded with type B colour film (see opposite). Both these methods allow greater control over the juxtaposition of images than superimposing when shooting. Further sources of information on techniques for photographing specific subject matter are included in the bibliography on page 297.

7. Making motion picture aids

ALTHOUGH still photographs allow close analysis and interpretation by students, that extra dimension offered by the moving image gives special teaching advantages. Subjects in which movement is an essential element immediately benefit—time scales can be reduced or extended to clarify actions. Techniques such as animation help to simplify information, and skilful editing offers possibilities such as emphasis and control of pace. Most of all, students readily identify with the realism of events in a well-made film.

In this chapter we are mainly concerned with the practical matters of planning, shooting and completing movie film. The aim is not to produce a major sound production with lip-synchronisation and all the professional frills, but a simple, straightforward informational aid.

Visual aid movies can be divided into single concept loops, and conventional silent or sound films. As discussed in Chapter 3, loop films are specially valuable for cyclic sequences and short visual demonstrations of a few minutes duration, viewed by small groups or individuals. Both loops and open spool conventional films are often just as valuable silent as when complete with a soundtrack. The teacher knows how the material fits in with his programme, and provides an ad-lib commentary anyway; authentic background noises can make a contribution, but may barely justify the additional time and hardware needed.

It is pleasant to be able to afford to shoot film on 16 mm for its extra image quality and handling ease in editing. However, for classroom audiences of only a few dozen the economics of 8 mm far outweigh its smaller image size disadvantages. We therefore concentrate on 8 mm in the pages that follow, mentioning 16 mm only when techniques differ significantly between the two gauges. There is also so little difference between the cost of black-and-white and colour reversal film that the latter will be considered the norm.

Subject treatment

Making a film involves a sequence of stages of which the actual shooting of film is only one part. Like the professional film-maker we can save time and expensive film stock by careful initial planning, and the working out of a basic shooting script first. After photography the editing stage is equally important in contributing to the pace and effectiveness of the finished production.

Having convinced ourselves that a motion picture will communicate the teaching material more effectively than, say tape-linked slides (see

TABLE 7.1

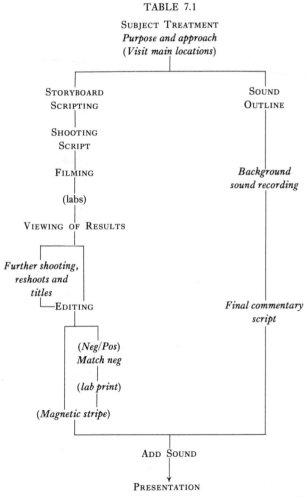

Table 7.1. The general pattern of production when making movie film aids.

page 108) analyse the key points to be covered and try to plan them in visual terms. Try to avoid a situation in which the result is merely a filmed lecture, recorded lesson or demonstration, which could just as easily be presented live. Plan to take full advantage of the medium to record movement, condense time, give close access to small, difficult or dangerous subjects, and offer other visual experiences beyond the scope of traditional teaching methods.

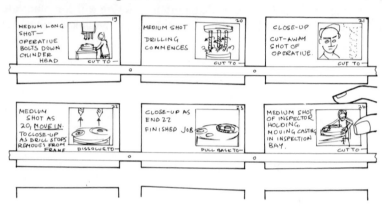

Fig. 7.1. Storyboard, using postcards carrying rough sketches and description of shots. When finalised, cards can be rearranged in order of locations, and so converted into a shooting script, Fig. 7.2.

Imagine that we need to make a short informational film covering metal casting—specifically the diecasting of aluminium cylinder heads in a local factory. Having visited the factory, the points which we decide must be shown might be:

1. Construction of the steel mould or die.

2. Preparation of the plaster cores which will form the interior cavity for each casting.

3. Positioning the core within the die, and ladling in the molten aluminium.

4. After a period for cooling, opening the die and removing the casting.

5. Breaking up and removing the remains of the plaster core and band-sawing rough edges off the casting.

6. Final precision machining of the valve and cylinder cavities, etc.

The easiest way to script these six stages visually is to use a *storyboard*—a series of cards, each containing a rough sketch with accompanying notes, for every shot. In this way proposed shots can be moved around and planned in a suitable order, bearing in mind that close-ups are very effective on a small screen and should be used plentifully. At the same time establishing and cut-away shots and over-all continuity are also important (see Fig. 7.1).

An *establishing shot* typically shows general environment before closing in on detail, and is usually necessary at the beginning of the film

SHOOTING SCRIPT. PAGE 3.

STORY BOARD Nº		LOCATION: M/C SHOP
19	L.S.	Multi-head driller—operative bolts down work. (CUT)
20	M.S.	Spinning drills contact casting pierce metal. (CUT)
22	M.S.–C.U.	As 20 but drill rise, out of frame. HOLD 5 SEC EXTRA FOR LAB DISSOLVE (DISSOLVE.)
21	C.U.	Cut-away shot of operative, looking down out of frame. Spinning drill right foreground (CUT)
		LOCATION: INSPECTION BAY
23	C.U.–M.S.	Finish casting held in inspector's arms. Framing & image size exactly as end of 22. BEGIN WITH 5 SEC HOLD FOR LAB DISSOLVE (Slow zoom back to:
24	MS	Inspector at bench, twists & examines casting. (CUT)

Fig. 7.2. Shooting script derived from storyboard, Fig. 7.1.

itself and at any other relevant change of location. For example, our film might open with a general view of a die machine shop before moving in to the actual die, which (mostly in close-up) will form the centre of the film. Similarly when the die is moved to the foundry for casting, or the casting taken to the machine shop, try to include a medium or long shot early-on to indicate the new environment before returning to detail. Re-establishing shots are also useful from time to time to break monotony and act as cut-aways.

Cut-away shots are used to cover necessary breaks in a sequence or the passing of time. For example, the full process of machining rough edges off the casting may take several minutes. By interspersing say, a close-up of the band-saw operator's face, we can return to the casting with the cutting job almost finished.

Smooth continuity of the image throughout the film relies upon factors such as following through an object or figure from sequence to sequence. (In this case the mould, and later the casting, fills the role conveniently.) If this featured object moves from one location to another try to include one shot at least showing it in transit. Watch out for obvious gaffs such as showing the hands working on the mould wearing dark cuffs one moment and light ones in the next, simply because the second shot was taken on another day.

Try to avoid sudden changes from long shots to close-ups and vice versa—try to soften the 'jump in space' which will occur on the screen by including a medium shot. Similarly zooms and dissolves (page 237) can be used in moderation to give smoother transition than is possible by a direct cut. Sometimes it is possible to move into close-up at the end of one sequence and then start the next sequence on a very similar close-up. For example, as shown in Fig. 7.1, the last shot of machinery may be a close-up of the drill withdrawing from the cylinder-head casting. This would cut to the next sequence (the completed product) opening with another shot of this aperture, making it about the same size and position on the screen but now in a finished state. The camera moves back to reveal the whole completed cylinder head. All these visual forms of punctuation can be observed every night in television films. They soon become familiar techniques.

As in the preparation of still images, prune the script ruthlessly to keep it simple and direct. Don't be tempted to include visual tricks for their own sake or the film may become too complicated and lengthy ever to be completed. In some films where the action is not controllable tight scripting is obviously a waste of time—although it is always worthwhile to formulate *some* idea of structure.

Organising a shooting script

We have one more important stage before actually exposing film. Where a finalised storyboard sequence has been prepared it can now be reshuffled into a shooting script (Fig. 7.2). This simply means laying out the shots in the most convenient order for photography, irrespective of final presentation. Each location is grouped separately, cutaways for each operation are all shot together and so on. Thus the most efficient use is made of shooting time, although of course this will mean rearranging most sequences by cutting and splicing later.

Splices *could* be avoided (each splice is a potential break in the film; loop films in particular should have minimum joins) by attempting to shoot everything in final order. From experience, however, we would be very lucky to film just the right length on each shot, never have to do a second take because someone does a wrong action, and handle the camera impeccably every moment. In practice then most shots will have to be spliced together, so that one might as well script for shooting convenience from the start.

Camera work

In the heat of the moment, with a rough shooting script in one hand and the subject ready for action, it becomes fatally easy to overlook some obvious technical point. The following check list for the technicalities of camera handling is suggested:

1. If the camera is electrically driven check that the batteries are in good condition; if spring-driven wind up the spring before loading and remember to rewind fully *after every shot.*

2. Check that the colour film is the correct balance for the illumination to be used. A correcting filter may have to be used, for example when shooting artificial light film in daylight (see Fig. 4.27). Avoid shooting in mixed tungsten lighting and daylight. Try to block or reduce all but one type of source.

3. Lace up the film quickly and competently. Loading a standard or double run 8-mm camera (Fig. 2.30) can be a fiddling operation. Practise with a length of scrap film until this job is handled reliably. Always run a few inches of film to check that everything is running through smoothly before closing the camera door.

4. Load and unload spools quickly and in subdued light. This is especially important when changing over spools after one-half of the width of a double-run 8-mm spool has been exposed. The makers include an extra foot or so to act as leader and trailer to protect the inner film on the spool, but too much exposure to light forms flashes of colour at the edges of the final image. For this reason shoot more film than usual on scenes right at the beginning or end of the spool. Super-8 film in cassettes avoids this risk of fogging; but must be firmly seated in the camera to run properly.

5. As with all colour photography, avoid very contrasty lighting if

detail is required in both shadows and highlights. For close-ups white reflectors are helpful in illuminating shadows.

6. Check lens aperture and focus controls. Using a normal exposure meter in the usual way (page 200) and set for the ASA film speed, the correct f-number appears opposite the camera shutter speed. For cameras running at the standard 18 fps this remains a constant $\frac{1}{36}$ sec. Unless the subject is only a few inches from the lens, focusing is not too critical, thanks to the phenomenal depth of field given by an 8-mm camera lens. Distance can mostly be guessed and set on the scale. In most cases, too, focus setting will not have to be 'pulled' (altered during shooting) when the subject moves closer to the camera. Lenses for 16-mm cameras require a more careful check on focus. A fixed focus camera with automatic exposure control does away with even these simple settings.

7. Remember to allow for parallax effects if necessary when shooting critically framed close-ups. If the cine camera is not a reflex type (Fig. 2.30) and therefore has a separate viewfinder, the difference between the scene observed through the finder and recorded by the lens could cause subjects to appear off-centre when closer than about 1–2 m. In most cases slight correction can be made empirically. However, titling and close-up copying call for more accurate corrections, as explained on page 226.

When setting up always try to film with the camera on a tripod, or a shelf or door clamp, or some other firm support. Resist the temptation to move the camera from side to side (panning) unless following a moving subject. Remember how blurred and irritating those home movies of panned landscape always appear. If panning or vertical tilting must take place make the action slow and smooth (use a pan and tilt head on the tripod). If a scene is too wide to include fully try to change to a wider angle lens—or shoot one part, then change the position of the camera slightly and record the other part as a separate shot.

Another cliche to avoid is over-use of zooming. A zoom lens, zoomed during shooting, gives an impression of moving forward into or backwards away from a scene (Fig. 2.32). Occasionally this is a useful continuity device for moving in on an important detail, but so often (as home movies again prove) the cameraman cannot restrain himself. The greatest value of a zoom lens is that it will substitute for a whole range of lenses—when setting up adjust the zoom until just the area of subject required is included. Thereafter the lens is used in the same way as any ordinary lens.

As a guide to begin with, try making the average length of each shot about 5–8 sec duration unless an action or process must be followed through. Even then it is often better to arrange that action over about 10 sec is divided between two shots with some difference of viewpoint or distance. If a moving figure is shown leaving the right-hand side of the frame try not to cut to a shot from such a viewpoint that the figure enters the frame from the right—this will look as if he is retracing his steps. Alternatively split the two shots with a brief head-on or rear view (Fig. 7.3).

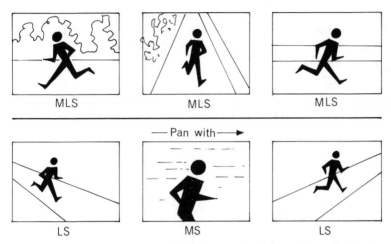

Fig. 7.3. Continuity. Two methods of allowing a moving figure to change his direction on the screen without seeming to be retracing his steps.

When making a film for the first time, using perhaps a hired or borrowed camera, it is sound policy to use up one roll of film trying odd sequences or checking the effect of camera controls. At the shooting stage even experienced film-makers throw away far more film than is finally used, and although we cannot afford the luxury of professional throw-away ratios, to be realistic we should expect to expose at least twice as much footage as the finished film.

As directors as well as cameramen, teachers have an advantage over the average amateur cinematographer in that we know our audience and the particular teaching job the film must fulfil. When looking through the viewfinder always try to visualise the final projected image seen perhaps from the back of the class. Does it make its point clearly (is the detail too small?), interestingly (is there enough variety in viewpoint and general visual treatment?), and concisely (can parts be cut without loss?).

Titling and close-ups

Apart from the simplest single concept loop, all films have a more finished appearance when given titles. It is also useful to be able to include in the film diagrams such as drawn artwork, illustrations from books, still photographs, etc., as well as big close-ups of various subject matter.

Preparation of artwork for filming follows the same general requirements as discussed at the beginning of Chapter 4. Transfer, magnetic or plastograph lettering, or even bold freehand drawing on card or the chalkboard can all photograph well. Keep titles and diagrams brief, simple and bold—remember the small size of the final image and also design within the height-to-width proportions of the 8-mm or 16-mm format (Fig. 7.4).

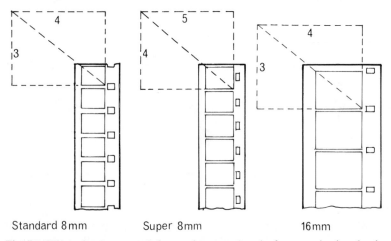

Standard 8mm   Super 8mm   16mm

Fig. 7.4. When planning artwork for movies remember the format ratio given by the particular size of film.

If the cine camera lens will not focus closer than several feet away, large title cards or a chalkboard will have to be used. A close-up lens, extension rings, or a camera lens designed to focus subjects down to a few inches away makes titling easier and big close-up work generally possible. However, unless the camera possesses a reflex viewing system parallax difference between viewfinder and camera lens will give off-centre images. Nothing looks worse than an unintentionally crooked or off-centre title (remember that, unlike still photography, it is impossible to crop or twist the frame to improve matters later).

A method of compensating for parallax error is to make up or buy a simple horizontal or vertical titler in which the camera slides along some form of rail, always at right angles to a title card holder (Fig. 7.5). With a piece of white card in the holder run the mounted camera right up to the card and mark the circular outline of the lens. The centre of this circle must now coincide with the centre of each title card—concentric rectangles can be marked out for convenience in placing. The camera viewfinder is simply used to assess the best size of image, not position.

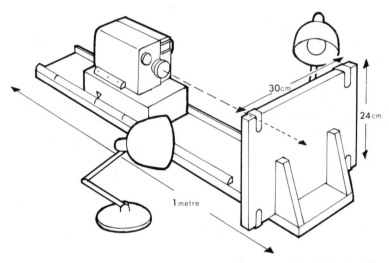

Fig. 7.5. Improvised titler made of wood which ensures camera is always centred on title card holder. One of a series of close-up lenses is fitted to the simple cine camera, which is then positioned at a pre-marked distance along the track.

Alternatively, prepare a correction card by making an impression on paper direct from the front of the camera lens barrel and viewfinder (Fig. 7.6). This paper should be the same size as the title card—say 10 × 8 in. Place the paper over the title to be photographed so that the hole made by the lens corresponds to the centre of the title card. Position the camera so that the impression denoting the centre of the viewfinder is now seen centred in the viewfinder.

Cards of 10 × 8 in. are a convenient size for titling because lettering on smaller cards tends to look rough when enlarged on the screen, unless exceptionally well done. Always leave a generous margin of card around the words to avoid any risk of the card edge showing. Flat artwork, clippings, etc., can be lit non-directionally by lamps at about 45° (page 147) or by diffused daylight. Remember to use the appropriate colour film or correction filter.

Three-dimensional lettering and other close-ups will record with emphasised texture if directional lighting is used, such as one oblique flood with a reflector on the shadow side. Try not to put the lamp too close to the subject, however, or it may overlight one side of the picture relative to the opposite side. Exposure readings are made using the same techniques as for still photography. Extra exposure to compen-

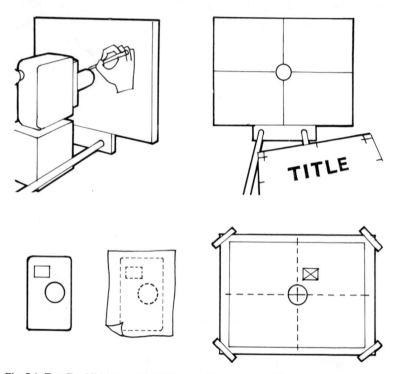

Fig. 7.6. *Top:* Establishing centre of filmed area by tracing outline of lens. This denotes the centre of each title card. *Bottom:* If camera has a separate viewfinder, trace positions of taking and finder lenses on paper and transfer to title board, making the lens mark central. When setting up, the rectangle must always be seen centred in the finder.

sate for working close-up does not occur with an 8-mm camera standard lens until the subject is less than 4 cm away. Shoot sufficient film on each title for the lettering to appear on the screen long enough to be read at normal reading speed for the audience age group, plus a little extra (say 10%). Cost of film alone therefore becomes one incentive for keeping titles concise.

Usually all titles and other flat copy are shot at the same time, and then inserted in their correct position in the film during editing. It is also possible to superimpose titles over moving images, as explained on page 236.

Editing

Having projected the raw results of our shooting as each processed film is posted back from the laboratory, we now have to edit out unwanted material and organise the remaining shots in correct order. A splicer (Fig. 2.33) is needed for cutting and joining film. A projector *can* be

Fig. 7.7. Improvised editing desk. A, Roll of polythene to protect everything from dust when not in use. B, Plastic strip to accept grease pencil number relating to each film clip. C, Wooden batten with headless pins, for individual shots and sections of film. D, Clean muslin bag. Note the muslin gloves on table, together with animated viewer, splicer, etc.

used to view and judge the juxtaposition of pieces of film but this is very inconvenient, and frequent lacing up causes film scratching. If possible use an animated viewer forming part of an editing desk (Fig. 7.7), perhaps at a teachers' centre.

If we are editing the original reversal film exposed in the camera we need to take special precautions against fingermarks, scratches and dust; cotton gloves are helpful. It is common practice to shoot 16-mm black-and-white film on negative stock from which the laboratory supplies a positive ('rush') film print. The negative itself is never projected

229

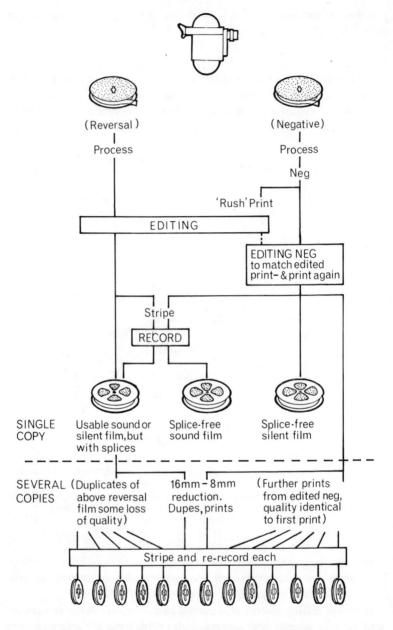

Fig. 7.8. The general pattern of operations between exposing film stock and the completed silent or magnetic sound film. (Editing reversal film is easier if a dupe is made immediately after processing. Like a rush print, this can be extensively man-handled and the original film finally cut to match.)

but the rush is run over again and again, and edited until it is absolutely right, ignoring any scratches or other handling marks it may accumulate. Finally the negative is very carefully cut and spliced to match the rush, and clean, splice-free prints run off by the laboratory. (At this stage too a change in film size can be made—16 mm being reduction printed on to 8 mm.)

A similar routine can be used for reversal colour or black-and-white 16-mm and 8-mm film. The laboratory will prepare a dupe which can

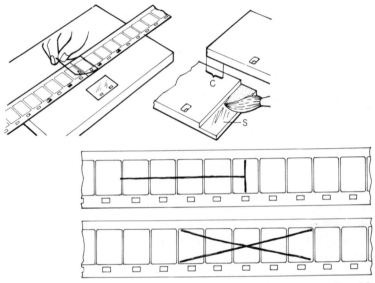

Fig. 7.9. *Top left:* Splicing butt-joined films with transparent adhesive tape. *Top right:* Cement splicing. Area S is scraped free of emulsion, and is cemented to roughened area C on back of other length of film. *Bottom:* Editing marks for position of cut, and of dissolve.

be manhandled for editing. The original film is then matched to the edited dupe and further dupes printed off. Naturally each laboratory stage increases costs pro-rata to the film footage.

Projecting original spliced film is really only satisfactory if we are using it for our own teaching, and are prepared to repair the occasional break. For all other purposes (and particularly for a loop film which is to be sealed into a cassette) a splice-free dupe would be advisable.

Splicing is not a difficult business if a good tape or cement splicer is available, but it does deserve to be done well. Practise on odd bits of scrap film. The tape splicer is the quickest and easiest to use, as the film does not then need scraping (see Fig. 7.9). However, long-term, tape splices are not quite as strong as good cement splices.

The first stage of editing is to make rough notes covering which sections of film can be discarded due to reshoots and which can be shortened in length. Marks for cuts can be made in white Chinagraph pencil on the back of the film itself (Fig. 7.9). The film is then cut with scissors and each shot (or series of shots if in sequence and usable as they stand) numbered according to the original script. The strips are stored either on a pin rack (Fig. 7.7) or in tins, and must be covered if left for any time as they are very vulnerable to dust and abrasion at this stage.

Now the film, including titles, is assembled in final order. This is where the creative side of editing lies—in establishing continuity, pace and visual relationships. Pace in particular must be geared to the age group of the envisaged audience. Usually the original script has to be modified in detail to make the most of images as actually shot. Cutaways are inserted where there would either be long-drawn-out actions or visual jumps.

If the same type of action (say pouring metal into the mould) takes place in both medium shot and close-up we might use the first half of one joined to the second half of the other—giving variety but with continuity of action. The length of time a shot appears on the screen also influences the tempo of action. Band-sawing a casting for example is a relatively active sequence which could be conveyed by a fairly rapid succession of short shots. Finally, editing is completed by splicing lengths of black leader film (available from Kodak) to form a leader and a trailer to the film.

Sound films

If the film is to carry sound this should be planned right from the start and the material shot at 24 fps rather than 18 fps to give better audio reproduction. Background noises and/or commentary points should be considered and written in outline form at the story-board planning stage. Make plenty of recordings in situ at about the time of shooting. When editing, some sequences may have to be kept longer than would be visually valid in order to give time for the commentary to make some particular point.

There are various methods of adding sound in low budget film making. We can have the final edited film (original or dupe) edge-striped * with magnetic oxide by one of several firms offering this service (see page 320). The cost of coating is a few pence per metre.

---

* Film which contains tape splices and is to be magnetic striped must have the tape width cut back so that the coating can be applied direct to the film base—it will not adhere satisfactorily to joining tape.

The film then becomes, for sound purposes, magnetic tape, and a recording is made on it through a magnetic projector of the type shown in Fig. 1.13.

Alternatively, link up an ordinary tape recorder with a film projector using a tape synchroniser to keep the two in step, and record sound direct on to the recorder. Some camera manufacturers (e.g. Bell & Howell) offer a 'package' of camera and linked battery tape recorder so

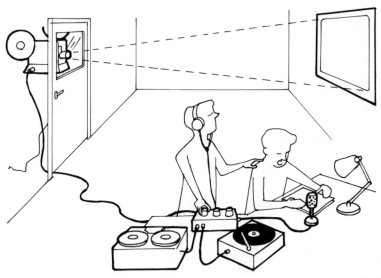

Fig. 7.10. An arrangement for recording music, effects and commentary on to striped film via a magnetic projector. The machine is located out in the corridor, to minimise mechanical noise. Sound recordist (operating home-made mixer unit) taps commentator as cue positions come up in film.

that lip-synchronised recordings can be made while shooting. This type of hardware is still expensive, however, and not necessary if one is content to use sound 'wild', i.e. commentary and general background noise spoken over pictures which do not actually show the speaker or detail of machines making definable sounds.

A rough and ready method is to use an unlinked tape recorder and projector. Put start marks on film and tape so that both are laced up at the same positions each time, and switch on both machines together. Try to ensure that the same projector and recorder are used for every presentation. In general the audio and visual content can be expected to run fairly acceptably in tandem for films up to about ten minutes duration.

As discussed on page 249, commentary recording should be carried out in an acoustically satisfactory area remote from projector noise. Background sounds and music* can be fed in separately through a mixer unit; or recorded throughout first and then erased away where the commentary is recorded later; or simply played near the commentator's microphone and faded up or down. Much depends on the hardware available (see Fig. 7.10). The great advantage of magnetic recording is that several attempts can be made until the sound track is just right.

Finishing loop films
If a loop film has been made it will have to be joined head-to-tail and encapsulated in a cassette, ready for use in a loop projector. Several software manufacturers (page 320) offer a cheap and reliable service splicing customers' film, waxing it against abrasion and sealing it into the cassette. This is a job well worth while having done professionally.

Special camera techniques and effects
Special effects have their own appeal. Be on guard against using them for their own sake rather than for specific educational purposes. Explore these techniques, but then deploy them with restraint.

TIME-LAPSE AND HIGH-SPEED CINEMATOGRAPHY. Both these techniques alter the time scale between subject action and the action projected on the screen. They are particularly useful for analysis purposes in educational material. At the same time learners need to be clearly informed of the manipulated time scale—particularly when the subject itself is unfamiliar. A clock face included in the picture is the best solution.

Time lapse involves the exposing of single frames with long time gaps between them, and then viewing the results at normal projection speed. The resulting speeding up of action is in direct ratio to the framing rates—hence a growing daffodil photographed at 1 frame every 2 min and projected at 24 fps has its growth rate increased by 2546 times.

Conversely, high-speed cinematography calls for the film in the camera to be exposed at a fast framing rate and then projected more slowly. A jumping horse photographed at 64 fps and projected at 16 fps has its action slowed down to one-quarter actual speed.

For time lapse we can use any cine camera which allows frames to be exposed singly—one for each push of the button. The camera is just set up on a support and the button pressed at regular intervals. This simple arrangement will do for subjects such as traffic flow at a roundabout

* A fee may be due to the Performing Rights Society, see page 342.

234

(filmed from a high building at one frame every few seconds). Plant growth, however, requires much longer intervals and the most practical arrangement is to connect the camera to a mechanical timer which switches on lights, exposes one frame, and switches off the lights again

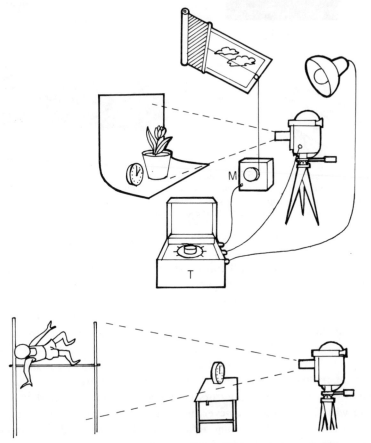

Fig. 7.11. *Top:* Time-lapse arrangement for filming plant growth. Every few minutes timer (T) closes window blind via motor (M), switches on lamp, and operates single frame exposure release on camera. *Bottom:* High speed filming of athlete's actions, using camera set to 64 fps. Note the inclusion of clocks.

hour after hour, day after day (Fig. 7.11). Such a timer can be hired (page 317) or made up from various ex-government surplus components. The camera should be electrically driven.

By standardising the subject lighting the exposure level remains constant. However, the camera shutter speed is often slightly slower when single frames are shot—usually working at about $\frac{1}{20}$ sec. Check

235

Fig. 7.12. Superimposing a title on the opening shot of a film sequence. The (white on black) lettering is filmed for 5 seconds and faded out. Then having wound this film back again in camera the opening shot is exposed, beginning on dark shadow area and panning up to the action after 5 seconds.

with the camera instructions. By taking a normal meter reading the *f*-number shown opposite this shutter speed is set on the lens.

Some cine cameras will run at 32 or 64 fps for modest high-speed photography. Beyond this a special high speed camera such as a 16-mm Fastax will have to be hired. Shutter speeds are usually faster at fast framing rates—typically $\frac{1}{130}$ sec at 64 fps—so the subject may need a high level of illumination. Also remember that a full cassette of film takes only a quarter of the normal time to pass through the camera, so that only relatively short periods of action can be recorded at one time.

SUPERIMPOSITION. Superimposition of two or more images can be handled by the colour laboratory if supplied with the various shots and told what is required. However, modest superimpositions are cheaper and quicker to achieve when actually shooting, provided the camera will allow the film to be run through twice.

Imagine we wish to superimpose a title on the opening shot of a film. The title would be set up and filmed as white letters on an absolutely black background (Fig. 7.12). (Take the meter reading off a white card held against the lettering and give twice the exposure indicated.) Next the film is wound back with a cap over the lens if the camera allows backwinding; alternatively the film will have to be removed in the darkroom and wound back to the beginning.* The opening shot for the film is now photographed, giving normal exposure. Try to open on a

* This may not be possible with Super-8 cartridge-loaded cameras.

fairly dark subject and, remembering where the lettering will appear, try to avoid odd highlights and detail which will confuse with the letterforms. Check off the number of seconds the title occupies on the film—after this the action can start, either by tilting the camera up to something happening, or by a figure, hand, etc., entering the frame.

Titles for superimposition should always be light-coloured lettering on a dark ground, allowing the scene to record in the latter area, making the title appear to 'float'. A really firm tripod is desirable for both sequences as any movement of one image against the other becomes very noticeable as 'wobble'. Sometimes superimposition of shots other than titles is needed, e.g. a face superimposed on a landscape. Each shot is then given two-thirds normal exposure and as far as possible the composition of each is arranged so that the highlights of one image do not cut into important areas of the other.

FADES AND DISSOLVES. Fade-outs into dark on the screen are useful at the end of a sequence or, followed by a fade-in, to suggest the passage of time. A fade-out can be achieved by simply closing down the lens aperture smoothly while shooting, and then covering up the lens completely. This method is fairly easy when lighting conditions are poor and the lens is used at wide aperture, as there is then plenty of diaphragm to stop down. In bright illumination where a small aperture is already in use and wherever a sudden increase in depth of field appears disconcerting on the screen a graduated grey fading filter (Fig. 7.13) is a better alternative. Some expensive cine cameras have built-in facilities for fades

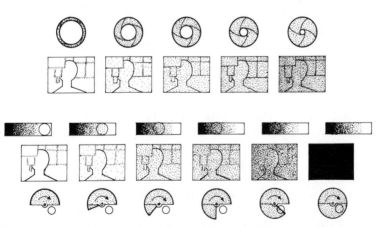

Fig. 7.13. Fading out. *Top rows:* Fading out by stopping down the lens aperture progressively sharpens the image of foreground and background detail, and finally never fully cuts off the light. *Bottom three rows:* Using a graduated grey filter over the lens (or an extra closing element in the rotating sector shutter) one can darken and finally obscure the image, without affecting depth of field.

237

in which the camera *shutter* gives a shorter and shorter exposure and then finally remains closed.

A dissolve from one scene into another really consists of a fade-in superimposed over a fade-out. Dissolves are useful for giving a smooth transition from one location to another. Having arranged a fade-out, the film is wound back and the next shot faded in. Dissolves are difficult to do empirically and really require a camera equipped for fading and backwinds. They can also be produced in printing by the film laboratory.

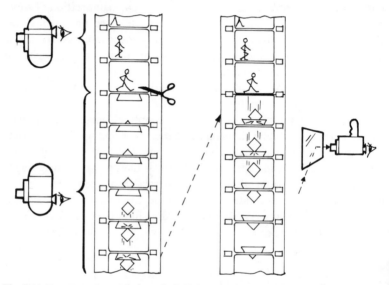

Fig. 7.14. Reverse action technique. *Left:* Using double perforation 16-mm film, camera is inverted to shoot brick falling on glass sheet. *Centre:* Processed film is reversed head-to-tail and spliced back in sequence. Brick now appears to reverse its action. *Right:* 8-mm camera may have to shoot via mirror, see text.

REVERSE ACTION. The basic technique for making people appear to walk backwards, cause water to jump into a glass etc., is simply to hold the camera upside down while filming. After processing the shot is cut from the film, reversed head to tail, and spliced back in again (Fig. 7.14). Unfortunately 8-mm film, having sprocket holes only on one side, must also be reversed left to right if the holes are to remain in the correct position. Thus, the emulsion is on the wrong side of the projected film, causing focusing changes. The image is also laterally reversed. A small front-surfaced mirror rigged in front of the camera when shooting (Fig. 7.14) can eliminate the lateral reversal but the change of focus remains. Some cameras allow the film to be run (or

238

hand-wound) in reverse. This facility is of course also useful for super-impositions.

Animation

The animation of models and series of drawings is a form of time-lapse cinematography requiring a steady camera, single-frame exposures—and a lot of patience in moving items a short distance at a time. Professional animators draw the moving parts of the image separately for each frame on acetate 'cells', which are placed over painted backgrounds and photographed. This is an expensive operation.

Much can be done, however, with cut-out figures and objects against static backgrounds—a sort of animated graphics. Wheels can be made to turn, toys walk, lettering write itself. The timing of each sequence can be planned mathematically remembering that 18 pictures must be exposed to occupy just one second of action on the screen. Animation is interesting and creative as an activity, but very time absorbing for the busy teacher. It can be valuable for short sequences in technical instruction films; for tasks such as illustrating stories for young children we should not forget the almost equal value of a filmstrip or slide set. Practical animation is discussed further in Chapter 9.

Animated transparencies and photographs

Motion simulation does not necessarily call for a cine camera and cine projector. Large line transparencies for display and for overhead projection can be made with sections which appear to move. 'Flicker books' and other simple mechanical devices can be used to make simple series of photographs move. Moreover, these are interesting projects for learners themselves to produce.

ANIMATED FLOW TRANSPARENCIES. At some time we have probably all seen large, diagrammatic display transparencies showing, for example, the flow of coolant through a nuclear reactor or circulation of blood through the human body, in which light patterns move continuously along the drawings of pipes and tubes. Usually the patterns appear like particles or bubbles of light moving in various directions in different parts of the diagram. In fact the display device is just simply a light box with a large motor-driven disc rotating just behind a coloured black-and-white transparency of the diagram. The transparency is either on high contrast photographic film or may be mechanically printed on plastic.* In each case the paths along which flow is to occur are transparent and all other areas, including background, are opaque.

* Commercial products such as Opticart illustration plates, E. J. Arnold & Son Ltd.

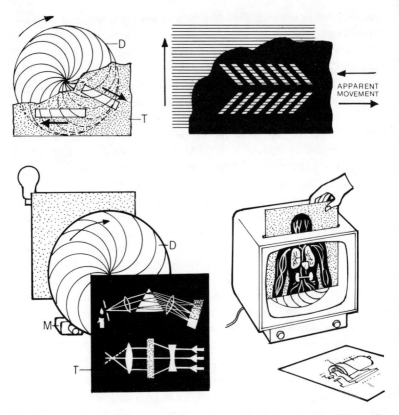

Fig. 7.15. Animated flow transparencies. *Top left:* Detail showing disc (D) carrying strong geometric pattern, rotating behind black and white line transparency (T). 'Movement' appears to flow in clear film parts, as indicated by arrows—speed and direction depending on their angle to disc lines. *Top right:* Variation using vertically moving endless band of regular parallel lines. *Bottom:* Commercial unit. Slot-in transparencies are printed in bulk or may be custom made (App. IV), or prepared oneself using lith film.

The front of both opaque and transparent parts of the transparency may be coloured.

Animation is induced in the flow channels by one of two methods:

1. The rotating disc has a strong black-and-white stroboscopic-type pattern which, passing behind the transparent channels, shows as a pattern of moving lines. The angle of the flow channel relative to the direction of the part of the disc which runs behind it determines the apparent speed of flow along that channel (Fig. 7.15). The diagram is carefully designed so that the general flow of movement is, say, clockwise—although this may not be obvious because channels at different angles will show differing rates and directions of flow.

240

2. The rotating disc is a sheet of polarising filter. Other small pieces of polarising filter are laminated in chains along the back of the various flow channels. As Figs 7.16–17 show, the pieces of filter are arranged so that their planes of polarisation alternate—for example at 90° to each other. Light virtually cannot pass through two polarising filters lying with their planes crossed, so that at any point in time alternate links in the chain block out the light. As the disc behind continues to rotate these same links begin to transmit light, while adjacent links grow opaque. The visual effect is one of small globules of light moving along the flow paths. More elaborate effects are possible using commercially

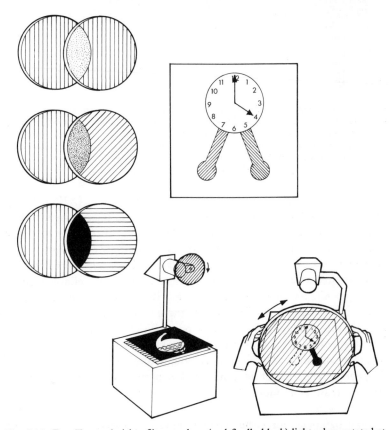

Fig. 7.16. *Top:* Two polarising filters reduce (and finally block) light when rotated at certain angles to each other. Simple clock OHP transparency with pola filters inlaid at differing angles shows pendulum appearing first left, then right, when viewed or projected through a rotating polarising filter. *Bottom:* On projector, rotating filter can be motor driven over lens or rotated by hand over transparency. Bottom left projector has crinkly Cellophane as 'liquid' in beaker and a second large filter *under* transparency. On screen beaker contents twinkle and change in colour and tone.

marketed Technimation polarising material (page 319). One advantage of motion simulation by polarisation is that by placing the transparency on the overhead projector and arranging the polarising filter to rotate across the lens (Fig. 7.16) the diagram can be projected in animate form on to a screen.

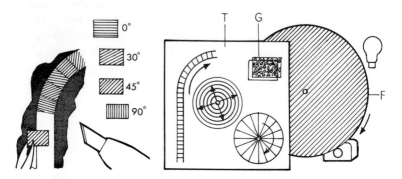

Fig. 7.17. Preparing polarised light flow diagrams. Pieces of appropriately orientated filter are laid in line over clear lines in the transparency. Viewed against rotating polarising filter (F) light 'bubbles' appear to move along channel. Similarly circle and sector mosaics suggest movement as indicated by arrows. Panel of small irregular chips of filter (G) wink and glitter. Transparency can be shown on OHP using single filter rotated over top surface or at lens.

Very interesting results are also possible using the OHP with an ordinary white-line-on-black transparency lying on top of a large polarising filter on the stage, and another rotating filter fitted over the lens. Lay crinkly Cellophane (the type used on cigarette packets) over some of the white areas—as the lens filter rotates colours appear and change in the treated areas. Similarly small irregular pieces of Cellophane give turbulent effects, and stretched or mutilated polythylene produces vivid-coloured swirling effects under these conditions. Motion simulation by this method has attractive possibilities, e.g. for giving a turbulent appearance to a solution in a beaker, gaseous combustion in a chamber and so on. The main drawback to any use of two polarisers is the general reduction of light output. The projected image will be much dimmer than usual unless kept small or viewed in efficiently blacked out conditions.

Transparencies for either stroboscopic or polarisation methods of animation should be prepared photographically. They should be planned to have black backgrounds, the diagrams being drawn with great care, particularly for the strobo pattern disc system, where direction and apparent speed of movements is greatly influenced by diagram design. Artwork is copied on to contrasty film (e.g. lith or general-purpose film processed in contrast developer) and the negative enlarged up on to lith sheet film.

Materials and information on laminating displays with polarising· filters is available from Polarizers (UK) Ltd, see page 319. Some producers of software for the OHP market motorised attachments.

ANIMATED SETS OF PHOTOGRAPHS. Simple subject matter, such as physical exercises, sports strokes, mechanical actions—in fact many of the subjects found in single concept loops—can be recorded effectively by a series of still photographs. As an alternative to displaying them as a story board they can be animated by making them into a 'flicker book' or mounting them into a form of Zoetrope or early motion picture viewer.

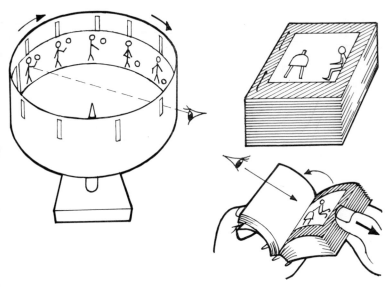

Fig. 7.18. *Left:* Zoetrope made out of biscuit tin to animate a strip of 6 × 6-cm contact prints. Eye sees prints in rapid succession through slits. *Right:* Contact prints arranged in action sequence and stapled to form flicker book.

One needs a 6 × 6-cm or 35-mm camera with a sufficiently fast wind-on to cover the action with a reasonable number of pictures (say a minimum of 2 per sec for physical education). This may mean hiring a motor-driven Leica, Nikon or 6 × 6-cm camera, or using a normal camera and either having the action repeated a sufficient number of times to build up the set of pictures, or posing one shot at a time, as in the case of a mechanical model.

The 6 × 6-cm format is probably the ideal for this work, because a sheet of contact prints made directly from the negatives can be given out to pupils. They can then cut out each print, put them in sequence with a long staple through the bottom margin (Fig. 7.18) and use them as personal flicker books. Alternatively, as a project, one or more Zoetropes can be made out of cardboard or tin and the contact prints mounted therein. Spinning the drum and looking through the slots animates the image.

When shooting the stills try to organise a plain (preferably light-toned) background and diffuse lighting of consistent brightness. Have the camera on a firm support and try to keep about the same distance from the subject throughout. Be generous about the number of pictures shot to cover the action—some of these negatives can be edited out later.

Some reference to films on film technique (including animation) and books and other sources of film making information are included in Appendix I, page 297. There are also several very helpful organisations for film-makers, see Appendix V.

8. Presentation of projected aids

MOST OF the planning and preparing of visual aids is thrown away if the material fails to be seen clearly by the learner due to badly managed presentation. Just as much know-how and care needs to go into this aspect of communication as traditional verbal or written means of teaching. Effective use of the new and improved media does call for a grasp of principles, a touch of showmanship and common-sense planning against disaster. Some effort is also needed to keep abreast of new presentation equipment and ways in which it can help one's teaching. The alternative is a kind of aggressive ignorance in which new gear is used in old ways and then discarded as unsatisfactory.

There are many gleefully related tales—one lecturer in education, for instance, wished to draw attention to a point in a transparency being shown on the overhead projector. Walking to the back of the room he found a chair, carried it to the screen, stood on it and using a ruler pointed at the image. When his behaviour was queried by students with another member of staff he replied, 'Oh yes, I noticed that too. He needed a longer stick.'

Basic technical knowledge of what one is doing leads to polished presentation and—even more important—smooth integration. There is obviously more chance of integration if presentation of aids to groups takes place in the usual teaching situation, rather than a special room. Even at the risk of some dilution of equipment and less than textbook projection conditions this use of home ground is much more satisfactory, particularly in primary and secondary education. The specially equipped room now has another role. Renamed a resources room and permanently equipped with simple visual aids hardware it can be opened for individuals or small groups to use at any time like a school library (see page 330).

The dual importance of presentation and integration will colour the content of this chapter, which is much concerned with the craft of projection, the art of showmanship in group teaching and the

245

disciplines of indexing and storage. To begin we should consider the finalising of self-produced aids ready for projection.

Finishing D-I-Y projected aids

MOUNTING SLIDES. The cheapest and quickest way of mounting black-and-white and colour transparencies is to use simple cardboard frames (latex self-sealing type). These are not very satisfactory for long-term heavy use because the picture area is unprotected and expansion of film base due to lamp heat during projection causes the slide to bow (pop) and require focus adjustment. Also card mounts easily bend, jam or split open when used in automatic magazine loading projectors.

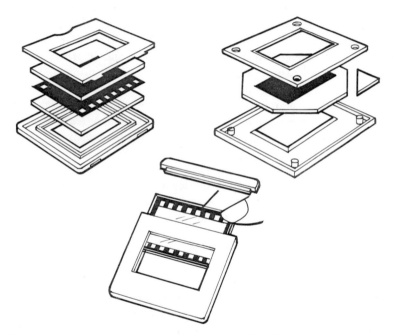

Fig. 8.1. Some plastic or metal mounts for 5 × 5-cm slides. *Top right:* glassless mount accepts transparencies already mounted in card. Similar mounts are made with apertures for other 35-mm formats, and for 7 × 7-cm slides.

Various mounts consisting of plastic frames with cover glass inserts are on the market—a good camera shop will have several types (Fig. 8.1). The most expensive are not always the most suitable. Choose a design which (a) will not jam in the magazine of the projector to be used; (b) does not hold the piece of film so loosely that it can shift its position and reveal perforations or allow entry of dust; and (c) allows the transparency to be loaded quickly and cleanly in the first instance.

Many of the mounts used by libraries consist of cover glasses in a thick card frame which is either self-adhesive or sealed by heat. They are quick to prepare and relatively dust-free, but the heat-type require an electric mounting press or at least the use of an iron (Fig. 2.29).

To mask off any unwanted part of the image use a piece of thin aluminium kitchen foil sandwiched in with the transparency. The foil is quite opaque, has a clean-cut edge and becomes less hot than black paper during projection. Rainbow patterns or Newton's Rings may appear in glass-bound slides unless care is taken (Fig. 8.2). They are

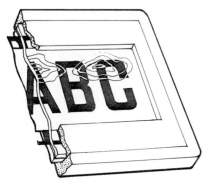

Fig. 8.2. Newtons Rings—ephemeral, contour like patterns, often in pale colours, caused by imperfect contact between cover glass and transparency.

caused by imperfect contact between the smooth surfaces of cover glass and film base. Avoid binding slides under conditions of high humidity and use cover glasses designed to avoid this defect. Such glass is lightly etched to give irregular contact, yet is fine enough not to show in the projected image.

All slides should be spotted so that they can be projected right way up and right way round without having to scrutinise the image every time they are used. The internationally agreed method of showing image orientation is indicated in Fig. 8.3.

A card mount can be spotted with a felt pen; self-adhesive coloured spots are satisfactory for plastic mounts (and can carry the reference number of the slide). Under normal (front projection) conditions the slide should be inserted into the projector or magazine so that when standing behind the projector facing the screen the spot is in the *top right-hand* corner facing you.

MOUNTING OHP TRANSPARENCIES. The purpose of mounting these transparencies is to prevent them curling out of focus and to prevent light escaping around the edges of the picture. Their large size makes them impractical to bind between glass. Educational stationers (page 320) supply rigid single boards or fold-over self-adhesive card mounts with cut-out apertures. As shown in Fig. 1.9, standard aperture sizes are 250×250 mm (10×10 in.) which uses the whole OHP stage, and 250×203 mm (10×8 in.) for transparencies produced by copying machine or photography. Apertures of 8×5 in. are also made. The outside dimensions of all these mounts are usually 305×305 mm (12×12 in.). Plastic one-piece mounts with a pin and stud system for securing transparencies are available.

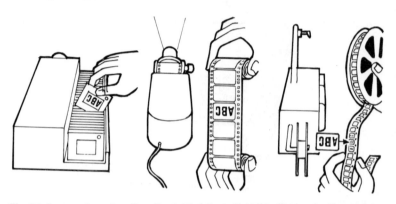

Fig. 8.3. Image orientation. Standing behind the projector looking at the (front projection) screen the picture on the slide/filmstrip/movie film should appear upside down (but not laterally reversed) if the image is to read correctly when projected. Note the position of the spot on the slide.

Most mounts have register holes punched near each corner—these will coincide with pins on some overhead projectors so that the image is centred quickly and accurately. Unfortunately there is not yet an accepted standard for register pin positions—unless transparencies are to be used on one machine only it will be wise to cut the corners off the mount. When the aid includes one or more overlay transparencies the base transparency can be mounted normally and each overlay registered and attached to the mount along one edge with a hinge of self-adhesive masking tape (Fig. 3.3). If the order in which overlays are introduced is likely to vary, attach each one to a different edge.

Care in choosing the tint used for coloured areas on overlays can give emphasis to overlapping zones by making additional colours appear. For example, some parts of an outline map may be overlaid with areas of cyan, denoting dairy farming. Another overlay with yellow areas shows arable farming, so that every part where the two overlap (i.e. combined dairy and arable farming) now appears as green.

248

The handling of self-adhesive tints and lettering for OHP transparencies is discussed on page 138. All these hand-finishing operations are most conveniently carried out on a portable light box (Fig. 4.12) which can be bought or made up.

ADDING SOUND TO PROJECTED AIDS. Think carefully before rushing in to add recorded sound to slides, filmstrips or film. As discussed on page 107, even when the user has planned the whole exercise himself, recorded commentary tends to become something of a Frankenstein— never as flexible as the teacher's own off-the-cuff accompaniment. Against this there are some subjects which benefit greatly from restrained factual commentary plus appropriate music or background sounds. There are also times when the originator of the material has to leave its presentation to someone else, or the aid may have been designed from the start for individual study. If the final aid is intended for pupils' own reference as individuals or in small groups (i.e. in a resources room) be careful to prepare the commentary with an open-ended approach very much in mind. The audio element must both direct pupils to the picture and lead them on to other resource material, such as books.

Don't write the commentary too much in advance. Design and shoot the visuals first: they have a habit of turning out slightly differently from the original plan. The commentary can then be prepared (and recorded) with the pictures actually on the screen as pupils will see them.

RECORDING. Choose a room for recording which is quiet and free from background noise. Locate the projector as far from the microphone as possible to avoid mechanical sounds (e.g. project the image through a glass panel in the door from another room). If necessary put the microphone in an open-ended box lined with blotting paper or papier-mache egg containers. As described on page 234, music can be recorded at the same time by having the loudspeaker from a record player near the microphone, and arranging for an assistant to control the volume as required. Alternatively use a mixing unit to control the volume of each channel separately.

Write and read the final commentary sparingly, so that students are not assailed by continuous and hurried speech (a failing in many American audio-visual aids). The cue to change the slide or filmstrip frame can be recorded along with the commentary by a single tap with a pencil on a convenient hard surface. Better still, if a slide synchronising device (e.g. Grundig, Philips and several others) is available, the commentator simply presses a button to record an inaudible signal on another track on the tape—on playback this triggers the picture change circuit in the projector. For information on adding sound to movie films, see page 232.

The craft of projection

Successful presentation requires good preparation in terms of room facilities, confidence in manipulation of hardware, and careful choice and timing of an aid within a class period.

FRONT-PROJECTION FACILITIES. If necessary almost any flat surface can be improvised as a front-projection screen. Even a dark chalkboard will serve for simple line diagrams (white lines on black), and of course additions and annotations can then be made in chalk. The usual matt-white-type of screen such as emulsion-painted wall, cartridge paper or a

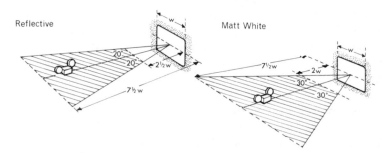

Fig. 8.4. Characteristics of silvered or beaded highly reflective screens, and matt white surfaces. The reflective screen returns a brighter image but over a narrow arc. In each case aim to contain the audience within the shaded area.

white canvas roll-up screen is non-directional in character. As Fig. 8.4 shows, matt screens are most useful for squarish rooms and any location where the projector delivers plenty of illumination.

Highly reflective screens such as 'beaded'* and (to a lesser extent) 'silver' surfaced types give a brighter image but only within a much narrower angle. These directional screens are excellent for long narrow rooms or where the projector gives modest light output. However, seating may have to be rearranged so that no one sits outside the cone of light from the screen, as here the image dims dramatically to almost nil. The angle of the screen needs adjusting too so that extraneous light sources are not reflected towards the audience.

Generally, least disruption of the classroom is necessary if the screen is placed near one corner and the picture projected diagonally across

* Contains a surface coating of thousands of glass beads which reflect light like miniature roadside 'cats' eyes'. Modern versions such as the Kodak Ektalite screen use a specially prepared aluminium sheet.

the room. The seats are then ready staggered (Fig. 8.5) and most of the class are located within a comfortable viewing zone from the screen. As shown in Fig. 8.4 this zone extends from about 2 matt-screen widths to $7\frac{1}{2}$ screen widths. A useful screen width for films, slides and filmstrips in a classroom of about 30–40 desks is 2 metres.

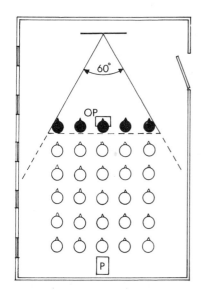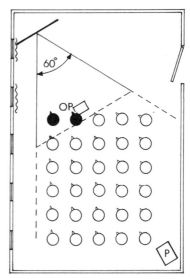

Fig. 8.5. Room arrangements for projection (matt white screen). OP, Overhead projector position. P, Slide/movie projector position. With left-hand layout front row of audience have to move back, most people's view is blocked by the person in front, image on screen is diluted by any light entering through windows or door. Right-hand arrangement automatically gives staggered seating, requires resiting of only two members of group, gives better screen shading and easier access to slide/movie projector.

A square-shaped screen enables vertical as well as horizontal rectangular slides to be shown without cut-off. A hood of matt-black plywood almost as deep as the width of the screen helps to shade it from other light sources. The hood can be made of hinged flaps which then fold over the screen surface to protect and hide it when not in use.

Projector distances needed to fill various screen sizes are shown in Tables 8.1–3. The *closer* the machine is to the screen or the *longer* the focal length of its lens the smaller and brighter the image will be. The rule is that if the image is too dim, make it smaller. With today's TV-conditioned audience a small bright image is considered better than a large dim one.

Tables 8.1–2 quote the focal length of standard lenses for various size projectors, film and slide, but alternative lenses are often available

TABLE 8.1

Projector distance and size of image—movie films

Visual aid	Projector lens	Distance from projector to screen				
		3 m	6 m	9 m	12 m	15 m
16 mm ⎧ 38 mm		0·7	1·4	2·1	2·8	3·5
⎩ 50 mm		0·5	1·0	1·5	2·0	2·5
Super 8 mm ⎧ 10 mm		1·5	3·0			
⎩ 20 mm		0·7	1·5	2·3	3·0	
Standard 8 mm ⎧ 12·5 mm*		1·0	2·0	3·0		
⎨ 20 mm		0·6	1·2	1·8	2·4	
⎩ 25 mm*		0·4	0·7	1·1	1·4	1·8

Width of picture on screen

* These focal lengths are generally the shortest and longest settings offered by the zoom (variable focal length) lenses now supplied with most standard 8-mm projectors.

and may be more suited to particular room conditions. Some slide projectors are equipped with zoom lenses—lenses which are continuously variable over a range of focal lengths. One simply sets up such a projector at the most convenient position in the room and operates the lens zoom control until the image is the correct size to fill the screen.

A large square screen is needed for the overhead projector which, although used at the front of the class fairly close to the screen, has the advantage of a much larger transparency than the slide or cine projector. A 2 m-square matt-white surface is quite satisfactory owing to the brilliance of the image from this projector. Table 8.3 shows image sizes for the OHP; interchangeable lenses are unusual for this machine. Of course, the one large screen can be utilised for all projectors, but where space permits, a separate highly reflective corner screen for cine films in particular will help give the brightest pictures, especially when some light is present in the room.

Many projectors, particularly the OHP, have to be tilted in some way to place the image centrally on the screen (overhead projectors

TABLE 8.2

Projector distance and size* of image—slides and filmstrips

Visual aid	Projector lens	Distance from projector to screen					
		2 m	3 m	4 m	6 m	9 m	12 m
24 × 36-mm SLIDE and DOUBLE FRAME STRIP	50 mm	1 m	**2·1 m**	**2·8 m**	**4·3 m**	6·3 m	6·7 m
	75 mm	80 mm	1·4 m	**1·9 m**	**2·8 m**	**4·2 m**	5·5 m
	100 mm	60 mm	1·1 m	1·5 m	**2·2 m**	**3·2 m**	**4·3 m**
SINGLE FRAME STRIP	50 mm	70 mm	1·4 m	**1·8 m**	**2·8 m**	4·2 m	4·5 m
	75 mm	55 mm	90 mm	1·3 m	**1·7 m**	**2·8 m**	3·7 m
	100 mm	40 mm	70 mm	1 m	1·4 m	**2·2 m**	**2·8 m**

Long side of picture on screen

have a tilting mirror and lens; the stage thus remains horizontal).
Unless the tilt is very slight visible 'keystoning' of image shape occurs
(Fig. 8.6) and to correct this the screen needs tilting forward at the top.
With directional screens this also helps to reflect a brighter image
down towards the audience. If a projector is being used in a large

TABLE 8.3

Projector distance and size of image—overhead transparencies

Visual aid	Projector lens	Distance from projector to screen					
		1 m	2 m	3 m	4 m	5 m	6 m	7 m
250mm	317 mm	75 mm	**1·6 m**	**2·4 m**	**3·1 m**	4 m	4·8 m	5·5 m
	355 mm	60 mm	1·3 m	**1·9 m**	**2·6 m**	**3·3 m**	4 m	4·6

Width of picture on screen

* In Tables 2 and 3 bold figures indicate recommended conditions of use.

253

lecture theatre with racked seating, locate it about halfway up the tiers of seats. Project on to a large vertically mounted screen above the chalkboard.

When sound films are projected, position the loudspeaker on top of a desk or cupboard near the screen where it can be seen by the whole group. If the loudspeaker is left on the floor, the front rows of the audience muffle the sound from the remainder, while the back rows only hear the noise of the projector.

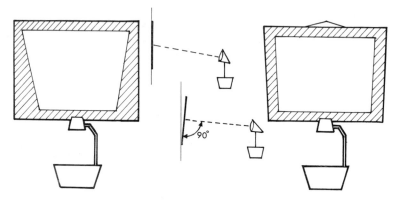

Fig. 8.6. Keystoning of image shape occurs if projector it tilted up to a vertical screen (*left and top centre*). Screen needs tilting forward.

BLACKOUT. Projected image quality will always be at its best when the room is completely blacked out. The richest black of the image can never be blacker than the screen's appearance with the projector switched off. The more ambient light present the lower the contrast of the picture. However, total darkness is often undesirable, as when students are being encouraged to take notes or refer to hand-outs; it is also difficult to achieve in the average classroom. The main thing is to minimise the amount of light reaching the screen surface. Use a hood or screens to keep this part of the room dark. Good plastic venetian blinds (blackout type) at the windows are ideal, as the amount of light entering can be fully controlled. In rooms fitted with light-tight roller blinds some artificial light may have to be left on to allow students to write.

Given a good transparency, the overhead projector is bright enough for the image to be adequate in full artificial lighting or daylight (but not with direct sunlight falling on the screen). Once again, however, the picture will gain in contrast if an effort is made to shade the screen.

Some teachers prefer to black out the room and work under controlled artificial light for the whole period if important sequences are to be explained via the OHP. When an episcope is used total darkness is more or less obligatory owing to its weak image intensity. A good blackout may also mean very poor room ventilation. Stuffiness and heat from the projector soon destroy concentration. Figure 8.8 shows various methods of creating air flow without introducing light.

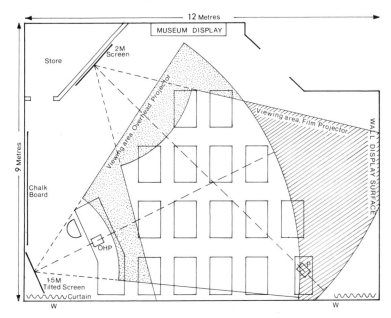

Fig. 8.7. A well laid out teaching area, with overhead projector and slide or movie projector (P). *Geography room, Trinity School, Croydon.*

BACK-PROJECTION FACILITIES. The projector can be set up on one side of a translucent screen so that the audience views the image, like a TV picture, on the other side. Back projection is pointless for the OHP, but for slide, filmstrip or film it offers the following features:

1. A picture with greater brilliance and clarity can be produced, particularly in a partly lighted room.

2. No equipment has to be set up within the audience, with attendant stands, wires, etc.

3. By folding up the light path with a mirror (Fig. 8.9) the teacher (or pupil) can be within easy reach of both projector and the image on the screen. A bigger image can be formed on the screen without necessitating a long space-consuming direct throw.

255

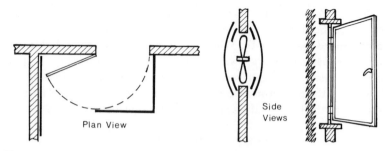

Fig. 8.8. Air circulation with minimum entry of light. *Left:* back-painted screen acting as a light trap at open door. *Centre:* Photographic darkroom type light-tight extractor fan. *Right:* Black plastic venetian blinds across open windows.

4. The image is laterally reversed unless the transparency is placed in the projector back to front. This is impossible with 8-mm films and 16-mm sound films which have sprocket holes along one side only, and so a mirror system becomes essential.

5. No rear-projection screen can be viewed from an angle of more than about 25° without severe fall-off in image brightness.

6. The system is not as flexible as front projection—adjustment of

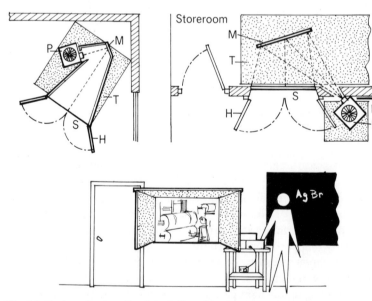

Fig. 8.9. Back projection. *Top left:* Self-contained tunnel unit on freestanding table. *Top right and bottom:* Space-saving by the use of an adjacent (blacked out) storeroom. P, Projector. M, Mirror. T, Table. S, Back-projection screen. H, Folding protective doors, acting as a hood when open. B, Blackboard.

image size is often limited owing to restricted space behind the screen and several projectors (slide, film, filmstrip, episcope) cannot easily share the one screen.

The most effective, easily improvised back-projection screen material is heavy gauge tracing paper. Ground glass is also good, and most suppliers of opaque screens make roll-up back-projection screens of matt plastic. If a mirror is used it should be a surface silvered or metal type, as an ordinary glass mirror tends to give a double image (minimised by keeping the angle of reflection small, see Fig. 8.10).

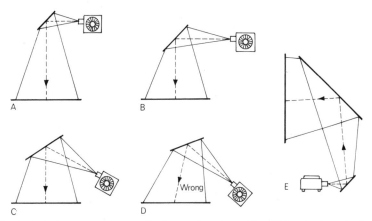

Fig. 8.10. Various arrangements of mirror and projector for efficient back projection. All (except D) deliver the image at 90° to screen surface. Arrangement E fits well into shelving or a console unit, but use of two mirrors calls for film inversion: avoid if projecting movies.

Arrange the system so that the central ray from the projector always reaches the screen perpendicular to its surface. Note how the further the mirror is from the projector the larger it must be.

One essential of back projection is complete blackout of the area between projector and the back of the screen. A tunnel made of hardboard sprayed matt black is satisfactory; some table units manufactured commercially fold away into a suitcase-size pack. A most effective and space-saving back projection method is possible if the classroom has an adjacent store or preparation room which can be blacked out. As shown in Fig. 8.9, a window can be built between the two rooms for the screen, plus a smaller aperture for the projector to reflect off a mirror located in the storeroom. Thus all the space and most of the mechanics are banished to the other room and the presentation resembles colour television. Note how the folding hood around the front of the screen closes to cover and protect it when not in use.

257

Back projection via a mirror is probably the most practical arrangement for a resources room (see page 330). The equipment can be permanently set up, and the characteristics of the back-projection screen suit close, small group viewing.

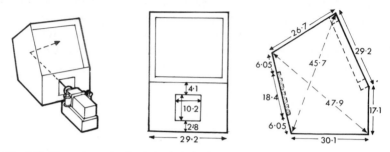

Fig. 8.11. Dimensions of a simple back projection unit for a slide or filmstrip projector. This might be constructed as a group project, using card or wood, a polished steel mirror and thick tracing paper. Dimensions are all in centimetres.

PROJECTION IN PRACTICE. The following points are worth remembering:

1. Know the projectors. Take any unfamiliar equipment home and thoroughly familiarise yourself with its use.

2. Prepare for accidents. Always have a spare lamp in the projector case (and preferably a cartridge fuse for the plug). Tie the mains lead to the leg of the projector table or have a simple plug and socket in the wire which will pull apart if anyone trips over it. Try to lay mains and loudspeaker cables along the bottom of the walls or high up, such as along a row of coat hooks.

3. Check that any transformers are set correctly for the school's supply voltage.

4. Check that the software is in the correct state for projection. Slides, filmstrips and cine film for front projection (or back projection via a mirror) must be orientated so that, seen from the back of the projector, the image on film is upside down but right reading (Fig. 8.3). For direct back projection the image is upside down and reversed left-to-right.

5. Have the image centred on the screen and sharply focused in advance. (A fixed shelf at the far end of the room for the filmstrip or slide projector facilitates its accurate positioning.) Check that the slide magazine is properly seated and the remote control is functioning.

When setting up a sound projector, first run the machine for light and sound without threading up the film. Remember that many amplifiers take about 30 sec to warm up—turn up the volume so that a hum is heard from the loudspeaker. Inserting a piece of card between the exciter lamp and sound head (Fig. 8.12) should create a sharp noise from the speaker. If much ragged 'foliage' appears around the edges of the rectangle of light on the screen stop the machine and clean the gate aperture with a small brush or cloth. If the machine is non-self-threading, the film can now be threaded up and moved a few inches through the machine by hand, using the inching knob. Check that the take-up spool is also turning. Now switch on motor and lamp long

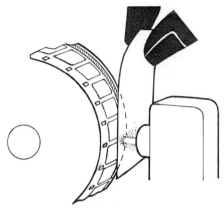

Fig. 8.12. Checking sound when setting up a sound projector by inserting thin card between exciter lamp and film (optical sound track).

enough to focus the main title, and switch off. If the film is to be shown shortly leave the amplifer on. If not *remember to switch the amplifier on* a moment or two before starting the film or the introductory commentary will be lost. A fault-finding list for projection appears on page 338.

Physical integration with teaching

Visual aids need to be smoothly integrated within a class plan, along with chalk-and-talk, note-taking and practical work by students. Here are some suggestions for teacher-presented aids.

1. Preview all material to be used (particularly sound films). Pick out the visual statements they make in order to inject each aid where it will give most support to the subject of study. Decide the best way to introduce and follow through the aid. Generally avoid describing an illustration before showing it. Putting up the aid first and then commenting engenders a response of interpretation which is more active than confirmation.

2. Avoid breaks in continuity caused by closing or opening window blinds. Try to arrange the room to have partial blackout which can remain constant throughout the teaching period, or full blackout with easy control of the room light. A single dimmer switch for room lighting is inexpensive and makes the change from one set of conditions to another almost imperceptible. Consider the need for room ventilation.

3. Don't overcomplicate a session by using several types of aid when one will do. Don't use a projector for just a couple of slides if the illustrations could equally be prepared for showing along with other material on an OHP. A turbulent teacher hustling from one box of tricks to another easily loses the subject in a technical steeplechase, with every student waiting (some hopefully) for something to go wrong.

4. Double check the state of the software and the mechanical functions of the hardware, especially if it is unfamiliar. Appendix VIII lists some technical hitches which can crop up in practice and ways of minimising their effect. Any of them *could* cause a hang-up long enough to break concentration.

5. Remove an aid from sight once it has made its point (this does not of course apply to pictorial wallcharts used to follow up a lesson). User-produced software can be planned to make one point at a time, but sometimes commercially made projection material contains too much information per frame. On the overhead projector this can be controlled by covering parts of the transparency with black card (Fig. 1.10) and so building up the image on the screen one part at a time.

6. When presenting a filmstrip or slides supplied with a written commentary try not to read this aloud to the class. The result is usually stiff, slow—even painful. Pre-read the material relative to the frames, making notes of the key points. Accompanying comments can then be improvised naturally and at a level appropriate to the group.

7. Learn from the ways visual aids are smoothly integrated into television programmes—news, current events, weather forecasts as well as educational programmes. We don't have the same funds available, but the presentation ideas and use of continuity need cost very little in the classroom. Borrowing of equipment naturally extends the possibilities of presentation. Twin slide projectors, for example, allow images (e.g. paintings) to be compared side by side, or by a simple electrical arrangement one projector lamp may be dimmed and the other brightened to 'dissolve' one image smoothly into another on a common screen (see also page 286).

8. Finally, a moment of truth. One can concentrate *too much* on presentation. A highly polished performance can lull students into a

form of false intellectual security. This applies particularly when aids are combined with formal lectures. Overprepared aids encourage *talking at* students instead of joint participation. Aids, indeed complete lectures, may be insufficiently open ended, and therefore seem remote to students, like a television or radio programme. An improvised aid (even an *apparently* improvised aid) can help to break this barrier (see Fig. 8.13). Try to assess objectively the effectiveness of aids in a teaching/lecturing session by inviting student reaction, or even the use of an occasional questionnaire.

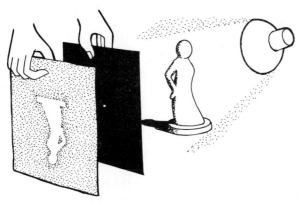

Fig. 8.13. Good improvised aids can be more effective than over-prepared ones. Here the actuality formation of a pinhole image via ordinary black card and tracing paper in a darkened room is more likely to be remembered than a filmstrip or loop film.

POINTS ON POINTERS. The old method of lunging at the screen with a stick to draw attention to some detail may damage the screen surface, and itself causes a confusing shadow. Special hand torches are made to project a small sharply focused arrow head or circle of light on to the screen from a distance. This is effective for both front and back projection except when the image floods the screen with light (e.g. a diagram with thin black lines on a white ground).

Several slide and filmstrip projectors contain a movable pointer arm in their carriers (Fig. 8.14). This can be moved to coincide with any part of the projected area. Similarly episcopes have an internal arm moved over the free surface of the glass pressure plate, controlled by an external 'joy stick'. Both pointers give a *black* silhouette on the screen. Unfortunately the teacher has to be standing right by the projector to use them. Pointer arms are not very effective when the projected image is predominantly dark, such as white lines on a dark ground.

On the overhead projector of course the teacher is already sitting at the machine facing the class, and can use a pencil or even a finger to

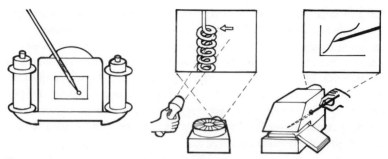

Fig. 8.14. Pointing devices. *Left:* sliding, pivoting arm built into projector filmstrip carrier. *Centre:* Special hand torch projecting a bright arrow-shaped patch of light on to screen. *Right:* Joy-stick swivelling pointer built into episcope.

point to detail in the transparency, just as naturally as to a page in a book. The pointer appears as a silhouette on the screen behind him.

When images are projected on to rigid back-projection screens such as ground glass, a grease pencil can be used to mark and draw on the smooth screen surface. (The ground surface should face the projector.) These marks rub off again with a dry cloth.

Storing and retrieving visual aids software

Software, like teaching notes, needs to be accessible. Storage in odd boxes and envelopes inevitably leads to mislaid items, particularly when the same material is used in various ways—say together as a lecture set and in individual reshuffled groups for seminar and laboratory periods.

If the sequence remains more or less fixed it can be kept stored in magazines ready for use in an automatic projector. By drawing a diagonal line across the pile of the slide set (Fig. 8.15) later absence or

Fig. 8.15. A diagonal line drawn across the top edges of a set of slides acts as an indicator to show whether an individual slide is missing, or wrongly orientated.

incorrect orientation of any slide is immediately apparent. Plastic sheets are available with pouches for 12–20 slides (Fig. 8.16). They can be filed in a ring binder or suspended from a bar in a filing cabinet, and enable the picture content of each slide to be seen. Filmstrips are most

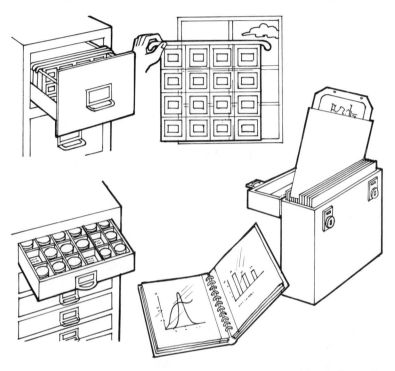

Fig. 8.16. Storage for projection transparencies. *Top:* 5 × 5-cm slides slip into a sheet of transparent pouches, suspended from a bar in an ordinary filing cabinet. *Bottom:* Filmstrips in compartmented drawers, and OHP transparencies in a ring binder (see also Fig. 3.3) or cardboard sleeves.

easily stored in their individual tins or boxes in shallow compartmented drawers. The title of the strip can be written at the bottom of its compartment, and so indicate the titles of strips which are missing.

OHP transparencies can be stored in damp-proof envelopes in a suspended system filing cabinet, in L.P. record sleeves (dummies obtainable from record stores), in Flipatran strip books, or punched and stored in ring binders.

Films, including short loops, should be stored upright in their boxes or cans, like books on a shelf. All film materials should preferably be stored in conditions of low humidity with temperature not exceeding about 24° C. Plastograph and felt board aids can be placed on sheets of

PVC and felt material respectively and sandwiched between card in a plan file.

INDEXING. Whether a collection of aids is for communal or personal use, some form of indexing soon becomes necessary. Equally, regular discard of outdated software and addition of good new material is educationally obligatory. (This is an effort sometimes, as having collected a set of aids one is tempted to keep using them indefinitely. Perhaps occasional mislaying of an aid—or class plan, or lecture notes—has a hidden value in forcing us into rethinking and rejuvenating such material.)

In practice, any retrieval system means having a reference number on each aid and indexing them in a book or on library file cards. Small self-adhesive numbered labels can be bought in sheets ready for attachment to slides, OHP transparencies, filmstrip cans, etc. The index might be cross-referenced so that any aid appears under chronological number, subject, particular lecture, topic and type of aid.

One feature card index system which is very suitable for a communal school collection of aids uses cards (Fig. 8.17) and an inexpensive punch. Each card has a printed lattice of from 200 to 10,000 tiny squares, enough for each visual aid held, and numbered serially.* A separate card is made out for every feature which may be the subject of search.

For example a 35-mm colour slide, No. 85, shows a model of Stephenson's Rocket locomotive. This is indexed by simply punching out No. 85 in six file cards headed: *Industrial Revolution*; *Railways*; *History of Transport Lecture*; *Steam Engines*; *Stephenson* and *Slides* respectively. Thus a particular feature card shows the numbers of all aids which possess the feature concerned, e.g. all the holes punched in the 'Steam Engines' card refer to material dealing with some aspect of steam power.

When seeking an aid one has only to stack all the cards covering the features required and hold them up to a lamp, whereupon light is transmitted through the whole stack only in places corresponding to the reference numbers of aids possessing all the characteristics required.

An interesting aspect of this system is that 'near misses' can be located. For example, we may be looking for *OHP transparencies* of *steam engines* used during the *industrial revolution* by registering these three cards. This may throw up several transparencies, but at the same time spots of diffuse light show the numbers of those aids which possess all but one of the features required. No. 85 would be one such spot, and by changing the OHP transparency card for the Slide card

* J. L. Jolley & Partners Ltd, High Wycombe, Bucks.

this aid would be picked out. Similarly cards for *Filmstrips*, *Films* or *Film loops* would each show which of these other forms of aid also cover the subject.

A good resources index could also cover *individual exhibits* in sets of material (i.e. *Jackdaws*) because many of these are capable of much

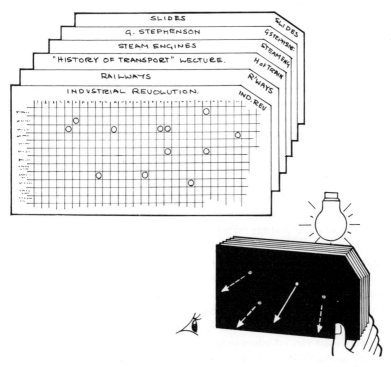

Fig. 8.17. A feature card indexing system using punch holes. Viewed against a lamp, a pack of wanted features reveals light spots denoting reference numbers of appropriate (and 'near miss') aids. See text.

wider application. For example there are plenty of scientific, geological and technological exhibits hidden away in kits based on humanities subjects.

Provided users always replace the aids under their proper index numbers (a requirement of any system) preparation of the index requires little effort and minimal writing. New features or characteristics can be added as required, making the system very open ended.

9. Photographic project work

So FAR we have been concerned with the use of photography and associated processes mostly as a *teacher's* aid—as a means of expressing concepts and ideas, and of disseminating knowledge. But almost everyone who has begun to explore the possibilities of still and movie photography will want to see how learners too can use the medium, either as a visual notebook or creative activity to express themselves. Its potential in this area has only recently begun to be explored in British schools, although in Germany and America the use of cameras by students has received active encouragement for some time. Manufacturers of photographic materials in all these countries have woken to the special needs of schools and are now active in promulgating the right technical information, sponsoring projects, competitions and exhibitions, and keeping educationalists using photography in touch with each other. More could be done, particularly in terms of reducing that great bugbear of photography—its cost.

The aim of this chapter is to discuss ways of organising photographic projects with various educational objectives. Much use will be made of practical case histories, which may in turn suggest ideas and applications for your own subjects.

The case for learner participation
As a curriculum activity, photography offers the following special advantages:

1. It breaks away from the 'print-dominated' approach to education. As a means of accomplishment, of making individual statements, photography is not limited by drawing, literary or linguistic skills. It offers a breakthrough for the student who is awkward and inhibited with the brush or pen, or one who is verbally inarticulate. This is particularly valid for children in the deprived areas or isolated rural localities, and for the sixteen- to eighteen-year-old group of lower ability range who may have already reached their academic ceiling. At the same time, photography offers very interesting creative possibilities and

adds a new dimension to science, fieldwork, etc., for more advanced groups.

2. Photography bridges several disciplines—notably science and art. It can be applied as a measuring instrument or visual notebook to subjects such as physics, maths, biology and geography. It can provide a major stimulus to visual perception in art and design and in English, helping students to see the world around in new ways. In short it helps to break down the old structure of isolated specialist subjects, and is well suited to learner-centred methods of education.

3. Most students identify easily with a photographic image as with a television image—it is outward-looking, contemporary and significant. Through photography schoolwork connects with one medium of their popular culture. After all, the use of a camera will eventually be accepted as a natural extension of the use of the ball-point pen and paper.

Organising photographic activities

The four main practical difficulties in organising photography are:
1. Cost of materials and equipment.
2. Provision of space and facilities.
3. The time factor in producing results.
4. The teaching of technicalities.

COSTS. Photographic materials utilise the metal silver; many cameras are precision optical instruments; unfortunately both are heavily taxed. However, the Local Education Authority is almost certain to have accounts with film and paper manufacturers such as Agfa, Kodak and Ilford. This allows professional trade discount off retail prices.

The school may be able to apply for a Value Added Tax exemption certificate which reduces material costs by a further percentage. (Strict records have to be kept by certificate holders showing when and how films and paper are used, and these books must be available for inspection. Some Authorities are unwilling to apply for exemption because of this extra bookwork.) Your Local Customs and Excise Inspector's Office will give details of procedure.

Educational establishments are also eligible to apply to the Board of Trade for exemption from import duty and to H.M. Customs and Excise for relief from particular taxes for items of photographic equipment, provided that equivalent equipment is not made by British manufacturers. Each application is judged on its merits, and can often be a great help in purchasing equipment such as precision single-lens reflex cameras and cine cameras, as these are not made in Great Britain. In most cases the retailer with whom your LEA deals for audio-visual photographic hardware will handle the whole application on the school's behalf.

Discounts and exemptions are of little assistance when a school department has virtually no funds at all available for photography. Some students at least will usually be able to borrow a camera from their family and friends if sufficiently motivated by stimulating projects. Equally whole classes can make their own simple still cameras out of film cartridges, cardboard and tape (see Fig. 9.6).

Photographic film and paper is more of a problem—particularly colour film, because of its high cost. Sometimes useful relationships can be established with local industry and commerce. Most big firms have photographic departments—similarly the police, hospitals and newspapers. Together with local commercial photographers and retail shops, these users do from time to time have small stocks of slightly outdated film which they are able to pass on to a school or college. This may also be a potential source of odd items of photographic lighting, dishes, etc., which after renovation still have a useful life. Investigate possibilities of buying government surplus materials or batches of slightly out-dated films. Membership of the local camera club brings one into contact with many willing sources of oddments and practical assistance.

Often one item of equipment can be adapted to fulfil several functions—for example the school's slide or filmstrip projector used as an enlarger or spotlight. Similarly some subjects can be photographed on to a strip of printing paper in the camera and prints then made from these cheap paper negatives. Where very limited funds are forthcoming for photography as an educational activity it is generally sound policy to purchase only the simplest equipment and concentrate most money on an adequate supply of films and paper. This will at least enable students to begin utilising the medium, and much can develop from the enthusiastic production of results.

SPACE AND FACILITIES. Most photographs will be taken out of doors or in 'studio' areas which can be quickly improvised in laboratories and classrooms. Apart from a dark cupboard (or changing bag) for loading a rollfilm tank, film processing can be carried out in normal lighting (see Figs. 2.25–6) providing a sink with water supplies is available. With care even the cupboard can be dispensed with and the film processed in its cassette (Fig. 9.1). This procedure, originally devised for Nuffield science, is not, however, recommended for general practice owing to the risk of scratches.

Rough contact printing can take place on a flatbed photocopier using continuous tone stabilisation bromide paper slow enough to be handled

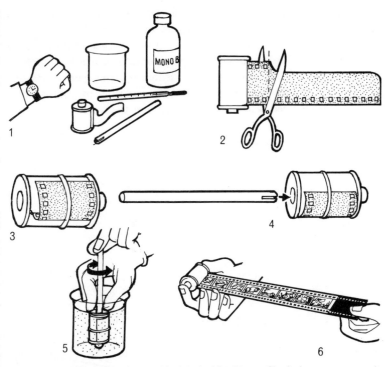

Fig. 9.1. Processing a 20 exposure black and white 35-mm film in its own cassette (no darkroom required). 1, Tools required are a watch, monobath developer and beaker, thermometer and piece of $\frac{1}{4}$ in. wooden dowelling slotted at one end. 2, 3, Shaped tongue of film is removed, 1 in. of film end looped over cassette casing and held by elastic band. 4, 5, Cassette plus dowelling lowered into 40 ml of Kodak monobath (20°C) and rod continually rotated fully one way and then the other while holding cassette body stationary. After 5 minutes drain, immerse in water, remove processed film and wash for further 5 minutes.

briefly in shaded room lighting. However, an improvised darkroom with orange safelighting is desirable for enlarging and serious printing. This can range from a modified 'Wendy House' to a permanent installation. For detailed layouts, see Appendix VI. It is even possible to buy an off-the-peg darkroom which simply requires connection to plumbing and electricity services (Fig. 9.3).

Of course, the provision for students of image production facilities and equipment has double justification when used for direct teaching visual aids making purposes too. Sometimes capital costs can be shared with groups such as the local Evening Institute or school Camera Club needing to use photography on the premises after school hours. Again, schools which decide to run a non-vocational CSE course in photography are likely to have more equipment and facilities made available.

The main facility required for cinematography is the provision of an editing bench and cutting rack which students can use at various times knowing that work will not be disturbed. A unit such as that in Fig. 7.7 which folds away into a cupboard or prep room is sufficient.

THE TIME FACTOR. As time modules, school-teaching periods do not lend themselves well to the conventional processing of photographs. Films and paper need washing and drying, and the teacher can be left

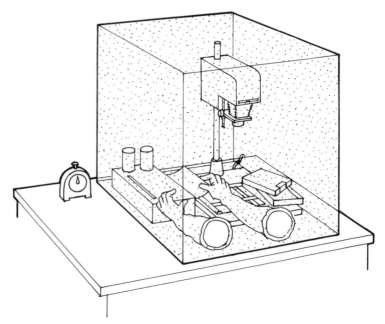

Fig. 9.2. Unit constructed from transparent red Perspex sheeting to allow enlarging on to projection speed stabilisation bromide paper. Long gloves of red or black material sealed to arm holes in wall allow items to be manipulated from outside, without letting in white light. Exposed prints are fed direct into processing machine, re-emerge damp–dry after 10 seconds. Perspex 'box' simply lifts from bench for changing negatives, retrieving processed prints etc.

burning the midnight oil finishing off what his students have so enthusiastically begun. As Fig. 2.26 shows, it takes about 45 min to process a black-and-white roll of negatives, excluding drying time. Despite these difficulties it is important to keep the momentum going by cutting corners at every opportunity.

The use of several triple tanks enables the work of a whole class to be processed at one time. If tanks are loaded up with the exposed films in darkness before the period begins small groups of pupils can be responsible for each tank—pouring solutions in and out, timing and checking temperature. Final washing should be 20 min but this can be cut to about 5 min by using a hypo-eliminator solution.

The easiest way to dry a film is to hang it up in a tall cupboard (e.g. a cleaned-out broom cupboard), leaving it there overnight. Alter-

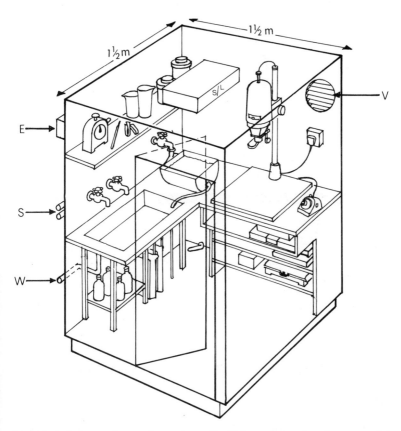

Fig. 9.3. A darkroom for one (or two) people which can be purchased as a complete free-standing unit from suppliers of timber buildings. Unit simply requires coupling up to school's electricity supply (E), hot and cold water services (S) and waste (W). Roof safelight and light-proof extractor fan (V) are built-in.

natively a forced air drier can be made out of one or more plastic drain pipes (Fig. 2.28) which will dry films in about 15 min.

Printing is interesting but time-consuming with conventional materials because the last prints still need 30 min wash before drying (7 min, using hypo eliminator). Prints are then laid out to dry on muslin tacked to a frame, or pegged on a line and left overnight (see

Fig. 2.29). Alternatively an electric flatbed glazer can dry or glaze wet prints in about 10 min.

This accumulated time needed to make prints and enlargements highlights the advantages of the roller processing machine and stabilisation printing papers. As discussed earlier on page 94, the prints are processed as quickly as they are exposed, and emerge damp–dry

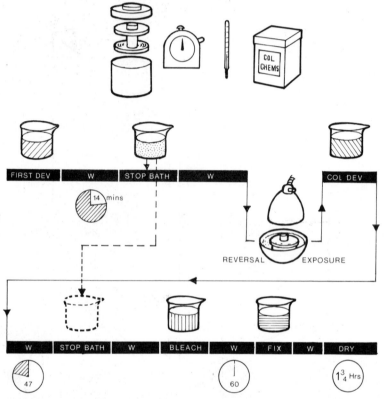

Fig. 9.4. Processing equipment and sequence for colour transparency reversal film, in this case 3M Ferranicolor. Five solutions are required. Film is fogged to white light part way through sequence (using white-walled bowl) and thereafter processing can take place with lid off tank. Other film brands use different chemical kits but similar sequence and timing.

from the machine. No sinks or plumbing are required, and the darkroom reduced to a booth, Fig. 9.2. As results are not fully permanent, those prints which are required long-term should be conventionally fixed and washed at some convenient time.

The biggest time-saver of all—Polaroid film materials—allow finished prints to be peeled direct from the camera. But demonstrations

272

PLATE 1 (*Top*): Photograph taken with a home-made pinhole camera, described on page 274. Exposure time needed was about $500\times$ the shutter speed at f8 indicated by meter, i.e. 6 seconds on Verichrome Pan given 20 per cent extra development time to improve low contrast image.

PLATE 2 (*Bottom*): Photogram of a skeleton leaf sandwiched between glass in the negative carrier and enlarged on hard grade bromide paper.

PLATE 3 (*Above*): Bas relief effect. Original Plus X negative is contact printed on to Ilford N8. 31 film. The resulting positive is combined (slightly offset) with the negative in the carrier of the enlarger and printed on hard grade paper.

PLATE 4 (*Left*): Editing photoplay transparencies (Kodak Ltd).

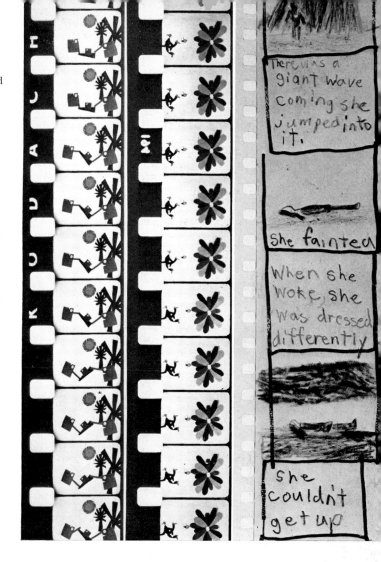

LATES 5, 6 and 7
Opposite): Clips
rom 8mm animated
lms made during
rt classes at *Sale*
irls Grammar
chool, Cheshire.
eft Eleven-year-
lds used symbols
ut from card to
epresent animals
nd landscape.
entre Design by
vo 16-year-olds
sing combinations
f drawings and cut
apes. Both films
ave striped sound-
acks. *Right* Story
rawn direct on
att-faced filmstrip
m with coloured
arkers by an
fant school pupil,
e page 192.

PLATE 8 (*Below*): Two frames from the photoplay *The Doctor and the Dormouse* by sixth-formers at *Gillingham School, Dorset.* Figures (coloured acetate), wire, fibreglass, etc., were arranged on an OHP stage and the projected image photographed off the screen using Ektachrome type B.

PLATES 9–15 (*Opposite*): High-speed photography of drops of salt water falling from burette (B) into a dish of milky water, through two wires which trigger xenon flash unit (F). Advancing the time delay on a relay between trigger and flash for each successive droplet records various stages in the life of a splash. By Lower Sixth physics group, *Abingdon School, Berks.*

PLATE 16 (*Above, left*): Ball thrown in the air and recorded during a time exposure by light flashes from a stroboscopic lamp. Velocity measurements can be made straight off the print, see page 293. *Mayfield School, Sussex.*

PLATE 17 (*Above, right*): Multi-image of a tennis player photographed indoors against a black background. A disc with cut-out sections is rotated rapidly just in front of the lens, see Figure 9.18.

PLATE 18 (*Opposite, top*): Aerial photograph from a radio controlled model aircraft, see page 292. Late afternoon sunlight emphasises vertical dimensions, but loses detail in deep shadows. *Harry Cheshire Secondary School.*

PLATE 19 (*Opposite, bottom left*): Mosaic of photographs received on equipment in the physics laboratory at *Plant Hill High School, Manchester* shows the day's weather from several hundred miles high as seen by an ITOS satellite. Coastline at bottom is North Africa; depression is centred over Britain. Transmitted pictures are recorded on domestic tape-recorder, replayed and photographed.

PLATE 20 (*Opposite, bottom right*): Testing a new aerial on *Plant Hill School* roof.

PLATE 21 (*Above*): A continuous tone negative enlarged on lith paper to give a line image. On lith film or translucent paper this could become a silk screen image (Figure 9.19) to be printed in inks of any colour. *Havelock School, Grimsby.*

PLATE 22 (*Right*): Frame from a tape-slide project for CSE (Art). Two transparencies projected by separate machines on to one screen, shading unwanted parts, and photographing the result. See Figure 9.11.

PLATE 23 (*Overleaf*): A sheet of contact prints from a student's 35-mm film exploring the effects of light on form by shooting a few sheets of paper. Much can be discovered and discussed from contact prints alone, without always going to the expense of enlargements.

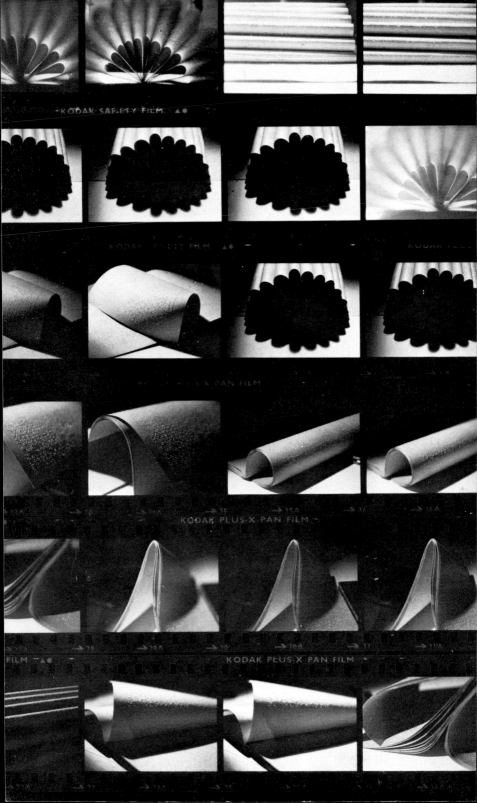

apart, this material is still too costly per exposure (Fig. 2.4) to justify much use by students themselves.

Processing colour films is a meticulous job, using expensive kits of chemicals. However, many younger students enjoy the practical routine of processing, say, Ektachrome, and it can be tackled as a team job with each individual responsible for one stage. Results are ready for projection in about $1\frac{3}{4}$ hours (Fig. 9.4) and this is encouraging to the photographer. Where the chemistry and disciplines of processing are of

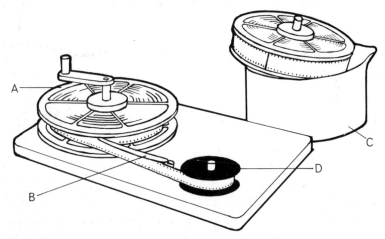

Fig. 9.5. Processing tank and loading unit for short (up to 50 ft) lengths of movie film. A, Large capacity plastic spiral. B, Automatic film guide. C, Tank body. D, Spool of exposed film. Once loaded, film receives same black and white or colour processing sequence as its still camera equivalent.

no educational value it may be cheaper (and often safer) to send them away for processing—even though results may not be returned for a week. Cine film is rather more difficult to handle owing to its length, and apart from odd camera tests, titles, etc., needed in a hurry (Fig. 9.5) it is advisable to have films processed professionally.

TECHNICALITIES. In general do not spend more time on teaching technicalities than is pragmatically justified. If the cameras the students are using allow picture making only under a modest range of conditions, set limited projects accordingly. Introductory explanations need cover only the most basic manipulation of the equipment and the main points raised in the packing note with the film. Later technical questions will arise as students become more ambitious, but to start with let them gain encouragement from producing simple images without too much inhibition.

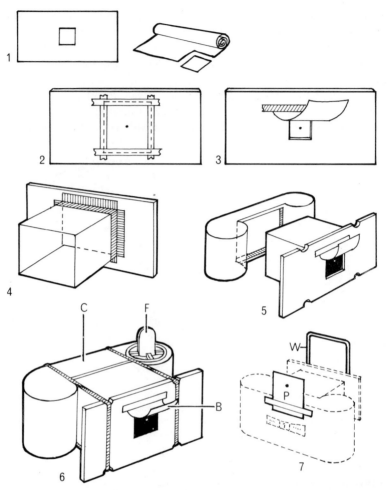

Fig. 9.6. Construction of simple pinhole camera. 1, Thin plywood with cut out aperture, and piece cut from roll of aluminium kitchen foil. 2, Foil, taped across aperture, is pierced by fine darning needle. 3, Black paper flap 'shutter' attached to other side of aperture. 4, Square tube of black card taped to (foil side) of wood. Ensure seal is light-tight. 5, Tube is pushed into square opening of 126 film cartridge and held by elastic bands. Piece of lolly stick (F) winds film. Lift flap B to make (time) exposure. 7, Peep sight made from wire (W) bent to same dimensions as picture format, and large pinhole (P) in card, centred at back of cartridge.

Making a simple camera is a good starting point for awakening an interest in photography, which can be harnessed to a whole range of subjects. Figure 9.6 shows a pinhole camera which could be made by twelve-year-olds for little more than the cost of one 126 film cartridge. A simple little sighting viewfinder can also be made from wire and attached appropriately to the top of the camera. The 126 cartridge contains enough film for twelve exposures, so that one camera can be made and shared by 2–3 pupils. The equipment is completed by a flat piece of wood to act as a film-winding key—an ice lolly stick is quite satisfactory.

With the flap obscuring the pinhole use the key to turn the film-winding knob until '1' appears in the rear window. The camera is supported on a firm surface and the flap lifted to expose the picture (give about 3 sec on 125 ASA film for outside scenes lit by sunshine, 9 sec if overcast). The film is wound on to the next number with the flap closed after each picture. As exposure estimation can only be approximate, try to expose two frames for each subject—giving the second frame about 3 times the previous exposure. If a 35-mm processing tank is not available the exposed film cartridge can be processed by the local chemist, ready for the following week.

Types of projects

The type of project set and its detailed planning is all important, the teacher forecasting just how far a particular group can be 'stretched'. Photographic manufacturers offer helpful technical information for schools and colleges through booklets and filmstrips, see page 298.

Worthwhile projects (still and cine) can be broadly divided into one or other of the following groups, although these have considerable overlap:

1. *Experimental images*—open-ended projects intended to encourage individual visual development and awareness. These may range from making shadow prints to sophisticated exploration of form and colour.

2. *Fictional material*—the planning, shooting, editing and projection of movie film or a series of stills, into a story-telling dramatic sequence, probably with the addition of sound.

3. *Documentary and technical*—records of group visits and excursions in sound and pictures, illustrations for individual written projects, or as by-products of modern methods of exploring science, maths, sociology, engineering, etc. Also the use of photography as a direct analytical or measuring tool, as for example in the tracking of earth satellites.

Experimental projects

PHOTOGRAMS. Experiments in visual development using photography may begin even in the infant school, although opportunities here are naturally restricted by considerations of safety and limited manipulative skills. At the Pheasey Infant School, Birmingham, five- and six-

275

year-olds have used photographic materials to make patterns and shapes as part of a perceptive investigation.*

Prints were made by light using simple opaque shapes positioned on photographic paper, and letting each child develop his result. A darkroom had first to be designed which would not be too obtrusive in a

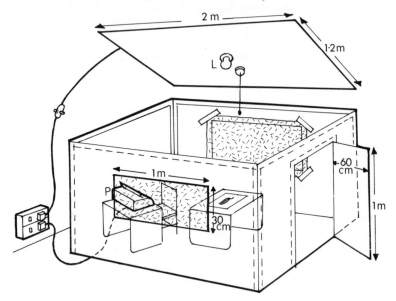

Fig. 9.7. Darkroom 'Wendy House', safe for young children to make photograms, etc. Constructed from Bristol Board on wooden battens, with orange gelatine sheeting over windows. Infants' tables inside carry stabilisation processor (P) and exposing area for continuous tone bromide paper, using lamp (L) on ceiling.

classroom situation and would accommodate a simple and rapid method of processing without risk of direct contact with chemical solutions, or require disciplines of timing and temperature.

The darkroom finally took the form of a portable adventure house (Fig. 9.7) built out of Bristol Board and 1 × 1-in. battening. Windows cut in the sides and covered with orange acetate acted as safelights and allowed supervision from outside. The darkroom housed a stabilisation roller processing machine,† plus a light bulb fitted to the ceiling and controlled by a pull-cord. Both light and machine could be switched off by the teacher from outside the darkroom.

The child positions cardboard shapes on a sheet of sensitive paper, gives a quick tug on the light cord to make the exposure, and feeds the

* By James Clement.
† On free loan from an industrial organisation.

276

paper into the machine. Ten seconds later the result is brought out to the classroom and the child asked his interpretation of the pattern. At first the children are encouraged to follow a prescribed programme of making these shadow pictures (photograms) of various patterns from uniform cardboard cut-outs. Later they make up their own pictures from uniform and non-uniform shapes supplied, and later designed themselves.

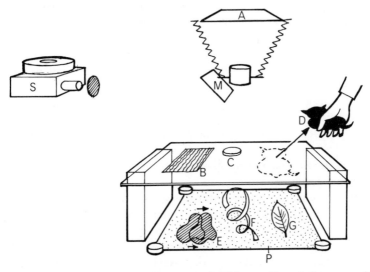

Fig. 9.8. Various arrangements for photograms. P, Light-sensitive printing paper with flat (G) or three-dimensional (F) objects casting shadows under light from the enlarger. Shifting object (E) during exposure gives two grey shapes, with a white overlap form. Patterned glass (B) and coin (C) on raised glass shelf have softer outlines. Removing cut-out (D) after part of exposure gives a *grey* image. Enlarger may itself contain silhouette material or a negative (A), or one can use a mirrored slide projector (through a grey filter to reduce intensity).

As an extension of photogram making for older children a slide projector or enlarger can be used as the light source. As shown (Fig. 9.8), shadow patterns can be cast on light sensitive paper in three ways:

1. Objects lie in contact with the paper, resulting in sharp, detailed, same-size shadows. (This can even be done on a flatbed photocopier.)

2. Flat objects are placed between pieces of clear film or glass in the projector slide holder (or enlarger negative carrier). This provides enlarged silhouettes, or detailed images if the objects are fairly transparent. By throwing the lens out of focus, outlines become diffused.

3. Three-dimensional objects are positioned on one or more glass or clear plastic shelves somewhere between the lens and the paper. The

angle at which the object is positioned determines its shadow outline and the height of the shelf above the paper gives increasing diffusion of detail.

If the objects used are opaque (leaf skeletons, grasses, cogs) give sufficient exposure time for the background on the processed paper to appear a rich black, leaving the shadows as clean white. Overexposure gives light 'creep' around the edges of shadows, giving a fogged or muddy outline. If opaque objects are removed after only part of the exposure time has been given (Fig. 9.8), shadow patterns in varying shades of grey are produced. In fact, by moving an object from place to place, multi-shadows are formed which, overlapping, create new outlines. Similarly combinations of 1, 2 and 3 can also be overlapped, to give new shapes.

Interesting photograms are also possible from semi-transparent objects such as glass marbles, rice, patterned glass and drawings in ink and pencil on tracing paper (or grease crayon on acetate). All these again give negative images so that familiar objects can be reinterpreted; the length of exposure time given determines how much of the subject is 'seen through'.

An ideal equipment line-up for this work is an enlarger connected to a timer (set by the teacher for the number of seconds needed to just give a good black background) and a stabilised paper processing machine. However, an adapted slide projector, a wall clock with a large second hand, Kodagraph Projection paper and three dishes for processing (Fig. 2.27) is a much cheaper alternative. The classroom needs a good blackout, or a Wendy house or a prep cupboard darkroom conversion in which light-sensitive paper can be safely handled between removal from its box and delivery into the processing machine. Orange acetate over an electric light source provides safelighting.

Photograms, apart from their obvious applications in developing awareness of shape and form in the art room, also offer interesting possibilities in subjects such as 'new' maths—for example, relationships between shapes devoid of form, and exploration of symmetry both in natural and man-made objects. Occasionally, photograms can be made direct on to photographic sheet film, or a paper print copied by heat on to film and then immediately projected on to a screen by overhead projector for general discussion.

IMAGE DISCS. A multi-textured or multi-coloured surface such as a tactile chart is built up and photographed in colour. The colour laboratory is asked to produce an enlarged film transparency, say 8 × 8 in., which is sealed against damage between two sheets of clear plastic. As a cheaper alternative build up a montage of rollfilm colour transparencies. The transparency is now fed through a slide projector (Fig. 9.9) very slowly, using an adapted electric clock or similar motor. If possible the transparency should feed the projector as a constantly rotating disc, but the design of some machines may require a long strip of image.

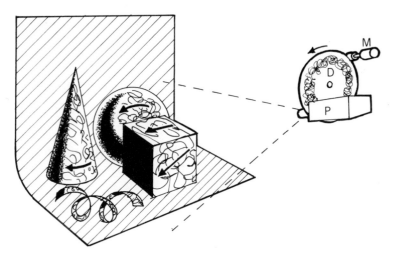

Fig. 9.9. Image disc. A ring of patterned/textured material, photographed and made into a 10-in.-diameter transparency (D) slowly revolves through projector (P). Image crawls at various speeds over matt white three-dimensional forms, but does not show on black velvet background.

The projector is arranged to throw a sharp image from one side on to the smooth white surfaces of various three-dimensional forms—cones, spheres, bowls—set on a black background. These forms therefore take on the projected 'textures', which slowly crawl across the surfaces at speeds and directions varying with their angle and shape. A disc may take half an hour to make one full revolution and during this time a tremendous variety of visual changes will take place. A second projector with an image disc of, say, faces enlarged from a football crowd might illuminate the forms from another direction, giving a wide range of permutations.

CAMERA PROJECTS. Still photography projects must be sufficiently open-ended for students to discover their own visual aspects and attitudes, which can then be developed through further individualised projects. Initially the requirement might be to produce a number of interesting images of one of the following:

People

Reflections

Parks and open spaces
Shops
Traffic
Anything below knee height.

Later, after discussion of results, some of these may be developed into more specific briefs, for example the people project might become:

People waiting—in bus queues, station platforms, laundrettes, etc.

Children—in schools, playgrounds, in the street.

People selling—in shops, street markets, newspaper stalls, icecream vans.

Evidence of people without showing people—graffiti, litter, wear marks, etc.

People in transit—in cars, trains, walking, cycling.

People in uniforms.

Human relationships—mother and child, boy and girl; suspicion, humour, insularity, comradeship.

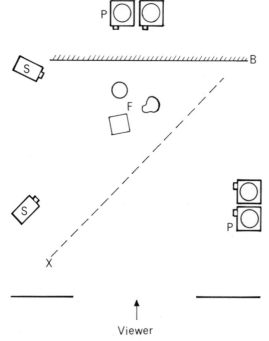

Fig. 9.10. 'Three-dimensional painting'. Plan view of one end of a darkened room separated off except for frame through which viewer observes staging area. X, Clear plastic screen or fine stretched muslin. B, Translucent back projection screen. F, Human figures and other three- and two-dimensional forms. S, Spotlights. P, Slide projectors. See text.

Alternatively the field may be narrowed down to a particular district, park or railway station.

At each stage, work (in the form of contact prints or slides) is discussed and the next stage mutually agreed. Technical problems are tackled as and when they crop up (often accidental blurring, misfocusing, light-flare or underexposure will suggest visual possibilities which can then be purposely invoked).

THREE-DIMENSIONAL PAINTING. As shown in Fig. 9.10 this is a visual 'happening' in which the viewer faces a frame not unlike a proscenium arch. Behind this is a blacked-out area containing a clear plastic sheet stretched at 45°, and a transluscent back-projection screen. Pairs of projectors present images on each of these screens—the use of pairs allows dissolves and superimpositions in each case. Between the screens, three-dimensional objects (including moving people) are lit by more projectors or spotlights from the sides, or are just allowed to form silhouettes against images on the back-projection screen. Working to sound pre-recorded on tape, a wide range of visual and audio effects are possible. Images can be photographic or painted transparencies, or even motion picture film sequences. Spatial relationships can be constantly changed and developed. Projectors can be hand-operated in a random fashion to give spontaneous results, or the whole thing programmed on tape.

MISCELLANEOUS TECHNIQUES. Other techniques well worth exploring for the interesting type of image they can produce include:

1. Hand-made colour transparencies using bits of gelatine filters, plastic, glass etc. Quite a thick sandwich of these materials can be made up and the projection lens then focused through to image one layer sharply at a time.

2. Sandwiching two or more colour transparencies in one slide mount to make a montage. Use overexposed images or subjects with predominantly light backgrounds. Apparently useless transparencies can combine to give spectacular results.

3. Project two separate transparencies on to the same screen (use images with dark grounds, or shade unwanted parts) and then photograph the screen (Fig. 9.11).

4. Print on to bromide paper with a fluorescent coloured base.* This gives a black image on colour. Bleached in a solution provided by the makers, the black will dissolve, taking with it the colour in image areas only. The result is a white negative image on colour, see Fig. 9.12.

5. Colouring black and white prints by Colorform (page 319).

* Kentint papers from Kentmere Ltd, see Appendix IV.

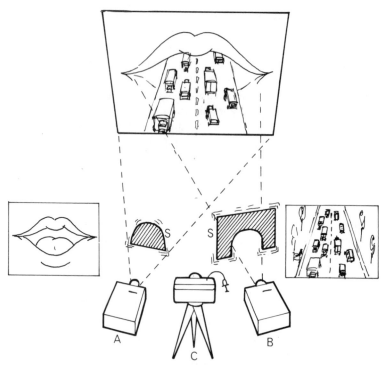

Fig. 9.11. Image combinations. Images from colour transparencies in projectors A and B are superimposed on a matt white screen. Shaders (S) block out unwanted parts of images. The composite is photographed with camera (C) using type B colour film. Shaders may be kept moving during exposure to further soften any edge effects.

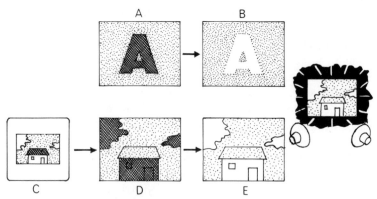

Fig. 9.12. Printing on fluorescent coloured bromide paper. *Top:* Black A printed on coloured ground (normal print processing). In maker's bleach black parts and *immediately underlying colour* become white. *Bottom:* Positive transparency (C) enlarged on to paper gives black on colour negative (D) or (after bleaching) white on colour positive (E). *Right:* Image shows up dramatically when lit by UV lamps in darkened room.

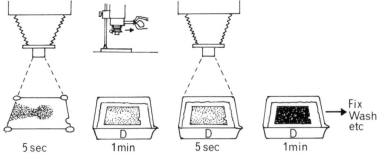

Fig. 9.13. Solarising. Neg is enlarged on to 5 × 4-in. line film, giving an exposure which would give a 'good' positive. After one minute in print developer, the processing film is fogged to light under same enlarger (less negative) and allowed to finish its two minutes development. This dense, solarised positive is dried and normally contacted on to another sheet of line film to give a thinner, negative image for enlarging.

Normal black and white prints are bleached and redeveloped in any of a range of image colours. N.B. Photostabilised prints *must* be conventionally fixed and washed before any chemical aftertreatments are performed.

6. Making negative images on paper by printing from black and white (Dia Direct) or colour transparencies, direct on to soft grade bromide paper.

7. Printing on to sheet film which is solarised by fogging during processing (Fig. 9.13) to give a final half positive-half negative print.

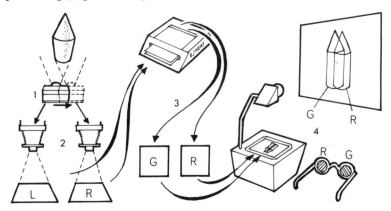

Fig. 9.14. Three-dimensional images. 1, Two pictures exposed with camera positions separated by 65 mm. 2, Equal size paper enlargements made from each negative. 3, Prints copied on any suitable copier to give contrasty OHP transparencies, one a red image, the other a green image on clear ground. 4, Transparencies are projected, slightly offset, and viewed through green/red filtered glasses to give three dimensional appearance.

8. Taking a stereoscopic pair of photographs, making enlargements which are heat copied to give two complementary coloured OHP transparencies. These are offset, projected and viewed through coloured spectacles. Fig. 9.14 shows details.

Techniques 5 and 6 can be arranged to give a final result on film, for adding to a slide series, e.g. photoplays, see below. Black and white negatives can of course be pressed into service as part of combines for techniques 1, 2 and 3.

Fictional projects

PHOTOPLAY. A visual approach undoubtedly encourages oral and written creative English expression work in young children. Discussing a child's pictures introduces description as a basis for writing. This may start with a few basic words added to the pictures, and later expanded into whole-story writing using the original picture simply as a stimulus and start point for further communication.

Developed into a group activity, this can encourage children to write story lines for commercially produced filmstrips (such as Lotte Reiniger's 'Puss in Boots'). The written matter is then adapted for transcription on to a tape recorder with the addition of background music. Going one stage further, instead of relying on a series of ready-made pictures the children can create the images for their own complete audio-visual presentation—a technique termed 'photoplay'.

For example, the story structure is first collectively discussed and decided. Every child is then expected to draw and paint one frame for the final production and work out his own written commentary on that frame. Continuity of picture and story line are again discussed as a class. When finished the paintings are photographed in order (perhaps by a member of staff) on to consecutive frames of a 35-mm colour film, using daylight. The work might even be completed by writing, playing and recording musical background, performing on a variety of 'instruments' including pop bottles and flower pots.*

One of the great advantages of photoplay is that, properly organised, it requires only modest funds for materials, and can involve pupils in the challenge of:

1. Formulating an idea or theme (factual or fictional).
2. Preparing a treatment.
3. Studying situations and locations.
4. Casting people.
5. Shooting.

* Based on work done at Gifford County Junior School, Essex.

6. Editing.

7. Producing and recording the supporting sound.

Photoplay is therefore not only valuable for the development and recording of dramatic work but is also a tremendous help in encouraging inarticulate children to express themselves generally. It can utilise and encourage the experimental visual work described earlier.

At Hampden Park Secondary School, Eastbourne, a fictional photoplay is being planned from scratch. The end result is to be a set of twenty slides and up to three minutes of sound. This means about two 36-exposure cassettes of reversal colour film plus a $3\frac{1}{2}$-in. reel of tape. A list of available locations and actors is decided first because it is easier to tailor a story to them rather than vice versa. A simple anecdotal storyline is chosen (the originality of the theme is less important than the way it is handled). A distinct structure of *beginning* or establishment of situation; *middle* or development of action; and *end* or rounding-off of story is used, thinking out the end first and working back.

Now the ideas are turned into concrete visual terms and the group reads and discusses the possible treatments. A storyboard (Fig. 7.1) can be made up at this point and tentative allocation of long, medium and close-up shots decided. The teacher emphasises the importance of plenty of close-up shooting.

While the storyboard is being broken down into a shooting script for each location other pupils are busy arranging permission to use these locations, preparing titles and props, and rehearsing actors and photographers (using empty cameras). Several sessions of shooting are planned, leaving the second session until the results of the first have been returned from processing and can be discussed. Production of 40–50% usable material from these first colour transparencies is considered quite good.

When all the visual material has been successfully shot and edited down the sound is planned in some detail. The commentary is evolved by discussion while viewing the slides. (Notes are made rather than written scripts and, having established this framework, several versions of the commentary are recorded. The best bits are then selected and the tape spliced together.) Finally music and effects—as much as possible recorded by the children themselves—are added. This is handled on the second track of a twin track tape recorder, or by 'dubbing'—re-recording commentary and accompaniment on to another recorder.

Using another form of photoplay children in the Art class at the Thomas Bennett School, Crawley, chose a track from a pop LP record. Everyone in the class painted pictures to illustrate different parts of the song. They then went through them, picked the ones which fitted the words best, took them outside and photographed them on colour film. The transparencies were then projected in time with the music on the record. The project was a success in that it provided an incentive to

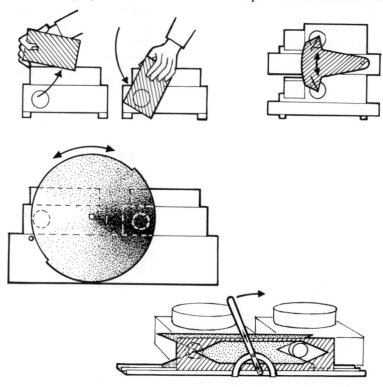

Fig. 9.15. Mechanical methods of dissolving one image into another on screen. *Top left:* Using two hands, masking one projector while unmasking another. *Top right:* Electrically operated swinging shutter. *Centre:* Rotating graduated grey filter. *Bottom:* Improvisation using two pieces of shaped plywood sliding in plastic channelling, operated by hand.

paint creatively. The children first identified with the music, found the necessary planning and organisation stimulating, and began to realise other possibilities in this combined use of media.

Another group made a more factual, documentary photoplay when they visited a local brick works to see how bricks were made. Hurried notes were made on everything as they went around (an unprecedented activity), together with tape recordings of all the sounds of machinery. The colour transparencies taken were edited, and a commentary re-corded with sound effects re-recorded as background.

Other, more open-ended photoplay projects worth tackling by older pupils include the portrayal of a particular area or part of town; a study of themselves in relation to their environment; and the illustration of stories in foreign languages for language teaching purposes.

PHOTOPLAY PRESENTATION. If two projectors are available the visual possibilities of photoplay are greatly extended. For example:

1. Make the slide series alternate between the two machines, both focused on the same area of screen. Superimpose or dissolve one image into another using two pieces of card, or various mechanical devices as shown in Fig. 9.15.

2. Give a multi-screen presentation by projecting images on different but adjacent parts of the screen. The projectors can then be programmed to give a single left- or right-hand picture; two side-by-side pictures; or one 'wide screen' picture in two halves joined at the centre.

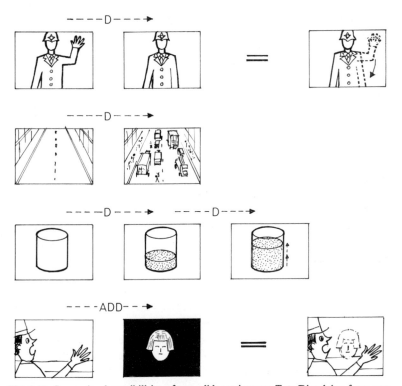

Fig. 9.16. Some visual possibilities of two slide projectors. *Top:* Dissolving from one transparency to the other makes figure appear to move arm. *Upper centre:* Dissolving here makes traffic materialise up out of the street. *Lower centre:* Dissolving twice to make beaker 'fill' with water. *Bottom:* Fading in one projector to superimpose on another image and so give 'ghost' effect.

3. As (2) but projecting from different directions on to facets of a three-dimensional white surface such as a curved screen, a cone or a sphere.

All these optical possibilities can be borne in mind in planning the photoplay. For example arrangement (1) allows a degree of animation: a sequence of transparencies taken nearer and nearer to a subject and then projected in sequence using dissolves gives the appearance of zooming in. Similarly a policeman on point duty can be photographed several times with his body occupying the same position in each frame but some with arms raised and some lowered. When these transparencies are dissolved the arms appear to move. (Fig. 9.16.)

Using similar techniques, faces can be made to loom in and out of landscapes. Captions and labels (shot against black backgrounds) can also be dissolved in and out of other pictures or even areas of colour (use coloured acetate in one projector instead of a slide). Two slides can be sandwiched together to give superimposition effects. These techniques are all natural stepping stones to film-making by children.

Fictional and experimental film-making

On the face of it, well organised film-making is not easy to equate with either standard class periods or the number of pupils in today's average classes. Nevertheless, under the guidance of their English teacher, a class of thirty-two third-year Walworth Comprehensive School children decided to make a film. Four months of $1\frac{1}{2}$ hours per week time-tabled periods were made available for the project. Some £45 from the School Fund bought a second-hand 8-mm cine camera, tripod and editing equipment. (The cost of film was recovered by showing the completed film to the school and societies for $2\frac{1}{2}$p per head.)

For practical reasons it was stipulated that the film should be silent, about 10 min long, with the children acting and all locations within 10 min of the school. Preparations then proceeded as follows:

1. Everyone individually wrote a script. Groups chose the best six of these scripts and favourite incidents from four of them were combined into one compromise script.

2. Several walks were taken together around the neighbourhood. Still photographs were taken and spontaneous incidents improvised—this heightened their visual sense of locality, and during discussions details in the script were filled in.

3. Having agreed the final story, a shooting script was enthusiastically written up for the form by one boy (previously notorious for his antipathy to written work). Parts and roles were then agreed and distributed throughout the class.

On the first day of shooting, their teacher accompanied them to the location (a street market) and pointedly left them to it. The students suddenly realised that it was all *their* film and their responsibility—they had to handle the people, obtain special permissions, remember to wind the camera and not shoot too much at once.

By the next week the film was returned from processing, provoking great discussion and argument. Shots were crooked, viewpoints were wrong, exposure erratic. After an hour they decided to throw away the whole first day's shooting and start again. But this time they knew what to avoid and had established standards among themselves.

During the next six weeks the teacher became producer rather than director—he organised administration in relation to school affairs, supervised the overall control of finance and watched the time factor. His other job was to ask pertinent and awkward questions occasionally and provoke continuous discussion. Often parts of the script were abandoned in favour of improvisation on the spot.

The job was completed in the following term by four boys who undertook all the cutting and editing during weeks of lunch hours. Finally a gala night was arranged by the children for their parents, at which they showed their film and talked about it at length, without notes.

Projects such as these prove that the wider the range of situations and demands the children experience, the more willing their attention and concentration. These children all had their response to film and TV at home affected by their film-making—schoolwork had connected with a medium of popular culture.

If one of the educational values of film-making for children can be to evoke a visual awareness of the local world, it can also encourage awareness of creative movement. In dancing, drama and physical education work filmed (or videotaped) records of group movements can be played back to the class for analysis. High-speed, time-lapse and reverse movement cinematography allow further experiments in movement. (For example, the class can all be asked to walk backwards while they are filmed in reverse.* The projected result is then compared with a normal film of the group walking conventionally.)

There are many interesting possibilities in the use of film inserts in school plays, teenage theatre productions, etc. Images projected on to a stage backcloth may be used to simulate exterior sequences—a character can be on the stage leaving the set one moment, and in the next on screen moving off into landscape. Similar transformation is possible back from screen to stage.

* Film with the camera held upside-down, see Fig. 7.14.

When using cinematography as part of drama teaching one has to face the very practical problem of how to equate a group of 30 or so pupils with one solitary camera. One method of organisation is to sit the students on chairs in a large circle in a room or hall well lit by daylight or by photofloods reflected off the ceiling. An idea is presented—for example, they are asked to improvise on the theme of 'meeting'. All the children present their efforts in the centre area in groups of two or three, and at the same time the 8-mm camera is passed around to give everyone the opportunity of filming one of these sequences. Each lesson consumes about one reel of film, and the results are viewed and discussed the following week. Film or video-recording therefore becomes an expendable commodity like paper.

In the Art department animation on film has obvious connotations for design drawing, but it often has a greater permanence and engenders more sense of professional achievement than painting. Simple animation requires few expensive materials, is not too difficult to organise and lends itself well to group work.

The project may for example start with the need to devise a strip cartoon series of related pictures making a simple story point. Pictures can be cut from magazines and related to form a series of actions in progression such as: Boy—football—greenhouse—breaking glass—boy running.

Other strip cartoons might feature metamorphosis—alphabet letters into insects, or a sequence of changes which both tells a story and gives experience in the transforming of one shape into another.

The actual film work may simply be single-frame recording of cut out figures—the aim for example being the creation of a new environment for an already existing character. The cut out figures are tacked on separate sheets of paper or acetate and combined with other cutouts, drawings, paintings or photographs. The result is jerky and without continuous flow, but involves plenty of variety and selection and problems of coherence if a thematic story is being followed.

Alternatively, very simple, direct drawing or scratching on clear * or black 16-mm film gives a fast-moving series of shapes (and colours) when projected. To start with, lines can simply be drawn down the film—dividing, combining and changing colour. Later simple registered images (Fig. 9.17) can be tried. Don't attempt animating a constant and definite form, as accurate registration of hand-drawn images at this scale is impractical.

To explore the scope of working by this method try a spot engulfed by a line, or a shape dividing. The projected images have continuously

* Use fixed-out film and write with Lumicolor 317 or similar OHP pens.

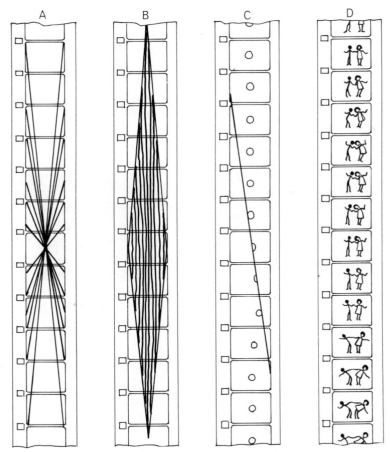

Fig. 9.17. Experiments in animation by direct drawing on clear 16-mm film. C is an attempt at a simple registered image. D is much more laborious and one must put up with a continuously changing outline to the figures.

changing outlines, and attempts should be made to design within this inherent characteristic rather than try to correct it.

Documentary and technical projects

The recording ability of still photography lends itself to a variety of projects, either general in character or linked for example to applied science. When senior pupils at a Secondary Boys School* were planning an exhibit for a British Association Science Fair they decided to attempt aerial photography, using a radio-controlled model aircraft. Members of the School's model aircraft club and photographic society

* Harry Cheshire School, Kidderminster.

pooled their interests, and a multi-channel radio transmitter was built to control a 60-in. wingspan aircraft. Elevator, rudder and motor could all be operated remotely and a separate signal was available to fire the camera.

Flight tests showed that the aircraft would lift a payload of 14 oz. The boys began searching for a camera not exceeding this weight, having a lens good enough to allow final exhibition size enlargements and a shutter operating at $\frac{1}{500}$ sec, in order to avoid image shake when flying at 30 m.p.h. In the end an old rollfilm camera with a good lens

Fig. 9.18. Arrangements for stroboscopic photography of moving subject (see Plate 28). Subject is set against black background. *Left:* Strongly lit with photofloods and shot through large disc with cutout sections rotating fast in front of camera. This can be built from a bicycle wheel. *Right:* Lit with stroboscopic flash-heads. In both cases the camera shutter is left open for whole of action. Speed of disc or flash frequency determines number of overlapping images.

was suitably strengthened and modified by substituting a black balsa wood box for the bellows, and adding a sheet film holder back. The photograph was exposed via a motor which simply wound in a thread attached to the shutter release.

After much experiment the best technique was found to be flying the model to a height of about 600 ft, switching off the engine to avoid vibration, and making the exposure on the glide. Successful black-and-white and colour photographs taken in this way include a survey of school buildings and part of a local housing estate, pictures of the River Severn for geographic purposes and attempts at archaeological research for the History Department (see Plate 18). Above all, investigation and the solving of problems by the team of pupils involved in this project made science a very real subject, and encouraged enquiry.

Photography and photographic equipment have direct application to optical and mechanical phenomena. Enlargers can be used to explore the image-forming properties of various lenses; photographs may be taken to record an apparently bent rod partly immersed in a tank of water, and prints used to provide quantitative evidence of the laws of refraction.

In the teaching of dynamics, a white sphere thrown in the air is photographed at regular time intervals along its path of motion. (The ball is illuminated from above with a stroboscopic lamp and shown against a black background, see Plate 16.) The parabolic trajectory described by the ball under the influence of gravity can be actually measured off the final photographic print or enlargement. This is an instance where the immediate results given by Polaroid camera equipment offer special advantages.

Mayfield School in Sussex, working in conjunction with Worcester College of Further Education, are using photographic methods of demonstrating photosynthesis in plants. Destarched leaves, together with a crucible of radio active sodium carbonate are placed in an evacuated flask. Dilute hydrochloric acid is dripped on to the sodium carbonate, and the flask left for some hours in a fume cupboard under a UV-rich light source.

The leaves are then removed and one or two taken to a darkroom where they are each pressed tight in contact with a sheet of photographic film. These sandwiches remain stored in the dark for a few days and the film is then developed normally. The film is found to carry a shadow image of the leaf, demonstrating how radioactive material has been absorbed into the leaf structure.

Several schools use photographic records of stamps as a link with school subjects. Themes such as historical buildings, costume, famous lakes and rivers, engineering achievements and foreign currencies are used. Children are encouraged to provide stamps which are turned into 35-mm colour transparencies with a standard copy set-up at school, and then projected for discussion. Similarly coins, cigarette cards, match box tops and many other items suggest themselves.

Other fruitful areas for documentary exploration are social studies projects involving students in individual research, taped/photographed interviews, etc.

Photo silk screen

Apart from photography itself forming a curriculum subject it also forms a technical part of several allied crafts and processes which give

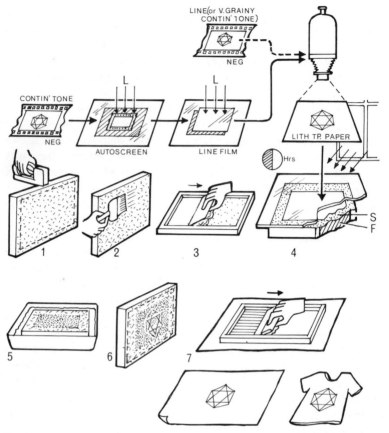

Fig. 9.19. Photosilk-screen. *Top:* Preparing the (final size) line or halftone positive print on translucent (TP) paper or film, under red safelighting. Silk screen preparation. 1, Stretching and mounting. 2, Degreasing. 3, Coating with emulsion (from underside) and drying, all under orange safelight. 4, Contact printing the photographic print on to front of sensitised screen (S) backed up with foam rubber pad (F). 5, Soaking in water to 'develop' image. 6, Drying print. 7, Squeezing printing ink through back of screen to print on to paper, fabric, etc.

scope for creative work, such as photo-silk-screen printing. This process allows line photographic images to be ink printed on to various surfaces in a variety of colours (Plate 21).

As shown in Fig. 9.19 the process requires little more than basic photographic equipment. There are four stages:

1. Select a negative* or part of a negative that is to form the basis of the design and enlarge this up to the required final size on translucent

* A contrasty line image. To reproduce continuous tones (1) contact print neg on Autoscreen film; (2) contact this on line film; (3) enlarge on to TP.

paper, such as Kodalith TP. This requires an enlarger in a darkroom with deep red safelight, and Kodalith high contrast developer.

2. Stretch nylon, Terylene or silk tightly over a wooden frame and degrease it with 5% caustic soda solution. Once dry, coat the inside of the screen with Seriset emulsion (see page 320) with a piece of stiff card and leave it to dry *in the darkroom* for 2–3 hours.

3. Place the screen over a block of foam rubber cut just to fill the frame. Position the line positive on top of the screen, pressed down tightly with a sheet of glass. Exposure is now made to daylight by leaving the sandwich near a window for 15–30 min. Film and glass are then removed and the screen soaked in water to reveal a negative image. The screen is allowed to dry overnight.

4. As in normal silk-screen printing the screen is placed in tight contact with the surface to be printed and ink swept across the back with a rubber squeegee. This produces a positive print.

Many variations are possible by multiple printing in various colours, forming repeat patterns, or superimposing strong positive and weak negative images.

A final word

It cannot be too strongly stressed that production of photographic images by students is a means to an end—most of its value rests in the discoveries and accompanying activities, and least of all in the polish of the finished product. Equally the work can be organised by anyone with a minimum of technical know-how, providing they can engender enthusiasm in a group of learners. Practical details given here are simply intended as a guide to future projects, because from experience requirements vary from one piece of work to another.

This chapter has tried to show the desirability of a photographic workshop in schools and colleges as a direct source of education, plus a secondary function for the production of visual aids. Much can stem from an active school camera club or film society. School publications and exhibitions too provide important showcases. Photographic manufacturers are sponsoring competitions for schools together with award schemes * open to teachers interested in applying photography, and teachers' courses (page 325). Publications such as *Visual Education* offer a regular exchange of ideas and examples of cross-discipline uses of the medium. In fact, having once got started, an impromptu course for one's fellow staff does wonders for future support and co-operation.

Prejudice—usually financially based—still exists on the part of

* Kodak Annual Award Scheme.

many Local Education Authorities. Yet there is surely as good a case for a photographic workshop as for many of the traditional crafts, particularly those which have ceased to have a social significance. A young person today is much more likely to have a still or cine camera than a weaver's loom or potter's wheel.

APPENDIX I

SUGGESTED FURTHER READING

On visual aids in education and training:

Communications and Learning, L. S. POWELL. Sir Isaac Pitman & Son Ltd, London (1969).

Aids to Teaching and Learning, H. S. COPPEN. Pergamon Press, London (1970).

Modern Teaching Aids, N. J. ATKINSON. Maclaren & Son Ltd, London (1967).

Audiovisual Aids and Techniques in Managerial and Supervisory Training, R. P. RIGG. Hamish Hamilton, London (1969).

Audio-Visual Aids in Higher Scientific Education. (The Brynmor Jones Report), H.M. Stationery Office, London (1965).

Projection for Teaching Purposes, Kodak Data Booklet ED-1. Kodak Ltd, London.

Diagrams, A. LOCKWOOD, Studio Vista, London (1969).

Designing for Visual Aids, A. WRIGHT, Studio Vista, London (1970).

Planning and Producing Audio-Visual Material, KEMP. Educational Foundation for Visual Aids, 33 Queen Anne Street, London, W1M 0AL.

8 mm Sound Film and Education, FORSDALE. Educational Foundation for Visual Aids, 33 Queen Anne Street, London, W1M 0AL.

Film Projection—Without Tears or Technicalities, M. SIMPSON. Educational Foundation for Visual Aids, 33 Queen Anne Street, London, W1M 0AL.

A Manual of Visual Presentation in Education and Training, E. A. TAYLOR. Pergamon Press, London (1966).

Teaching by Projection, R. S. JUDD. Focal Press, London (1963).

Projecting Slides, M. KIDD and C. LONG. Focal Press, London (1963).

A Guide to the 8-mm Loop Film, G. H. and L. S. POWELL. British Association for Comm. & Ind. Education (BACIE) 16 Park Crescent, Regent's Park, London (1968).

A Guide to the Use of Visual Aids, L. S. POWELL. British Association for Comm. & Ind. Education (BACIE) 16 Park Crescent, Regent's Park, London (1968).

Producing Slides and Filmstrips, Pamphlet S-8. Eastman Kodak, distrib. Kodak Ltd, London.

Audio-Visual Planning Equipment, Pamphlet S-1. Eastman Kodak, distrib. Kodak Ltd, London.

Multiple Screen Showmanship, Pamphlet S-28. Eastman Kodak, distrib. Kodak Ltd, London.

Integrated Teaching Aids, R. MURRAY THOMAS. Longmans Green & Co., London (1970).

Letraset System for Practical Visual Aids, Letraset Ltd, 195 Waterloo Road, London, S.E.1.

The New Technology of Education, M. J. APTER. Macmillan, London (1968).

(See also the many occasional papers, surveys, monographs and critical reviews published by the Educational Foundation for Visual Aids, Appendix V.)

On photography as an activity for learners:

Basic Still Photography,* Kodak Ltd, London (1969).

Notes on Photo-Play,* Kodak Ltd, London (1968).

How to Animate Cut-outs, C. BARTON. Focal Press, London (1969).

Film Making in Schools and Colleges, Edited by P. HARCOURT and P. THEOBALD. British Film Institute, Education Department, London (1960).

How to Make Films at School, J. BEAL. Focal Press, London (1969).

Young Film Makers, S. REES and D. WATERS. Society for Education in Film and Television Publications, 81 Dean Street, London W1V 6A.

A Film Society Handbook, Edited by R. C. YANNOCY. Society for Education in Film and Television Publications, 81 Dean Street, London W1V 6A.

(See also various free monographs available from the British Film Institute Education Department and the Society for Education in Film and Television.)

On photography and cinematography in general:

Commonsense Photography, L. GAUNT. Focal Press, London (1972).

All-In-One Camera Book, W. D. EMANUAL. Focal Press, London (1972).

All-In-One Cine Book, P. PETZOLD. Focal Press, London (1972).

Photography Hints and Tips, G. KNIGHT. Fountain Press, London (1969).

* No charge.

Camera Close-up, O. CROY. Focal Press, London (1970).

Photography—Materials and Methods, HEDGECOE and LANGFORD. Oxford University Press (1971).

Making Photograms, V. HAFFER. Focal Press, London (1970).

Design by Photography, O. CROY. Focal Press, London (1967).

How to Make 8 mm Films, N. BAU. Focal Press, London (1969).

*The Fundamentals of Film Making,** Kodak Ltd, London.

*Making Titles, Diagrams and Animated Effects,** Kodak Data Booklet AV-3, Kodak Ltd, London.

*Legibility Standards for Projected Materials,** Kodak Data Booklet AV-6, Kodak Ltd, London.

Magazines, Newspapers and Periodicals regularly featuring developments in photography and visual aids applied to education:

Visual Education. The Magazine of the National Committee for Audio-Visual Aids in Education. (Monthly) And particularly the Yearbook (July), 33 Queen Anne Street, London, W1M 0AL.

Times Educational Supplement. (Weekly), Times Newspapers Ltd, Printing House Square, London, E.C.4.

Screen. Journal of the Society for Education in Film and Television (bi-monthly), 81 Dean Street, London, W1V 6AA. SEFT also publish Screen Education Yearbooks.

News for Education. (Three publications annually), Kodak Ltd, Dept. 73A, Kingsway, London, W.C.2.

Practical Photography. (Monthly). East Midland Allied Press, Ounde Road, Peterborough, Hunts.

Film User. (Monthly), P.O. Box 109, Croydon, Surrey.

Film News. (Quarterly), Rank Audio Visual Ltd, P.O. Box 70, Great West Road, Brentford, Middlesex.

Audiovisual Communications Review. (Monthly), 1201 16th Street, N.W. Washington, DC, U.S.A.

Audiovisual references:

Painting with Light. 16-mm, 20 min. Agfa Gevaert Ltd, Great West Road, Brentford, Middlesex.

Window on the World. 16-mm, 18 min. *Life Magazine*, Time/Life Building, New Bond Street, London, W.1.

Music for your Movies. (12-in. LP Record, including dubbing fees), Twenty-four pieces of mood music, published Fountain Press, 46 Chancery Lane, London, W.C.2.

* No charge.

Filmstrips and the Teacher. 18 frames 35-mm F/S. National Film Board of Canada, distributed Guild Sound & Vision Ltd, page 318.

Fundamentals of Photography. (Teaching kit—manual, slides and demonstration material), Kodak Ltd, London (1969).

Fundamentals of Film Making. Series of 16-mm 20 min films. Distrib. British Film Library, 81 Dean Street, London, W.1.

Also various filmstrips available at nominal charge from Kodak Ltd and Philips Electrical Ltd, London. An invaluable range of film and television extracts for film-teaching purposes can be hired from the British Film Institute Education Department library.

APPENDIX II

GLOSSARY OF TECHNICAL TERMS

A4. International paper size $8\frac{1}{4}$ in. $\times$ $11\frac{3}{4}$ in.

Acetate (or tri-acetate). Clear, non-flammable film base.

Activator. Chemical—usually a strong alkali—able to cause rapid development in light sensitive materials manufactured with developing agents already in their emulsion, e.g. photo-stabilisation paper. Will not itself develop conventional photographic film or papers.

Actinic (light). Light to which the particular material is sensitive.

Ambient light. Existing or residual light (e.g. after inefficient room blackouts have been drawn).

Angle of view. Indicates the amount of a subject included by the lens/camera combination. The longer the focal length of the lens the narrower the angle of view on a given format.

Animated viewer. Machine like a simple low magnification movie projector with easily variable film speed, used to give a convenient moving picture when editing (see Fig. 2.33).

Animation. Imparting movement to a drawing or model, e.g. cartoon films.

Aperture (of lens). Size of the lens opening through which light passes. Normally calibrated in f-numbers, being the diameter of the beam of light incident on and allowed to pass through the lens, divided into its focal length. Widest apertures have lowest f-numbers. All lenses set to the same f-number give images of a (distant) scene at equal brightness.

Artwork. Hand prepared drawings, paste-ups, lettering, etc., in two-dimensional form.

ASA. American Standards Association. Applied to photographic materials, an arithmetic scale of numbers denoting relative sensitivity to light. (Half the ASA number = half the sensitivity or 'speed'.) See also **Uprating.**

Aspect ratio. Width-to-height proportions of image area.

Autoscreen. A Kodak high contrast lith film, factory fogged behind a 133 line screen, so that when correctly exposed to an image and processed the result is a direct half-tone picture (q.v.).

B shutter setting. Stands for Brief—shutter remains open for as long as the release button remains pressed.

Balance, colour. The relative proportion of different colours present in a 'white' light source. Colour films are made in different types, each giving accurate reproduction when the subject is lit with a particular light source. See Fig. 4.27.

Balancing stripe. When a magnetic stripe is coated along one edge of a movie film to allow sound recording a second, narrower stripe on the opposite edge reduces film distortion and curling. See Fig. 1.14.

Bracketing. Taking several pictures of a scene at different exposure times or aperture settings—usually half and double as well as the estimated correct exposure ($\frac{3}{4}$ and $1\frac{1}{2}$ with colour film).

Bromide paper. Light-sensitive photographic paper for enlarging (or contact printing). Most types must be handled under appropriate safelighting conditions.

Carrier. Holder for the slide, film strip frame (or negative) in a projector (or enlarger).

Cartridge. Single unit container housing both feed and take-up spools. Made for small-format still and 8-mm movie film cameras. Container for an open spool of movie film—complete cartridge being 'plugged into' a self-threading projector.

Cassette. Light-tight container for 35-mm camera film (Fig. 9.1). Ready to use container for loop movie film (Fig. 1.19).

Claw. Device which, engaging in one or more perforation (sprocket) holes in the film, transports it one frame per stroke. Usually in film or filmstrip projector, or movie camera.

Coarse screened. A half-tone illustration made up from a coarse pattern of dots easily discernible to the eye, i.e. about 80 lines per inch or less (Plates in this book are screened at 133 lines, and can be regarded as fine).

Colour Balance. See **Balance**.

Contact printing. Making a photographic print by laying the light-sensitive material in tight contact with the negative and exposing (to light). Print is therefore same-size.

Close-ups. Movie or still photographs in which the picture area is filled with a relatively small part of the subject (e.g. a single head). Usually photographed from close to the subject, but may be shot from afar using a telephoto lens.

Continuous tone (original, or film). Containing (or able to record) a range of tones between dark and light, such as a conventional photograph, painting, etc.

Contrast developer. An energetic developer giving contrasty images, particularly on line film, such as concentrated print developer. See also **Lith developer**.

DIN. German-based system of film speed rating. Doubling of sensitivity indicated by an increase of 3 DIN.

Density. In its generalised sense term synonymous with the darkness or depth of tone of a photographic image.

Depth of field. Distance between nearest and farthest part of subject sharply imaged at the same time. Greatest with short focus lenses and small apertures (high f-numbers). See Fig. 6.1.

Development. Causing the image imprinted (by light, heat, etc.) on sensitive material to become visible.

Diapositive. Transparency, e.g. a slide.

Diazo materials. Diazonium salt coating which is destroyed upon exposure to intense ultra-violet or blue-rich light.

Diffuse lighting. Illumination reaching the subject from many different directions, resulting in gentle modelling and mild or non-existent shadows, e.g. quality of light from an overcast sky, a lamp reflected off a white ceiling, etc.

Dissolve. Simultaneous fade-out of one image and fade-in of another on the same screen.

Dry mounting. Mounting by means of shellac-coated tissue placed between paper base image and mount, and subjecting the sandwich to heat and pressure.

Dual spectrum copiers. See light/heat copiers.

Dubbing. Recording sound accompaniment to movie (or series of still) pictures after shooting.

Dupe. Abbreviation for duplicate.

Dye line. Synonymous with diazo.

EP recording. Extended play (45 rpm) recording.

EVR. Electronic video recording. Patented process of special motion picture film with magnetic sound track sold for replay through any TV set. See Fig. 1.17.

Easel, enlarging. Flat board with adjustable flaps placed on the enlarger baseboard to hold paper flat during exposure. Edges of paper masked by the flaps receive no light, so giving white borders.

Electronic flash. Equipment which gives a brilliant flash of light by discharging a powerful capacitor through a small gas-filled tube. Discharge usually triggered by contacts in the camera shutter itself.

303

Emulsion. The light-sensitive layer on photographic films and papers, consisting primarily of silver halides in gelatine.

Enlarger. Optical projector to give enlarged (or reduced) size images which can then be exposed on to light-sensitive film or paper.

Exciter lamp. Component in a sound projector. Lamp used to produce a small beam of light to read an optical sound track. See Fig. 1.13.

Exposed. A light- (or heat-) sensitive material which has received exposure to an image. Usually relates to the stage after exposure and before processing.

Exposure increase. When working very close to the subject, e.g. macro-photography, exposure read with a (non through-the-lens) meter should be multiplied by $\dfrac{\text{lens to film distance}^2}{\text{focal length}^2}$. See Fig. App.7.2.

Extension rings. Rings or short tubes attached between camera body and lens, to allow the sharp focusing of very close subjects—i.e. macrophotography.

f-**numbers.** See **Aperture.**

fps. Frames per second.

Fade. Fade-away of the image, usually into white or (movies) black.

Filmholder (large format cameras). Light-tight holder for sheet film, loaded and unloaded in the darkroom. See Fig. 2.16.

Film speed. Measure of sensitivity of film to light. Usually expressed as ASA or DIN figure.

Filmstrip. Sequence of still pictures on a length of (normally 35 mm) film.

Filter, lens. Sheet of (usually dyed) gelatine or glass used over lens to absorb particular wavelengths from the light beam.

Fixed focus. Camera having lens permanently set for a fixed subject distance, e.g. set for 3 metres but, using a small fixed aperture, giving a depth of field from infinity down to 2 metres.

Fixer. Chemical (basically a solution of sodium thiosulphate) used after development to make soluble or otherwise neutralise those parts of a photographic image unaffected by the developer. Photograph can thereafter be handled in normal lighting.

Flash-bulbs. Small bulbs containing inflammable zirconium wire and an electrical igniting filament. Contents burn out in a (once only) brilliant flash when a few volts are applied—usually triggered by camera shutter. Most small bulbs are blue dyed to give daylight colour balance.

Flashcube. Assembly of four small flashbulbs in common unit—which is simply rotated 90° (e.g. automatically, by spring) between pictures, so allowing four pictures without bulb changing.

Flatbed copier. Genetic term for all copiers which use a flat glass-topped light box to expose the original document, so allowing bound books and magazines to be copied.

Flat copy. Substantially two-dimensional subjects such as drawings, photographs, paintings, textiles, etc.

Floodlamp. Wide reflector lighting unit usually containing a lamp such as a photoflood. Produces diffuse quality lighting.

Focal length. Distance between lens and position of sharp image for a subject a great distance away. (Strictly does not apply to special lens designs such as telephoto.) For a given format, focal length determines camera's angle of view.

Focusing. Varying the distance between lens and image (and/or lens and subject) until a sharp image is formed. Distance needed between lens and image = $(M + 1) \times$ focal length, where M is height of subject divided into the height of its image.

Focusing screen. Finely ground glass screen or similar ridged material on which the lens may focus an image, viewable from behind the screen. Used in all reflex and stand cameras for focusing and viewfinding combined.

Fogging. Submitting light- (or heat-) sensitive material to random active light (or heat). As in opening the back of a loaded camera or a box of enlarging paper, in white light.

Format. Dimensions of image area.

Frame. Each separate image area formed on a film.

Gate. Smooth channel in which film is held (and intermittently moved) during projection or movie shooting.

Glossy paper. Photographic printing paper with an extra top coating of gelatine. If dried in contact with a highly polished surface (e.g. a chrome glazing sheet) the paper takes on this same gloss surface. When simply air dried the paper gives a semi-gloss finish.

Half-frame images. 18×24-mm format pictures on 35-mm film.

Half-tone. Pictures printed in newspapers, magazines etc. which appear to be continuous tone but in fact are made up of black and white dots whose distribution gives an *impression* of greys.

Half-tone screen. Fine-ruled transparent screen used to convert continuous tone originals into half-tones. See also **Course screened**.

Halogen lamps. Small intense tungsten lamps which do not blacken with age. Available as photofloods, spotlight bulbs, etc., which they match in colour.

Heat filter. Glass filter able to absorb a high proportion of infra-red (heat) wavelengths. See Fig. 1.1.

Hecto masters. See **Spirit masters**.

Hypo. Popular name for sodium thiosulphate. Colloquial name for fixing bath.

Hypo eliminator. Chemical (normally 0.3% hydrogen peroxide solution) able to convert residual hypo in film or paper into inert salts. Photographic images can then be given a very curtailed wash and remain reasonably permanent.

Inching. Moving film through a projector very slowly, by means of a hand-turned knob coupled to the transport mechanism.

Incident light attachment. White plastic attachment for meter cell which diffuses incoming light from all directions. For measuring light from the subject position.

Infinity. A distance so great that light from a given point reaches the camera as virtually parallel rays. In practice, distances of about 1000 times the lens focal length and over.

Intermittent movement. The mechanism (activating a claw) able to transport film in a series of jerks, one frame at a time, in between brief pause periods while it is exposed (or projected).

Keystoning. Distortion of image shape in projection, due to screen not being at right-angles to the light beam.

Lacing up. Threading the film through a movie camera, projector, animated viewer, etc., ready for use.

Laminating. Sealing one material over another, e.g. thin heat-sealed plastic to cover and protect the face of a wallchart.

Leader. Length of blank film (usually black) proceeding and attached to the main movie film. Serves to protect main film and facilitate lacing without losing opening images.

Line film. High contrast photographic film. Most line films are sensitive only to blue and can be handled under an orange printing room safelight.

Line original. Drawing, lettering, etc., consisting of solid and clear areas only—no greys—such as the diagrams in this book.

Lith developer. Extreme contrast developer when used with lith materials.

Lith film/paper. Very high contrast materials capable of extremely dense blacks when processed in lith developer. Most lith materials can be handled under a deep red safelight.

Long focus lens. Lens having a focal length much longer than the diagonal of the image format for which it is used. Provides large images of subjects a great distance away; gives flattened perspective; has shallow depth of field.

Long shots. Shots showing the general scene, distant figures, landscapes, etc.

Loop film. Movie film attached head to tail as a long loop, thus allowing continuous repetition.

Loop projector. Movie projector designed for loop films (usually in cassettes).

Macro lens. Specially designed for close subjects, usually has a mount allowing it to focus well out from the camera. See also **Exposure increase**.

Macrophotography. Photography at very close subject range (often giving an image larger than the subject) but without the use of a microscope or other special instrument.

Magnetic stripe. Narrow band of zinc oxide coated on non picture area of movie film, on which sound may be recorded magnetically.

Master. An intermediate from which copies may be run off in quantity on an appropriate machine, e.g. by diazo, ink or spirit duplicator or offset lith.

Mixer unit. Equipment for fading and mixing sound from microphone, gramophone, tape-recorder, etc.

Monobath. A single solution able to develop and fix black and white films in one stage. (Fixer component is slower to act than developer.) Impossible to overdevelop, but solution gives fixed degree of development.

Monochrome. Single coloured. Usually implies black image, but equally applicable to a dye image of one colour such as those produced by heat or diazo.

Negative image. Image in which blacks, whites and tones are reversed, and (colour negatives) colours are complementary, relative to the original subject.

OHP. Overhead projector.

Open spool film. Movies film wound on a conventional open-flanged spool, as opposed to permanently housed in a cartridge or cassette.

Overlay. Flap of transparent material on which may be drawn parts of a map, diagram, etc., which will then immediately register with the main drawing underneath.

Panchromatic. Light-sensitive materials which are sensitive to all visible colours, recording them in appropriate shades of grey. Should strictly be processed in total darkness—no safelights.

Panning. Rotating (the camera) about a vertical axis.

Photocell. Electronic cell able to convert light signals into electrical current flow.

Photocopier. Copying machine using the action of light- and photo-sensitive materials. Normally uses liquids for processing.

Photoflood. High-intensity, short-life light bulb run direct off the mains. Cheaper than 500 W photographic lamps. Has a colour temperature of 3400 K and can be used with Type A colour films (Table 4.27).

Photographic (or photopearl) lamps. 500 W (and above) pearl lamps and spotlight bulbs having a colour temperature of 3200 K. Standard for Type B colour film.

Photomicrography. Photography through a microscope.

Photopearl lamps. See **Photographic lamps.**

Photo-stabilisation materials. Light-sensitive materials (printing paper only, not films) designed to be processed by brief application of activator and then stabiliser solutions—usually by motorised roller machine.

Polarised light. Light restricted to vibrate in one plane only.

Polarising filter. Grey filter used (*a*) to polarise light and (*b*) when suitably orientated, to block the path of already polarised light. Some plastics, crystals, etc., exhibit coloured stress patterns when placed between a pair of such filters. Also used to eliminate (polarised) reflections.

Polaroid process. Patented process using special photographic film, paper and jellied chemicals. Must be used in a camera with a Polaroid back. Allows finished black and white print, transparency or colour print to be pulled from the camera within seconds.

Positive film. 35-mm black and white film with slow, bromide paper-like characteristics and originally used for printing motion picture film. Useful (and cheap) for making positive transparencies from negatives, and vice versa, using enlarger or camera.

Positive image. Image in which blacks, whites, tones and (colour film) colours approximate those of the original subject.

Processing. General term covering one or a sequence of physical or chemical changes required to make a reasonably stable image in appropriately exposed sensitive material.

Projection speed material. Term sometimes used to distinguish paper etc. sensitive enough to be exposed under the enlarger (must be handled under safelighting) from document copying (contact printing) materials.

Raster pattern. The pattern of horizontal lines making up the image displayed on a television screen. In Britain 625 lines are used for each picture.

Reduction printing. Making a print which is *smaller* than the negative. Most enlargers offer this facility.

Reflex printing. Copying (an opaque-based or double-sided original) by placing it in face contact with light sensitive paper which is then exposed to light *through the back*. See Fig. 2.4.

Reversal film. Film designed for reversal processing.

Reversal image. A direct positive image produced without requiring a separate negative stage.

Reversal processing. Processing (usually more stages than negative processing) to give a reversal image. Chemicals and procedure vary somewhat with each type of colour and black and white material.

Rewinding. Winding back movie film from take-up to feed spool, ready for projecting next time.

Right-reading copy. A copy which, if it contains text, can be read normally from the front.

Roller processor. Motorised machine for rapidly processing photo-stabilisation materials.

Rollfilm. Photographic film, usually $2\frac{1}{2}$ in. wide (known as 120 or 620) attached to numbered backing paper and rolled on a flanged spool. See Fig. 2.15.

Rotary copier. General term for copiers engineered to accept the original through a feed slot, passing it around a drum. Such machines cannot handle bound or stiff based originals. See Fig. 2.1.

SLR. Single lens reflex.

Safelight. Darkroom light source filtered to emit colour to which photographic material is insensitive. Required colour varies with type of emulsion.

Sans serif. Genetic term covering type styles without little 'feet' to the bottoms of upright letters, etc.

Screened illustrations. See **Half-tone illustrations**.

Shutter. Mechanical device to control the *time* light is allowed to reach the film. Used in cameras and movie projectors.

Silver halides. Light-sensitive chemicals found in photographic films and papers.

Single lens reflex. Camera design which allows the user to observe the image through the actual taking lens up to the moment of shooting (see Fig. 2.16). No parallax error.

Slide. Image on a transparent base, intended for projection. Traditionally on glass but now normally on film sandwiched between glass. (Sizes see Fig. 1.2). Term sometimes applied to a sheet film or plate holder for a large format camera.

Slow motion. Movie filming at a fast framing rate, the result being projected at slower speed.

Solarising. Technique of fogging film or paper to light during development, giving an image which is positive in some areas, negative in others.

Sprocket holes. Regular holes punched into film outside picture area. These engage with sprocket wheels and claw mechanism on the projector or camera, in this way transporting the film through the machine.

Sprockets. Rollers carrying teeth which engage with film sprocket holes. Used on projectors, cameras, animated viewers, etc.

Stabilisation. Instead of fixation, photographic images may be left in a state of reasonable stability in light by passing through a stabilisation bath (typically 35% Ammonium thiocyanate) and squeezing dry without washing. Results tend to fade chemically after some months (see page 95). Owing to whitish deposit left in emulsion is more acceptable for paper than film materials.

Stabilisation materials. See photo-stabilisation.

Standard-8. 8-mm-wide movie film with frame format, and frame and sprocket-hole positions as originally designed in 1935. Gradually being superseded by Super-8.

Stencil. Intermediate from which copies can be run off in quantity on an ink stencil duplicator.

Super 8. 8-mm-wide movie film with redesigned sprocket holes which allow each frame to be larger in size, leading to a sharper, brighter picture on the screen.

Synchroniser. Device for linking separate items of equipment—tape player and projector, two projectors, etc.—so that they work in tandem.

T setting on shutter. Stands for 'time'. Shutter remains open until release is pressed a second time.

Telephoto lens. Long focus lens of compact design. Lens is physically shorter than its focal length.

Thermal copier. Heat copier.

Time lapse. Movie filming allowing an appreciable time to elapse between exposing successive frames. When projected at normal speed this gives a greatly speeded up record of the subject, e.g. growing plants.

Trailer. Blank film forming the last few feet of a movie film or film strip to protect the image-bearing film and to facilitate lacing for rewinding, etc.

Translucent. Transmitting but also diffusing light, e.g. tracing paper.

Transparency. Image (normally positive) on a transparent base. Term is now broadly synonymous with slide.

Tungsten lamps. Electric lamps using heated tungsten filaments, e.g. photofloods, household lamps, halogen lamps.

Twin lens reflex. Camera design using two lenses—one for focusing and viewfinding and another to expose film. See Fig. 2.16.

Uprating. Shooting film at more than the manufacturer's suggested speed rating, e.g. exposing 400 ASA film as if 800 ASA. Film is then given modified processing. There is a distinct limit to the degree of uprating possible before image quality suffers.

VTR. Video tape recorder.

Videocassette. Easy-loading commercially produced software (on tape, film, etc.) intended for playing out sound and vision through an ordinary television set. Also known as videocartridge or telecartridge.

Videotape. Magnetic tape able to reproduce the sound and vision of a television programme.

Videodisc. Special gramophone record-type disc able to play commercially prepared sound and vision through a television set.

Wide angle lens. Lens with a focal length much shorter than the diagonal of the format for which it is designed to be used. Gives a wide angle of view and considerable depth of field.

Zoetrope. Simple Victorian apparatus to view short series of pictures in rapid succession, so giving the impression of one moving image (see Fig. 7.18).

Zoom lens. Lens which can be made to vary its focal length (so changing image size) without altering image sharpness, f-number or other factors. See Fig. 2.32.

PHOTOGRAPHIC MATERIALS FOR STILL AND MOVIE PHOTOGRAPHY SUGGESTED IN TEXT

TABLE APP.3.1

Still Photography	Size				Speed (ASA)	Notes
	35.	C.	R.	Sh.		
B & W Neg Films						
Agfapan 25	✓				25	These films are extremely fine grain— but slow speed makes tripod essential
Panatomic X	✓	✓			32	
Ilford Pan F	✓	✓			32	
Verichrome Pan		✓	✓		125	Low cost. Wide exposure tolerance
Kodak Plus X	✓		✓	✓	125	General purpose under good lighting
Ilford FP4	✓		✓	✓	125	conditions; fine grain
Kodak Tri X	✓		✓	✓	400	General purpose; can be uprated by
Ilford HP4	✓		✓	✓	400	100% if given extra development
Agfapan 1000	✓		✓	✓	1000	Grainy; more expensive; use under poor
Kodak Recording	✓				1250	lighting conditions; can be uprated
Royal X pan			✓		1250	50–100%
Ilford N.5.50				✓	6	Use under enlarger for line printing on
Kodak Process				✓	6	film, solarising, etc. (Orange)
Kodalith	✓			✓	10	Very contrasty. Lith dev. (Red)
K'lith Autoscreen				✓	3	As above, gives screened results
K'lith Pan				✓	10	V. contrasty. Lith dev. For copying coloured originals
Kodak F.G. Positive	✓				6	Normal contrast bromide emulsion on film. For printing slides from B & W negs. (Orange)
Col Neg Films						
Agfacolor CN17	✓			✓	40	Use in daylight or (filtered tungsten).
Kodacolor X	✓	✓	✓		80	Self processing fairly simple
Ektacolor			✓	✓	100	
Colourslide (Reversal) Films						
Kodachrome II	✓				25	Use in daylight, etc; processing by lab
Kodachrome X	✓	✓			64	only; lowest cost col trans
K'chrome II Type A	✓				40	As above, but photoflood lighting
Agfacolor CT18	✓		✓		50	Use in daylight etc; processing by user
Ektachrome X	✓	✓	✓		64	or lab; H.S. film can be uprated 100%
Ektachrome				✓	50	
H. Speed E'chrome	✓		✓		160	
Ansco 500	✓				500	Grainy, useful for poor light

Still Photography	Size				Speed (ASA)	Notes
	35.	C.	R.	Sh.		
Ektachrome Type B				✓	32 ⎫	Use with photopearl lamps. User or lab
H.S. E'chrome Type B	✓		✓		125 ⎭	processing
Agfacolor CK	✓		✓		80	Use with photofloods
Infra-Red E'chrome	✓				100	Colour distorting film. User/lab processing
B & W Reversal Film						
Agfa Dia Direct	✓				32	Direct, low cost B & W slides. Processing included in price

Movie Photography	Size		Speed (ASA)	Notes
	16 mm	8 mm		
B & W Neg				
Plus X neg	✓		80 ⎫	Similar characteristics to Plus X and
4X neg	✓		500 ⎭	Tri X still film
B & W Reversal				
Plus X rev	✓		50 ⎫	
Tri X rev	✓		200 ⎬	Processing not included in purchase price
Fuji R200		✓	200 ⎭	
Col Reversal				
Kodachrome II	✓		25 ⎫	Processing incl in price, Daylight
		✓	64 ⎭	
E'chrome EF7241	✓		160	User/lab processing. Can be uprated. Daylight
K'chrome II Type A	✓	✓	40	Photoflood. Processing incl in price
E'chrome EF7242	✓		25	Photopearl. (Otherwise as 7241)
E'chrome 160		✓	100	Photoflood. Processing incl in price

Rapid Processing Films For Still Photography	Size			Speed (ASA)	Notes
	Pk.*	R.*	Sh.*		
Polaroid Type	107	37	57	3000 ⎫	All give contin tone B & W print, in
		46-L		800 ⎬	15 secs (46-L in 2 mins)
			52	400 ⎭	
		42		200	
		146-L		200	Line B & W trans
	88	48	56	75	Col print (60 secs)

All films are panchromatic unless safelight colour (e.g. Orange) quoted in notes. All Ektachrome films (E3 & E4 types) can be processed by user in E3 chemical kit.

Key. 35: 35 mm cassette. C: Cartridge. R: Rollfilm. Sh: Sheetfilm. Pk: Packfilm.

* Fit Polaroid cameras or special camera backs only.

SUMMARY: RECOMMENDED MATERIALS FOR EXPLORING STILL PHOTOGRAPHY

Plus-X/FP4/Verichrome Pan. Requires least exposure accuracy and is therefore excellent for beginners' black and white photography; also cheapest per exposure. However, its slow speed imposes limitations in poor lighting conditions with simple cameras. Tripod may be needed.

Tri-X/HP4. Good all-round-use film, which can be used at 800 ASA if development increased 10%. More grain than Plus-X.

Recording Film. Useful for (*a*) Grainy image effects, particularly when enlarged on hard (e.g. Kodalith LP) paper; (*b*) Shooting under extremely dim conditions. Little exposure latitude; and rather expensive.

High-speed Ektachrome. General purpose (daylight) colour transparency film for photo-plays, etc. Can be rated 100% faster (or more if colour deterioration acceptable) and development increased accordingly. Class can process in E3 kit of chemicals. Similarly **High-speed Ektachrome type B**, for photopearl lighting.

Kodachrome X. Lower cost than Ektachrome, remembering that processing included in price. Virtually grain free colour transparency film, not so impractically slow as Kodachrome II. However processing only by Kodak (about one week) and no speed uprating. Similarly **Kodachrome II type A**, for photoflood lighting.

Infra-red Ektachrome. 'False colour' transparency film giving dream-like effects (photo-plays, etc.). Green living foliage records magenta and crimson, faces and lips yellow. Should be exposed through deep yellow or green filter, and rated at 100 ASA, or 200 with through-the-lens meter. Works most dramatically in Spring (young foliage). Very contrasty; requires accurate exposure.

Agfa Dia Direct. Extremely useful V–A material—the only film giving black and white slides by direct reversal processing (by makers in 2–3 days). Low cost. Good medium contrast—also give acceptable results from line artwork etc.

Kodalith. Extreme contrast. Critical exposure. Needs lith developer for fullest (rich black) effect. Can be used in camera (e.g. for 35 mm negative line slides from artwork, diagrams), but more often as a printing material under the enlarger, using 35 mm or sheet films forms. Kodalith LP paper gives contrasty dramatic prints with lustre surface finish. TP paper gives identical image but has a translucent base for silk screen printing, page 293. Autoscreen film has the characteristics of Kodalith, but gives an image consisting of fine dots when correctly exposed, page 186. Used as intermediate for silk screen, lith or document copying reproduction. Minimum size 10 × 8-in—smaller sizes must be cut from this. All lith materials require deep red safelighting.

Ilford N5.50. Roughly equivalent to grade 3 bromide paper, on film. Excellent for solarisation effects and printing images as OHP transparencies. Orange safelight.

Bromide Paper Glossy Single Weight. General-purpose enlarging paper. Can be glazed or air dried (semi-matt). Supplied in grade 1 Soft; 2 Normal; 3 Hard; 4 Extra Hard. Hard paper for normal prints from 'soft' (flat negatives) and vice versa. For classwork all four grades are really required. As with all enlarging (projection) paper, an orange safelight is essential. Wide range of sizes, including rolls.

Kodagraph Projection Paper. Similar to grade 4 bromide paper but 20% cheaper, matt surface, less intense 'blacks'. Useful for photograms and line handouts.

Kodak Contact Paper C145. Medium contact paper, too slow for enlarging but satisfactory for contact printing to bright light source (e.g. 100 watt bulb). Owing to this insensitivity can be handled and processed by children in dim artificial lighting.

Kentint Bromide Paper. Enlarging paper on range of 6–8 coloured bases. Gives black-on-colour image (page 281). Paper behaves as if grade one—requires contrasty negative.

Monobath. One solution developer/fixer for black & white films. Convenient but not flexible—contrast set by formula of solution.

Kodak D76, Ilford ID11. General purpose developer for black and white films. Keeps for many weeks; can be used repeatedly; moderately fine grain.

Ilford P.Q. Universal. Concentrated liquid developer for prints.

APPENDIX IV

MANUFACTURERS, SUPPLIERS AND HIRERS
OF HARDWARE AND SOFTWARE; SERVICES

To keep this list within manageable proportions only a cross-section of manufacturers are mentioned by name. However, the hardware suppliers listed (prefixed '*supp.*') maintain a comprehensive stock of products from all current sources and can usually offer a wide range of descriptive literature. Try to make a point of visiting the National Audio-Visual Aids Centre * (page 321) before choosing a major item of audio-visual equipment. Here direct working comparisons can be made between various makes and informed, unbiased guidance obtained from people conversant with the problems of teaching.

SOURCES OF HARDWARE

Audio-Visual Projectors, etc.
E. J. Arnold & Son Ltd, Butterley Street, Leeds 10.
Rank Audio-Visual, P.O. Box 70, Great West Road, Brentford, Middlesex.
Newman & Guardia, Edinburgh Way, Temple Fields, Harlow, Essex.
Bell & Howell A-V Ltd, Bridgewater Road, Wembley, Middlesex.
(*Supp.*) Paul Plus Ltd, 28 King Street, Newcastle, Staffs.
(*Supp.*) M. R. Warner & Co.,* 26 Chapel Ash, Wolverhampton, Staffs.

Copying Machines
Heat
'Bandaflex'. Block & Anderson Ltd, Cambridge Grove, Hammersmith, London, W.6.
Light-Heat
'Dual Spectrum' Minnesota Mining & Manufacturing Co. Ltd, 3M House, Wigmore Street, London, W.1.
Photocopiers
'Verifax', Kodak Ltd, Kingsway, London, W.C.2.
'Copy-Rapid', Agfa Gevaert Ltd, Great West Road, Brentford, Middlesex.

* Hardware is available for hire from this source.

Diazo
Ozalid Ltd, Langston Road, Loughton, Essex.
Electrostatic
Rank-Xerox Ltd, Marylebone Road, London, N.W.1.

Duplicators
Spirit
'Banda', Block & Anderson, Cambridge Grove, Hammersmith, London, W.6.
Ink Stencil
Gestetner Ltd, Gestetner House, 210 Euston Road, London, N.W.1.
Litho
Multilith Ltd.

Photographic Equipment
(*Supp.*) Dixons Photographic Ltd,* Soho Square, London, W.1 and 22 St Anne's Square, Manchester.
(*Supp.*) Pelling & Cross Ltd,* 104 Baker Street, London, W.1.
(*Supp.*) Edric Films Ltd,* 34 Oak End Way, Gerrards Cross, Bucks.
(*Supp.*) Greenaway & Morris Ltd,* Swindon, Wilts.
Film editing
Robert Rigby Ltd, Northington Street, London, W.C.1.
Screens
Clearvue Projection Co., 92 Stroud Green Road, London, N.4.
Back-projection matt plastic
Autobates Learning Systems Ltd, Lutterworth Road, Nuneaton.
Photo-stabilisation processors
John Blishen & Co. Ltd, 75 Kilburn Lane, London, W.10.
Lighting
Malham Photographic Equipment Ltd, 65 Malham Road, London, S.E.23.

SOURCES OF SOFTWARE

Ready-to-use aids
Filmstrips, slides, filmloops, OHP transparencies, wallcharts, etc.
Catalogues from:
 Educational Productions Ltd, East Ardsley, Wakefield, Yorks.
 Encyclopaedia Britannica International Ltd, 18 Regent Street, London, S.W.1.
 Transart Ltd, East Chadley Lane, Godmanchester, Huntingdon.

* Hardware is available for hire from this source.

Diana Wyllie Ltd, 3 Park Road, Baker Street, London, N.W.1.

Woodmansterne Ltd, Holywell Industrial Estate, Watford.

Ealing Scientific Ltd, 15 Greycaine Road, Watford, WD2 4P.

Industrial & Commercial Education—Macmillan Ltd, Little Essex Street, London, W.C.2.

Daily Telegraph Magazine Colour Library, Fleet Street, London, E.C.4.

ITL Vufoils Ltd, 109 Clifton Street, London, E.C.2.

B.B.C. Publications, 35 Marylebone High Street, London, W.1.

Sunday Times Filmstrips, 200 Gray's Inn Road, London, W.C.1.

Films

Gateway Educational Films Ltd, 470 Green Lanes, London, N.13.

Film Libraries

National Audio-Visual Aids Library, Paxton Place, Gipsy Hill, London, S.E.27.

Guild Sound & Vision Ltd, Kingston Road, Merton Park, London, S.W.19.

Petroleum Films Bureau, 4 Brook Street, London, W.1.

Rank Film Library, P.O. Box 70, Great West Road, Brentford, Middx.

Central Film Library, Government Buildings, Bromyard Avenue, London, W.12.

Educational Foundation for Visual Aids, 2 Paxton Place, Gipsy Road, London, S.E.27.

British Film Institute, 42 Lower Marsh, London, S.E.1.

Connoisseur Films Ltd, 167 Oxford Street, London, W.1.

Open University Film Library, 25 The Burroughs, Hendon, London, N.W.4.

Video cassettes
Hire & Sale

EVR Partnership, 1 Hanover Square, London, W.1.

Do-it-yourself materials mentioned in text
Photographic films, bromide paper

Kodak Ltd, Kingsway, London, W.C.2. Kodachrome, Ektachrome, Tri-X, F.G. Positive film etc.

Agfa-Gevaert Ltd, Great West Road, Brentford, Middlesex. Dia-Direct, etc.

Ilford Ltd, Ilford, Essex. FP4, Pan F etc.

Lith films, papers, developers
Kodak Ltd. Kodalith and Autoscreen.
Ilford Ltd. Ilfoprint.
Coloured base, and cheaper bromide papers
Kentmere Ltd, Stavely, Westmorland. Kentint.
Stabilisation papers and chemicals
Kodak Ltd. Ektamatic.
Ilford Ltd. Ilfoprint.
Heat copying materials
Minnesota Mining & Manufacturing Ltd, 3M House, Wigmore Street, London, W.1.
Agfa Ltd. Transparex.
Direct positive, chemical diffusion transfer and dye diffusion transfer materials
Kodak Ltd. Autopos, Instafax CT, Verifax.
Duplicator masters, foils etc.
(See makers of appropriate hardware, and Kodak Ltd.)
Diazo material, developers etc.
Ozalid Ltd, Langston Road, Loughton, Essex
Criterion Ltd, Venesta International, 1 Hanover Square, London, W.1.
Electrostatic materials, developers etc.
Rank Xerox Ltd, Marylebone Road, London, N.W.1.
Ozalid Ltd. Ozafax.
Criterion Ltd. Arkwright transparency film.
Developers, fixers, monobaths, photo-tints, bleachers, toners, hypo eliminator, rapid fix, colour processing kits, liquid opaque, 'colorform'
Johnsons of Hendon Ltd, Hendon Way, London, N.W.4.
Kodak Ltd.
Polaroid films, backs, cameras
Polaroid (U.K.) Ltd, Huggins Lane, Welwyn Garden City, Herts.
Polarising filters
Polarizers (UK) Ltd, Lincoln Road, Cressex Estate, High Wycombe, Bucks.
Louis Newmark (Technamation) Ltd, 101 Bell Street, Reigate, Surrey.
Colour filters, safelights
Kodak Ltd.
'Write on' film
Rank Audio Visual Ltd, Great West Road, Brentford, Middlesex.
Kodak Ltd.
Transfer lettering, shading, symbols etc.
Letraset Ltd, 195 Waterloo Road, London, S.E.1.

Photoflood and photopearl lamps
Philips Electrical Ltd, Century House, Shaftesbury Avenue, London, W.1.
Dry mounting tissue
Ademco Ltd, Lincoln Road, High Wycombe, Bucks.
OHP Markers, plastic, pens etc.
Matthews Drew & Shelbourne Ltd, 78 High Holborn, London, W.C.1.
Transart Ltd, East Chadley Lane, Godmanchester, Huntingdon.
Hook and loops materials
E. J. Arnold & Son Ltd, Butterley Street, Leeds.
Emulsion for photo silk screen, and trial silk screen kit
Selectasine Silk Screens Ltd, 22 Bulstrode Street, London, W.1.
Stroboscopic Lamps
Dawe Instruments Ltd, Renault Estate, Western Avenue, London, W.3.
PVC Covered flat bottomed sinks
Pelling & Cross Ltd, 104 Baker Street, London, W.1.

Services—tailor-made aids, photographic processing, duplicating, etc.
OHP transparencies
Mallographic Ltd, 6 Chandos Street, London, W.1.
General Photography
See register pub. by Institute of Incorporated Photographers, Ware, Herts.
Movie film processing and sound striping, cassetting and filmstrip printing
Humphries Fotofacilities, P.O. Box 2HL, 71 Whitfield Street, London, W.1.
Filmatic Laboratories Ltd, Colville Mews, Lonsdale Road, London, W.11.
Kay Laboratories Ltd, 49A Oxford Road, Finsbury Park, London, N.4.
Rank Film Laboratories Ltd, Denham, Uxbridge, Middx.
Kodachrome processing, duplication of transparencies, low cost colour printing
Kodak Ltd, Box 14, Hemel Hempstead, Herts.
3 Hour transparency processing and colour printing
Museum Colour Laboratories Ltd, 259 Tottenham Court Road, London, W.1.
Camera repairs
Bowens Camera Repair Service, First Avenue, Bletchley, Bucks. (Also regional agents.)

HELPFUL ORGANISATIONS
SOCIETIES AND ORGANISATIONS FOR THE DEVELOPMENT OF VISUAL AIDS: SPECIAL COURSES

THE NATIONAL AUDIO-VISUAL AIDS SERVICE

Operated jointly by *The Educational Foundation for Visual Aids* and *The National Committee for Audio-Visual Aids in Education*. Both the Foundation and National Committee share administrative headquarters at 33 Queen Anne Street, London, W.1, and jointly operate The National Audio-Visual Aids Centre at 254 Belsize Road, London, N.W.6 (described below).

The Educational Foundation for Visual Aids was established in 1948 by the then Ministry of Education in consultation with the LEAs. It is concerned with the distribution, production and cataloguing of educational films and filmstrips, supply of equipment and the provision of technical services. The EFVA Catalogue of Visual Aids therefore gives details of material produced specifically for teaching purposes from all sources. All material described can be hired direct from the Foundation's National Audio-Visual Aids Library at 2 Paxton Place, Gipsy Road, London, S.E.27.

The National Committee for Audio-Visual Aids in Education was set up by the Ministry, teachers organisations and LEAs to promote and offer practical information on all audio-visual matters, and operate an educational advisory service to teachers and commercial producers of educational equipment and materials. It does not act as a direct producer itself. The National Committee:

1. Organises training facilities for teachers at the National Audio-Visual Aids Centre, and various National and Regional conferences and exhibitions.

2. Publishes the monthly journal *Visual Education* and a wide range of booklets on various audio-visual developments. Also organises a regular national information service for schools.

3. Offers a personal enquiry answering service on educational matters.

At *The National Audio-Visual Aids Centre* the Foundation and National Committee offer teachers the following:

1. A *demonstration centre*: a permanent working display of audio-visual hardware and materials, where, for example, every current overhead projector model can be compared side by side and discussed with unbiased educationalists.

2. A *technical service* for the sale and servicing of hardware.

3. An *experimental development unit* staffed by engineers to assess new equipment and research methods of approaching teaching problems with manufacturers.

4. A *training department* offering various courses for teachers covering new methods and techniques.

5. A *reference library* of audio-visual publications.

The centre at 254 Belsize Park, London, N.W.6, is open to callers during normal office hours; nearest station Belsize Park.

THE NATIONAL COUNCIL FOR EDUCATIONAL TECHNOLOGY

Acts as a central agency for the promotion of research, the initiation of development, co-ordination of training of teachers in the application of educational technology, and dissemination of information. Government departments sponsoring the Council include the Department of Education and Science, University Grants Committee, the Schools Council and Ministry of Defence. The Nuffield and Gulbenkian Foundations also act as sponsors and there is an overlap in membership between the Council and the NCAVA (above) to assist co-ordination. However, members of the Council are appointed by the Secretary of State for their expertise in educational technology rather than as representatives of other bodies. NCET is responsible for:

1. Initiating and establishing research projects, feasibility studies, etc., much of which is carried out under contract in universities and colleges.

2. Publication of books and pamphlets on learning systems, through their official publishers Education Press Ltd. Also their regular *Journal of Educational Technology*.

The National Council for Educational Technology operates from 160 Great Portland Street, London, W1N 5TB.

THE BRITISH FILM INSTITUTE

The national body for the encouragement and development of the film as an art and as a mode of expression; runs the National Film Theatre and National Film Library. The BFI Education Department has done much pioneer work in the educational field, and operates the Society for Education in Film and Television as a subsidiary body. Government grant-aided, the BFI is responsible for:

The National Film Library, custodians of valuable historical copies of the world's films. A lending section is available to schools and film societies—for example feature film extracts capable of detailed study within a normal teaching period.

The National Film Theatre, on the South Bank, London—a centre offering international programmes of particular value to the student of the cinema and the general public.

BFI Education Department Publications which produces books on film teaching at all levels by teachers, and books supplying information and serious comment on the cinema.

A Central Booking Agency which will book all film material for the teacher, regardless of source.

An Information Service free to all enquirers on film matters.

Support to film societies all over the country and to specialist organisations such as the British Industrial and Scientific Film Association.

Further information from the British Film Institute, 42 Lower Marsh, London, S.E.1. (BFI Publications are at 81 Dean Street, London, W.1.)

THE SOCIETY FOR EDUCATION IN
FILM AND TELEVISION

A voluntary organisation of teachers interested in practical film-making and the promotion of screen education. Membership costs a few shillings and is open to individuals and institutions such as Schools and Colleges. Members receive the Society's bi-monthly *Screen*, and various other publications—mostly documented case histories of school projects and handbooks. The SEFT is of particular value to teachers interested in introducing film societies and time-tabled screen education periods into their schools. A Summer School, a London Conference and various regional Conferences are organised each year. The Society works in close collaboration with the BFI Education Department and is a grant-in-aid body of the BFI. Further information from the General Secretary at 81 Dean Street, London, W.1.

THE BRITISH ASSOCIATION FOR COMMERCIAL
AND INDUSTRIAL EDUCATION

BACIE is a voluntary organisation with a membership including indus-trial and commercial firms, industrial training boards, LEAs, universities, colleges, trade associations, etc., as well as individuals. It offers the following:

BACIE Journal (quarterly) covering training practice and policy, and including a useful bibliography on publications in the field of education and training in industry.

Publications and memoranda (seven times a year)—handbooks, training manuals and reports.

Courses, conferences and exhibitions.

An information service to members, including library and loan facilities.

There are eleven Regional Groups. BACIE headquarters is at 16 Park Crescent, Regent's Park, London, W.1.

NATIONAL REPROGRAPHIC CENTRE FOR DOCUMENTATION

Part of Hatfield Polytechnic, Hatfield, Herts. Independent centre for testing and evaluating reprographic and micrographic equipment. Provides technical information and short courses for educationists interested in applications of reprography. Enquiry Service and regular Bulletins on an annual subscriber basis.

INSTITUTE OF REPROGRAPHIC TECHNOLOGY

Largely supported by manufacturers of document copying and office printing equipment and materials, IRT offers an information service on reproduction techniques. It is also concerned with the training and qualifying of technical personnel in this field. Information from 157 Victoria Street, London, S.W.1.

ROYAL PHOTOGRAPHIC SOCIETY

An independent learned society founded for the advancement of photographic science and its applications. Members (mostly amateur photographers) can attend meetings, lectures and exhibitions in the Society's house. The RPS has a library of great historical interest and publishes two regular and very dissimilar journals—*The Photographic Journal* and *The Journal of Photographic Science*. Secretary's address: 14 South Audley Street, London, W.1.

The RPS is also associated with the Photographic Alliance of Great Britain (121 Shawhurst Lane, Hollywood, near Birmingham), a federation of camera clubs which will provide lectures, judges, taped film strips and slide talks, leaflets and inter-club competitions.

INSTITUTE OF AMATEUR CINEMATOGRAPHERS LTD.

Founded to assist individual amateur cinematographers by disseminating technical information and offering exchanges of views and experiences. Publishes *IAC News*; offers scripting advice; has film and book libraries; and organises an annual film competition and Film Festival. Address: 8 West Street, Epsom, Surrey.

SPECIAL COURSES FOR TEACHERS

Type of course	*Held at*	*Organised by*
Two-week block courses in practical still photography and in film making	Kodak Training Centre, Ruislip	Kodak Ltd, Educational Service, Victoria Road, Ruislip, Middlesex
Courses ranging from one weekend to two full weeks on the educational application of audio-visual aids (including CCTV)	The National Audio-Visual Aids Centre, 254 Belsize Road, London, N.W.6	The National Audio-Visual Aids Service
Summer schools in film education	Various centres	British Film Institute
Various practical courses on aids to teaching in an overseas context	Overseas Visual Aids Centre, Tavistock House, 31 Tavistock Sq., London, W.C.1	Overseas Visual Aids Centre
One year full-time course for University of London Institute of Education Diploma in the theory and practice of Visual Aids	London University and OVAC	Overseas Visual Aids Centre
One term course on film, television and photography in schools. For serving teachers	Hornsey College of Art, London	Hornsey (for the Department of Education and Science)
Short courses for education and training officers in Industry	Various Colleges and Universities	British Association for Commercial and Industrial Education
Technical short courses (and day-release courses preparing audio-visual Technicians for City and Guilds examination 419)	Various Local Technical Colleges and Polytechnics (e.g. Wandsworth Technical College)	The Local Education Authority

APPENDIX VI

LAYOUT, FACILITIES AND EQUIPMENT
FOR PHOTOGRAPHIC WORK AREAS

Local conditions such as available floor space, services (and of course money), as well as a school's particular requirements, all mean that recommendations can only be generalised. However, lay-outs and schedules of equipment are suggested for three types of facility:

1. A one-man darkroom/workroom for user-preparation of visual aids.

2. A photographic workshop for up to six learners at one time.

3. A resources centre serving all the audio-visual production, storage and retrieval needs of a large school, and staffed by one or more full-time technicians.

The Appendix also includes a list of suggested camera equipment for students tackling photography.

A ONE-MAN PHOTOGRAPHIC PREP ROOM

A room used by only one person at a time can serve the dual role of darkroom and workroom (Fig. App.6.1). A 'dry' bench is required for the enlarger, paper storage and the loading of film spirals. The sink forming the 'wet bench' should be about 9 in. deep with 24-in. splashback and a flat bottom; this can be constructed in wood lined with thick PVC sheeting or bought ready made (page 320). Chemicals and dishes are stored underneath. Hot and cold water supplies are essential and the sink should contain duckboards on which dishes containing chemicals can stand.

The dry bench also carries a document copier and permanent camera support and lighting rig for copying on 35-mm film. One safelight is wallmounted over the sink for use when printing; at other times a white light on the ceiling gives illumination. Both benches have power points adjacent. Prints can be dried on muslin stretched over horizontal wooden frames, and films can hang from a simple clothes line or be dried in a home made cabinet.

The room must be really light-tight, yet ventilated—with a light

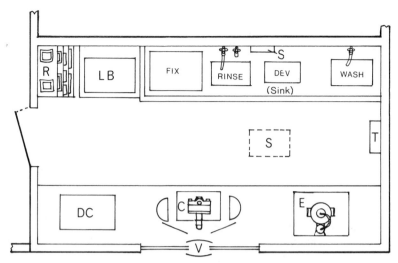

Fig. App.6.1. One-man photographic prep room. R, Muslin racks for drying prints.
LB, Light box. S, Safelight. T, Towel. E, Enlarger. C, Copying set-up. V, Ventilating
fan (light-tight). DC, Document copying machine.

trapped extractor fan or at least a window which can be opened when
darkness is not needed. Walls are finished in white emulsion or gloss
paint; floor in PVC sheeting or quarry tiles.

Hardware (make-do alternatives in brackets):
Daylight film processing tank(s) and spiral(s) (or beaker for processing
film within its cassette).
Thermometer for combined dish/tank use.
Clock with luminous face and large secondhand. (Or wristwatch.)
Enlarger to accept largest negative size used.
Masking frame.*
Two dishes to suit the largest prints to be made; one a size larger for
the fixing solution. (Or use processing unit of photo copying
machine, below.)
Print washing tank (or one further dish).
Muslin racks for print drying. (Or use clothes line.)
Home made vertical column and movable clamp for 35-mm camera (or
adapt enlarger).
Two simple flood reflectors. (Or desk lamps.)
Light box with glass over a diffused strip tube, for binding slides.*
Light/heat copying machine for OHP transparencies and spirit or ink
masters.
  * Desirable but not essential.

Photo copying machine for continuous tone and line originals (or motor processing section only—use light box above for exposing).
Wall safelight with orange filter screen.
Extractor fan.*
Negative drying cabinet. (Or nylon clothes line.)
Print drier/glazer.*
Dry mounting press.*

A PHOTOGRAPHIC WORKSHOP FOR STUDENTS

This is a communal workshop area which can be used by four to six pupils for processing and printing their own still photographs and editing movie films, and (at other times) by teaching staff or technicians preparing visual aids materials. The space is broadly divided into areas requiring light exclusion and those areas where work can be carried out in white light.

Two schemes are shown in Fig. App.6.2: (A) using conventional dish processed printing materials and (B) using roller processed (stabilised) materials. Scheme B is more expensive in terms of hardware but money is saved by reduced plumbing and darkroom area, and very much less time is taken up in producing prints.

The previous suggestions on wet and dry benches and room finish still apply but here access to the darkroom should be possible without spoiling other people's work by allowing entry of white light. A doorless light-trap is the best solution as it also allows excellent ventilation, but this takes up more space than a door-plus-curtain or pair of doors. For Scheme A it is also helpful to have a simple light-tight hatch through which wet prints can be transferred from safelighted to white light areas without wetting the floor. The small loading room allows individuals to load rollfilm tanks in darkness without having to disturb their colleagues in the printing darkroom.

The Scheme B roller processing machine obviates the need for a wet bench; little else is needed for printing and greater space can be allocated to the white light work area.

Basic Hardware for Scheme A:
The list of items suggested for a one-man workroom, in appropriately greater quantity *plus*:
Additional clock in workroom—to time film processing.
Large safelight suspended from ceiling over print processing sink (the wall safelight is used near entrance).

* Desirable but not essential.

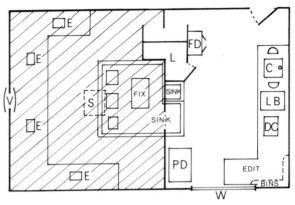

Scheme A

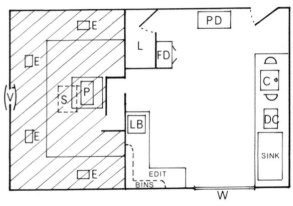

Scheme B

Fig. App.6.2. Photographic workshop for students. E, Enlarger. V, Ventilation. S, Safelight. L, Loading room for processing tanks. FD, Film dryer. PD, Print dryer. C, Copy camera. LB, Light box. DC, Document copier. W, Window. P, Processing machine for stabilisation bromide paper. See text.

Film drying cabinet—now essential to avoid passing damage and dust, and to speed production.

Additional sinks in workroom:

(1) To accommodate film tanks during processing.

(2) For washing prints. This can either accommodate a print washing tank, or be designed as a cascade washer.

Flatbed print drier.

Cine rewind arms (for movie editing).

Animated viewer (for movie editing).

Splicer (for movie editing).

Pin or clip board over muslin lined bins, to accommodate sections of film during cutting (for movie editing).

Basic Hardware for Scheme B:

The items suggested for a one-man workroom, adjusted in quantity *plus*

Print processing machine—Ektamatic, Ilfoprint, Agfa Rapide, etc.

Film-drying cabinet.

Movie editing hardware as for Scheme A.

(N.B. The only sink is now in the workroom, for film processing and fixing and washing stabilised prints required permanently, page 272).

A SCHOOL AUDIO-VISUAL RESOURCES CENTRE

The function of a comprehensive and well equipped centre of the kind shown in Fig. 6.3 is to offer a service of software preparation and hardware loan and operation for a school of 1000 plus pupils. The centre is staffed by technicians, with teaching staff directing the content of visual aids material and (if they wish) carrying out its preparation. Pupils are also encouraged to make use of the resources centre darkrooms and movie areas when working on photographic projects, under technical supervision. Note the centre's physical links with the

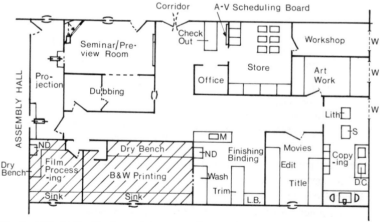

Fig. App.6.3. Audio-visual resources centre for a major school. Note how projection room also serves assembly hall. Dubbing room has sound-proof window into preview room, used when recording. Technician at check-out desk organises loans of projectors etc on trolleys located in rear storeroom, reserves time on machines, darkroom, etc. S, Spirit duplicator. DC, Document copiers. LB, Light box. M, Dry mounting press. ND, Negative dryer.

Assembly Hall. Similarly it might be linked to the library (Fig. App.6.4) via a slide/filmstrip/loop-film reference room always available to learners for individual access to audio-visual aids. This reference room also issues strips and certain other software for home study, and is staffed by a teacher's aide who is in effect an audio-visual librarian.

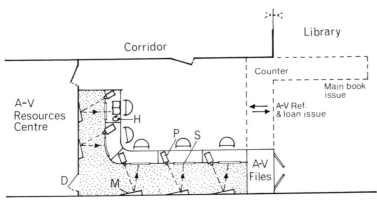

Fig. App.6.4. An A-V reference room, forming part of the library, but linked to (and serviced by) a school's resources centre. Each booth has a user-operated back-projection arrangement into a darkened 'tunnel'. P, Projector (slide, strip, or loop movie). M, Fixed mirror. S, Small back-projection screen. H, Headphones for sound-track material. D, Door for servicing.

The following list of hardware is suggested for a centre serving a school of this size, and would probably have to be built up over a period of years. Television equipment is not included:

2 16-mm 1000-W sound projectors* with optical/magnetic sound heads with record/replay facilities and speakers. To be based in the projection room but available elsewhere if needed.

2 16-mm 1000-W sound projectors* with optical sound heads and 12-in. speakers with at least 6 m of speaker lead.

1 Super 8-mm sound projector* and speaker.

1 Dual gauge Standard/Super-8-mm silent projector.*

10 Super-8-mm cassette loading silent projectors* (four for permanent use in reference room).

12 Overhead projectors (some permanently located in teaching departments).

5 5 × 5-cm automatic slide projectors* with remote control.

3 Filmstrip projectors* with remote control.

* Tables 8.1–3 on pages 252–3 show the lens focal length required.

6 Dual slide/strip hand operated viewers or projectors (permanent as in reference room).

1 Episcope (25 × 25-cm platen).

1 Microprojector.

6 Projector stands with lockable wheels, and easily adjusted for height and level.

1 Synchroniser for 8-mm film projector/tape recorder.

1 Synchroniser for slide or filmstrip projector.

3 Two-track transportable tape recorders (mains).

2 Portable cartridge loading tape recorders (battery).

1 Three speed high quality stereo tape recorder.

3 Record playing decks with amplifiers and speakers.

1 VHF radio receiver permanently in department for taping broadcasts.

1 Portable radio receiver (battery).

2 Movie cameras for Super-8, with reflex viewfinder and zoom lens.

1 Movie camera for 16 mm, with reflex viewfinder and standard lens.

2 35-mm SLR cameras, each with standard lenses and close-up bellows attachments.

1 Wide angle lens to fit above.

1 5 × 4 in. plate camera with standard lens and four film holders.

2 Exposure meters.

4 Really firm tripods with pan and tilt heads.

1 Copying stand with two floods.

2 500-W spotlights on stands.

3 500-W floodlights on stands.

Film-editing equipment for 8-mm and 16-mm film.

Darkroom processing and printing equipment.

(See suggestions for students' photoworkshop.)

1 Thermal document copier for making OHP transparencies, and spirit master and ink stencil making.

1 Photo copier (flatbed type) for copying all types of original on to paper and offset master making.

1 Spirit duplicator—for moderate runs.

1 Offset office duplicator—for long runs.

3 Portable cine/slide screens about 2 m. square, matt white.

1 Portable cine/slide screens about 2 m. square, directional.

(Other 2 m.-square screens for OHP use, located within departments.)

3 Portable back-projection screen units.

Workshop tools including power drill, power saw and a small metal turning lathe.

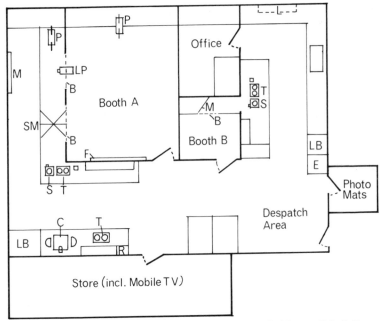

Fig. App.6.5. Plan of audio-visual department staffed by technicians at Exhall Grange School. P, 16-mm sound projector. LP, 8-mm loop projector. S, Slide projector. T, Tape recorder. M, Fixed front silvered mirror. SM, Swivelling mirror (serves either of two projectors). B, Back-projection screen. F, Front-projection screen. LB, Light box. E, Slide/strip files. R, Radio receiver. L, Translift. *Visual Education.*

BASIC HARDWARE FOR STUDENTS TO TAKE AND PROCESS PHOTOGRAPHS

The following equipment enables a group of twenty students to undertake quite a wide range of projects such as photoplays, assuming that some of the team will be organising people, acting, co-ordinating continuity, and doing other non-technical jobs. Equally this pool of equipment allows a smaller number of students to shoot, process and print photographs for their own individual projects.

1 35 mm SLR camera of modest * price with standard lenses.

1 35 mm inexpensive * direct vision camera with standard lens.

1 Close-up bellows attachment for SLR camera.

2 Exposure meters.

1 Tripod with pan and tilt head.

2 Daylight film processing tanks with spirals.

1 Thermometer.

* Price ranges—see Table 2.3 on page 84.

1 Set of plastic pegs and nylon line.
1 35-mm enlarger.
3 Print processing dishes.
1 Small dry mounting iron or press.
(Plus use of a slide projector and tape recorder.)

Desirable camera extras:
1 Wide-angle (28 mm) lens for SLR camera.
1 Telephoto (135 mm) lens for SLR camera.
1 Slide copying attachment for SLR camera—see Fig. 4.23.
1 Flash (bulb) attachment.
2 Colour filters—yellow and red.
1 Cable release.

FOCUSING AND EXPOSURE DATA FOR
CLOSE-UP CAMERA WORK

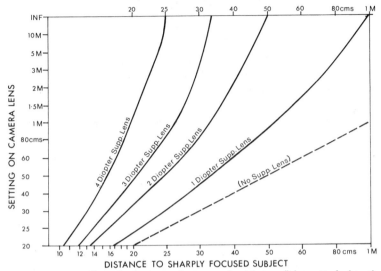

Fig. App.7.1. The effect of using a supplementary (or 'close up') lens attached to the camera lens. Strength of lens is indicated by its diopter power, which is additive. Thus, 1D plus 2D lenses equal a 3D lens. However, too many supplementary lenses used together will reduce image contrast and definition.

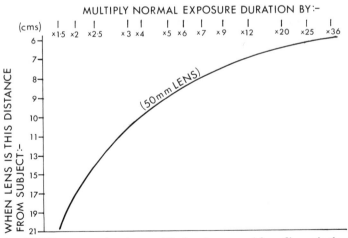

Fig. App.7.2. When camera lens is spaced farther than normal from film, as in the case of extension rings or bellows, image is made extra dim. Exposure should be increased (e.g. longer shutter open time) as shown here.

335

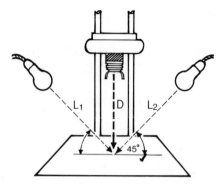

Fig. App.7.3. When copying using two No. 1 Photofloods and the camera lens appropriately extended by rings, etc., the table below suggests necessary exposure times.

Lens—55 mm. Each lamp—N °1 Photoflood 275 W

D	L_1 and L_2* (each)	Exposure time † (lens set to f. 8) on:			
		Dia Direct	Plus X	K'chrome A	E'chrome B + 81A filter
30 cm	60 cm	$\frac{1}{8}$ sec.	$\frac{1}{30}$	$\frac{1}{15}$	$\frac{1}{30}$
	40	$\frac{1}{15}$	$\frac{1}{60}$	$\frac{1}{30}$	$\frac{1}{60}$
20	60	$\frac{1}{4}$	$\frac{1}{15}$	$\frac{1}{8}$	$\frac{1}{15}$
	40	$\frac{1}{8}$	$\frac{1}{60}$	$\frac{1}{15}$	$\frac{1}{60}$
15	40	$\frac{1}{8}$	$\frac{1}{60}$	$\frac{1}{15}$	$\frac{1}{60}$
10	40	$\frac{1}{2}$	$\frac{1}{15}$	$\frac{1}{4}$	$\frac{1}{15}$

* Sufficiently distant to illuminate whole original evenly. Assumes lamps are not in reflectors.
† To nearest marked shutter speed.

APPENDIX VIII

CHECK LIST FOR TECHNICAL FAULTS—
STILL PHOTOGRAPHY AND FILM PROJECTION

STILL PHOTOGRAPHY

Symptoms and probable causes of the most common faults:

Image unsharp:

Faulty camera focusing—is foreground or background sharper than the main subject?

Camera shake—are there signs of directional overall blur?

Subject movement—are stationary parts of the picture sharp?

Faulty focusing or shaking of enlarger—this will make the grain pattern unsharp too.

Negative not lying flat in enlarger, or document not in tight contact in document copier—is the image unsharp in patches?

Image generally too dark (negs) or too light (reversal colour transparencies):

Overexposure—are the shadow parts of the subject more acceptably recorded than the highlights?

Overdevelopment (negatives)—are the highlights very dense relative to shadows, giving a contrasty result even with flatly lit subjects?

Light fogging—is the effect *overall*, degrading shadow detail more than highlights? If the fog extends beyond the boundaries of the picture area light probably reached the film through a faulty camera back or outside the camera, e.g. processing under the wrong safelight.

Image too light (negs) or too dark (reversal colour transparencies):

Underexposure—is shadow detail indecipherable?

Underdevelopment (negs)—is shadow detail present but weak in contrast, highlights also lacking strong density?

Obstruction—are both shadow and highlight details lost in patches? Probably caused by a camera strap in front of the lens (or very uneven development).

Colour cast (reversal colour transparencies):

Daylight film used in artificial light—strong orange cast.

Daylight film used in very overcast conditions or with some types of electronic flash—bluish cast.

Daylight film used in light from fluorescent tubes—greenish cast.
Artificial light film used in daylight—strong blue cast.
Artificial light film used with domestic lamps—orangish cast.

Image crooked or off-centre:
Parallax discrepancy—maybe you are shooting close-up with a direct vision or twin lens reflex camera.
Faulty viewfinding—viewfinder damaged, or camera knocked between setting up and shooting.

Line film images high contrast but black subject lettering 'eaten away' and meally (negatives):
Overexposure.

Line film image records black lettering clean and clear but white paper as grey (negatives):
Underexposure.

Line images too lacking in contrast, whatever exposure is given:
Film not sufficiently contrasty—subject blacks begin to grey over before subject whites reach strong density.
Wrong developer or insufficient development.

'Half moon' marks (about 5–10 mm wide) in white or black, usually on rollfilm:
Kink marks—the film has been buckled, probably when loading into a film processing spiral.

Black 'tram-line' scratches along the length of the film:
Abrasion—probably grit caught at the mouth of the film cassette or in 'clenching' (tightening the spool while holding the end of the film).

Purple patches (prints) and milky patches (negatives):
Insufficient fixing—refix immediately.

Image begins turning sepia and bleaches:
Insufficient washing—fault may only be apparent some weeks after processing.

Fingerprints on films:
Damp or chemically contaminated fingers in direct contact with the emulsion. Hold film by the edges only.

Scum marks on films:
Chalky deposits in tap water—often these will polish off the back of the film with a clean cloth, but fit a water filter.

SOUND FILM PROJECTION

If a projector is defective consider all the most likely causes before abandoning it to the service engineer. Often the trouble can be easily remedied by the user (but not to the extent of dismantling the machine unless he knows what he is doing). The golden rule is always to set up and check the projector before the presentation.

Different machines vary in their mechanical detail, but the following symptoms and their probable causes are common to most 16-mm sound projectors. For explanations of the parts of a projector, see Fig. 1.13 on page 34.

No sign of life when all switches 'on'—not even pilot light:
Is mains lead properly connected; is the wall socket working; check fuse in mains plug.

Motor and lamp blower working but no light on screen:
Check for an obstruction such as a lens cap; projection lamp needs replacement.

Lamp and blower working but no movement of film:
Projector set to single frame; film jammed.*

Lamp and motor working but no sound from speaker:
Is amplifier switched on; loudspeaker connected?

As above, speaker hums but no reproduction of soundtrack:
Check if exciter lamp alight (optical sound); is film threaded around sound head; maybe film is silent or recording starts later; film may be threaded back to front;* maybe scanning slit is obstructed.

Sound reproduction is 'mushy' and indistinct:
Film is not tightly threaded around sound drum.

Image on screen unsharp:
Is lens focused; is gate fully closed; check for grease or finger marks on front or back of lens.

Image is upside down and actions appear backwards:
Film is running tail first (i.e. has not been rewound after last showing).

Image is reversed left to right (back-projection screen):
Projector must be used with a mirror. See page 256.

Image is too big (or too small):
Position projector nearer to (or further from) screen; change to a longer (or shorter) projection lens.

Image breaks up into a fast-jerking flicker like faulty framehold on TV:
Loss of top or bottom loop,* due to a torn sprocket hole or poor threading.

Ragged black edges to projected image instead of clean rectangular frame:
Dirt and debris accumulated in film gate aperture—clean with a soft brush.

* Danger; film may be irreparably damaged. Switch off and check visually, using inching knob if necessary.

Instead of winding on to take-up spool projected film feeds on to floor:
Film not attached properly to take-up spool; spring band driving take-up missing or slipping; bent spool pinching film and preventing the spool filling completely; projector set to 'rewind' (some makes).

Any projector first aid kit should contain a spare mains lamp and exciter lamp (optical sound machines); fuses for plug and machine; a screwdriver and a torch.

APPENDIX IX

THE COPYRIGHT POSITION

THE PHOTOCOPYING OF PUBLISHED MATERIAL

Most modern books (this one is no exception) begin with a rather daunting notice from the publishers warning against copyright infringement by reproduction '... in any form or by any means, electronic, mechanical, photocopying ...'. The fact is that regard for copyright is essential to the continued publication of works of all kind. If free copying so reduces sales of the original commodity that publication becomes uneconomic, then in the last resort important publishing in many fields must wither away.

However, on one hand we have a situation in which the law sets general limitations on photocopying, and on the other the total impracticability of seeking written permission for each and every copy made. Developments in the technology of copying machines have proceeded so rapidly that making an OHP transparency or paper copy need take no longer than setting up a book in an epidiascope—yet the former is strictly infringement of the law, while the latter is not.

The Society of Authors and The Publishers Association appreciate the practical difficulties of this situation, and particularly the needs of teachers and lecturers. They suggest limits which authors and publishers generally would not regard as unreasonable for photocopying purposes. For example a single copy of a single extract not exceeding 4000 words or a series of extracts up to 8000 words (provided this does not exceed 10% of the whole work) would be considered reasonable. It would also be an unusual publisher who would regard the reproduction of single illustrations for classroom or lecture hall projection as infringing his copyright. *Multiple* copies of text or illustration (e.g. a copy for each individual in communal class studies) is another matter, and prior permission should be sought.

Under Section 41 of the Copyright Act 1956, copyright cannot be infringed by reproduction or adaptation in a course of instruction, where the copy is made by teacher or student *other than by use of a duplicating process*, or when as part of a question or answer in an examination. Of course there will often be occasions when reproduction of a couple of dozen copies of an extract will not endanger the economic viability of the work at all, and usually a publisher will give permission. The point is that such multiple copies of copyright work are illegal without permission, and so permission should be sought.

For fuller information on Photocopying and the Law, The Society of Authors publish a Guide for Librarians and Teachers, obtainable from 84 Drayton Gardens, London, S.W.10.

DIRECT USE OR RE-RECORDING OF COPYRIGHT MUSIC

The Copyright Act also covers music, and views the public performance of copyright music in a similar light to the duplication of a copyright publication. Where music is performed or reproduced in school as part of a school concert or entertainment given by parent–teacher associations, youth clubs, etc., royalties are normally due. However, 'Public performance' is *not* involved if the audience is limited to teachers or pupils in attendance at the school, e.g. as in class work.

Of course it would be impractical to seek permission separately from every copyright owner of every piece of music on each occasion and most Education Authorities take out an annual (tariff 'N') licence with the Performing Rights Society Ltd, covering specific buildings. This blanket licence then covers all public performances in the locations specified. The Performing Rights Society is responsible for distributing the proceeds of such fees to performing copyright owners.

For further information contact The Performing Rights Society, 29 Berners Street, London, W1P 4AA, and Phonograph Performance Ltd, 62 Oxford Street, London, W.1.

Index